WHOLE TRUTH

THE TAINTED PROSECUTION OF AN AMERICAN FIGHTER PILOT

BY BOB HARVEY

To Catherine,

Bob Harvey

Viper Pilot Press

Cocoa, Florida

Published by Viper Pilot Press, Cocoa, Florida

ISBN: 978-0615933634

Also available in e-book editions

F-16 image on front cover by Andrew Howe, iStockPhoto
F-16 image on back cover by Val Gempis, U.S. Air Force
Flag image, author photo and cover design by Chris Kridler

Learn more at ViperPilotPress.com

CONTENTS

Notes

The names of the people in this story are accurate. If their names were used in the official Record of Trial on the Air Force Freedom of Information website, I used them here. I protected the privacy of those not listed by the Air Force.

Kimberly Hanks, the accuser in this case, went public with her name in a television interview with NBC News' "Today Show" on March 13, 2013. She chose to put her name into the public eye and, as a result, it is used in this book.[1]

In a military court-martial, jurors are called court-martial panel members. In this book, I refer to the five Air Force officers who sat on the court-martial panel simply as jurors.

An "Article 32 hearing" is similar to a civilian preliminary hearing in the civilian judicial system. Its purpose is to decide if there is sufficient evidence to proceed to court-martial. The Investigating Officer (IO) of the Article 32 hearing conducts the hearing and makes a recommendation to the Convening Authority (usually a senior officer) whether to proceed to court-martial.

When referring to a general in the Air Force, regardless of rank, it is proper protocol to address him or her simply as "General" in speech and "Gen" in writing. Similarly, a Lieutenant Colonel is addressed as "Colonel" in speech and "Col" in writing. In an effort to insure clarity, I have left the abbreviation for Lieutenant — Lt. — in front of each reference to the rank of Lieutenant General or Lieutenant Colonel and Brigadier — Brig. — when referring to a Brigadier General.

Captains Tanya Manning and Dawn Brock were both promoted to the rank of major prior to the trial. Consequently, their statements and Article 32 testimony state "captain," while their testimony during the court-martial used "major." I used their Captain rank throughout the book to avoid confusion.

Lt. Col. James H. Wilkerson had been selected for promotion to full Colonel prior to the allegations against him. The effective date of that promotion was designated as March 1, 2013. However, the Air Force not only did not promote Lt. Col. Wilkerson; they instead continued to punish him despite the overturned verdict. They forced him to retire at the rank of Major effective January 1, 2014.

At the time of this writing, the complete Record of Trial for U.S. v. James H. Wilkerson is on the U.S. Air Force Freedom of Information website at http://www.foia.af.mil/reading/thewilkersonfoiacase.asp. This site provides a video and multiple photos of the Wilkerson home that the defense entered into evidence in the trial, including views of each bedroom in the home and the stairs leading to the guestroom on the lower level.

All references in the endnotes that refer to statements, summarized Article 32 testimony or trial testimony are from the Record of Trial downloaded from this website.

A listing of the stories printed by the *Stars and Stripes* about the Wilkerson case is available at: **http://www.stripes.com/news/stories-related-to-the-lt-col-james-wilkerson-case-1.218209**, "Stories related to the Lt. Col. James Wilkerson case."

Testimony often referred to times in military twenty-four-hour clock time, rather than civilian, twelve-hour clock time. I attempted to write all of the times in the twelve-hour civilian time method.

To help the reader understand the rank system in the military, the chart below lists the hierarchy for enlisted and officer ranks:

Title	Abbreviation
Enlisted Ranks	
Airman Basic	AB
Airman	Amn
Airman First Class	A1C
Senior Airman	SrA
Staff Sergeant	SSgt
Technical Sergeant	TSgt
Master Sergeant	MSgt
Senior Master Sergeant	SMSgt
Chief Master Sergeant	CMSgt
Command Chief Master Sergeant	CCM
Chief Master Sergeant of the Air Force	CMSAF

Officer Ranks

Second Lieutenant	2nd Lt
First Lieutenant	1st Lt
Captain	Capt
Major	Maj
Lieutenant Colonel	Lt Col
Colonel	Col
Brigadier General	Brig Gen
Major General	Maj Gen
Lieutenant General	Lt Gen
General	Gen

PRINCIPAL
CHARACTERS

Captain Benjamin Beliles, USAF — Assistant trial counsel; stationed at Ramstein Air Base, Germany, but detailed to Aviano Air Base, Italy, for the court-martial

Suzanne Berrong — Civilian employee of the Medical Group at Aviano Air Base, Italy; Kim Hanks' best friend at Aviano; had never met the Wilkersons prior to the trial

Colonel Joseph Bialke, USAF — 3rd Air Force Staff Judge Advocate; Lt. Gen. Franklin's command attorney; stationed at Ramstein Air Base, Germany

Captain Dawn Brock, USAF — One of three women from the Aviano Medical Group, including Kim Hanks, who met Col. Ostovich at the club and rode in his car to the Wilkerson home; Captain Brock did not know Col. Ostovich or Lt. Col. Wilkerson prior to meeting at the club

Colonel (Judge) Jefferson Brown, USAF — Presiding Judge in U.S. v. Wilkerson; a U.S. Forces in Europe circuit judge

Colonel Don Christensen, USAF — Prosecuting attorney, Chief of the Government Trial and Appellate Counsel Division and Chief Prosecutor for the Air Force, stationed at the Air Force Legal Operations Agency at Joint Base Andrews, Maryland. Col. Christensen said he "detailed himself" to the Wilkerson case

Colonel Scott Cusimano, US Army, Retired — Former Director of Staff for the wing commander at Aviano Air Base, Italy

Master Sergeant Danielle Dunnivant, USAF — Enlisted woman from the Aviano Medical Group; friend of Hanks

Lieutenant General Craig Franklin, USAF — 3rd Air Force Commander, Convening Authority; F-16 pilot; stationed at Ramstein Air Base, Germany

Major Gerremy Goldsberry, USAF — F-16 pilot in the Aviano Operations Group; friend of Lt. Col. Wilkerson; was with Col. Ostovich and Lt. Col. Wilkerson in the car and at the Wilkerson home

Kim Hanks — Accuser, physician's assistant and civilian employee of Aviano Medical Group

Major Albert Lowe, USAF — F-16 pilot in the Aviano Operations Group; friend of Lt. Col. Wilkerson; was with Col. Ostovich and Lt. Col. Wilkerson in the car and at the Wilkerson home

Captain Tanya Manning, USAF — One of three women from the Aviano Medical Group, including Kim Hanks, who met Col. Ostovich at the club and rode in his car to the Wilkerson home. Captain Manning testified she knew who Col. Ostovich was but had not met him prior to meeting at the club. Captain Manning was granted testimonial immunity.

Captain Jeffrey Martin, USAF — Military Area Defense Counsel (ADC); Air Force-appointed defense attorney; stationed at Lakenheath Air Base, England

Lieutenant Colonel Paula McCarron, USAF — Air Force appointed Investigating Officer (IO); conducted Article 32 hearing and authored report recommending court-martial; stationed at Pope Field, North Carolina

Brigadier General Pamela Milligan, US Air Force Reserve (USAFR) — Current spouse to Kim Hanks' former husband; defense witness whose testimony challenged the truthfulness of Hanks under oath in a previous court proceeding. Testified via video teleconference from Kialula, Hawaii; her testimony was not permitted in front of the jury.

Captain Vy Nguyen, USAF — Assistant trial counsel, JAG attorney stationed at Aviano, Air Base Italy

Major Michael O'Keefe, USAF — Medical technician at Aviano Medical Group; friend and co-worker of Hanks and the technician who interviewed Hanks the morning after the alleged incident

Colonel Dean Ostovich, USAF — Vice Wing Commander at Aviano Air Base; friend of Lt. Col. Wilkerson; F-16 pilot; driver of the car to the Wilkerson home. Col. Ostovich was granted testimonial immunity.

Frank Spinner — Civilian Defense Attorney

Colonel David Walker, USAF — Operations Group Commander; Lt. Col. Wilkerson's supervisor

Lieutenant Colonel Bryan D. Watson, USAF — Staff Judge Advocate

Lieutenant Colonel James H. Wilkerson, USAF — F-16 pilot and Inspector General at the Aviano Fighter Wing; the accused

Beth Wilkerson — Wife of Lt. Col. Wilkerson

Two visiting boys — Two young boys who were overnight guests at the Wilkerson home. Their names are not critical to the telling of this story. I refer to them as visiting boys. I have not used their names, or their mother's name, to maintain their privacy.

Brigadier General Scott Zobrist, USAF — Aviano Air Base Wing Commander; F-16 pilot

Acronyms and Definitions

3rd AF — 3rd Air Force: a "numbered" Air Force; the higher unit of command, which contains one or more wings; 3rd AF was commanded by Lieutenant General Craig Franklin, the Convening Authority in the Wilkerson case

ADC — Area Defense Counsel: defense attorney appointed by the Air Force to represent the accused in military cases, similar to a public defender

AFOSI — Air Force Office of Special Investigations or Office of Special Investigations — OSI: the investigative law personnel of the Air Force

CC — Commander: the senior officer in command

CJCS — The Chairman of the Joint Chiefs of Staff: the senior military officer in the United States Military

DoD — Department of Defense

FW — Fighter Wing: the basic fighting unit of the Air Force; traditionally a wing occupies a base with one commander, the wing commander

JAG — Judge Advocate General: an Air Force officer who is also an attorney and who is designated as a judge advocate

SARC — Sexual Assault Response Coordinator: the victim's rights advocate

SECDEF — The Secretary of Defense

TLF — Temporary Lodging Facility: an on-base building similar to a hotel, with rooms for rent by the night

UCMJ — Uniform Code of Military Justice: the Congressional Code of Military Criminal Law, which is applicable to all military members

USAF — United States Air Force

USAFE — United States Air Forces Europe: all U.S. Air Force personnel in Europe

USAFR — United States Air Force Reserve

USO — United Service Organizations, Inc.: provides morale-boosting programs, services and live entertainment support to American military members around the world[2]

PROLOGUE

"Cry 'Havoc,' and let slip the dogs of war."
— *William Shakespeare, "Julius Caesar"*

Throughout history, nations have fought wars, and it is usually the strongest nation that wins, the nation with the best fighting forces. In times of war, a nation calls on the strongest and smartest to fight its battles — these are called "warriors." Warriors are necessary, but only to fight wars. In times of peace, time and again, populations have turned on their warriors.

A nation at war needs all kinds of warriors, some who fight on land or on the sea, and some who fight in the air. This book focuses on one who fought in the air. This story is about the prosecution and wrongful conviction of a U.S. Air Force fighter pilot, Lieutenant Colonel James H. Wilkerson. More than that, it is also a story about the prosecution of the U.S Air Force fighter pilot culture. The fighter pilot culture is prominent in this story because attacking it was a key element of strategy used by the prosecution to convict Lt. Col. Wilkerson.

The ideal fighter pilot is the perfect blend of discipline and aggressiveness:

> "Fighter Pilot" is an attitude ... it is cockiness, it is aggressiveness, it is self confidence ... it is a streak of rebelliousness, and it is competitiveness. But there's something else, there's a spark, there's a desire to be good, to do well in the eyes of your peers, and in your own mind. I think it is love, of that blue-vaulted sky that becomes your playground, if, and only if, you're a fighter pilot. You don't understand it if you fly from A to B and straight and level. You merely climb and descend. You're moving through the basement of that vault of blue. A fighter pilot sees not a cloud, but beauty, not the ground

but something remote from him, something that he doesn't belong to as long as he's airborne. He's a man who wants to be ... second best to no one.
— Robin Olds, Brigadier General,
USAF, Triple Ace

These same characteristics — aggressiveness, rebelliousness, self-confidence — that make a great fighter pilot sometimes rub others the wrong way. Similar to what happens to the best athletes in colleges, their real or perceived special treatment inspires jealousy. Flying a high-performance fighter aircraft is glamorous, exciting and downright fun.

Historically, fighter pilots are an elite group. Theirs is a special calling. They risk their lives, almost daily, in defense of their country whether in training or in combat. In my twenty-seven years of flying F-16s, more than a dozen of my friends were killed in training accidents. Others were lost in combat. The nature of a fighter pilot's calling, joining the military and flying a high-performance fighter, is high risk. Each time a fighter pilot "straps on a jet," he or she knows, somewhere in the back of their mind, there is a risk of not coming back today. It is an unspoken but shared risk happily accepted in order to be one of the best. Because of that risk, the excitement and the danger, fighter pilots are a band of brothers (and sisters). They trust one another daily with their lives.

Not everyone has what it takes to be a fighter pilot and to live the military life. The military is known for long deployments, many years outside the United States and frequent separations from family. Today, our military is stretched thin and often sacrifices time and family for frequent combat deployments. Fighter pilots sacrifice for various reasons, similar to other military servicemen and women. But they get to fly, too. And they love it.

From this day to the ending of the world,
But we in it shall be remember'd —
We few, we happy few, we band of brothers;
For he to-day that sheds his blood with me
Shall be my brother ...
— William Shakespeare, "Henry V"

Blood spilled in battle makes Shakespeare's soldiers brothers — a family — in their struggle and comradeship,[3] and the same can be said of fighter pilots.

The story you are about to read is about Lt. Col. James H. "Jay" Wilkerson, call sign "Roscoe." A career Air Force officer and a spirited fighter pilot, he and his wife, Beth, were going about life in a typical way, enjoying their assignment to Aviano Air Base in northern Italy. After a fairly normal Friday evening socializing with friends, Beth reluctantly offered a place to sleep to a female stranger, left behind at the Wilkerson home by her friends. Neither Jay nor Beth could ever have imagined how their kindness could lead to a chain of events that would wrongfully convict and imprison the up-and-coming fighter pilot and tear their family apart.

In a case with zero evidence and contradicting accounts by the accuser, the Air Force sent its senior prosecutor from Air Force Headquarters in Washington, D.C., to prosecute the case. Joined by investigators who ignored evidence of innocence and a commander who violated guidance against unlawful command influence, this prosecutor threatened and intimidated witnesses and handpicked a jury of officers predisposed to dislike fighter pilots to get a conviction.

THE WHOLE TRUTH exposes corruption in the military justice system and unlawful influence by the highest levels of our government. Political correctness is driving the military to imprison innocent men. THE WHOLE TRUTH explores in-depth the case against fighter pilot Lt. Col. James Wilkerson from the first witness statements through the cover-up and eventual acquittal. But the acquittal was not the end. Politicians using the case for personal gain continued to persecute Lt. Col. Wilkerson despite his full acquittal. And the Air Force went along with the persecution despite its questionable legality.

THE WHOLE TRUTH proves Lt. Col. Wilkerson's innocence and exposes a one-sided, Salem-witch-trial mentality inside the U.S. military. It is, unfortunately, only one of many wrongful conviction stories. Research shows there are other warriors facing similar circumstances. These false accusations and wrongful convictions are indicative of a system that has turned on some of those warriors who defend our nation. Political correctness has invaded and corrupted the military justice system.

1

BEYOND A
REASONABLE DOUBT

"All things are subject to interpretation.
Whichever interpretation prevails at a given time
is a function of power and not truth."
— *Friedrich Nietzsche*

As on many other Friday nights, this was a casual outing — four guys going to see the band Seether on its USO tour at the American Air Base in Aviano, Italy. It was a semi-official appearance, required as ancillary duty to their positions as pilots and leaders in the fighter wing. The four men met early in the evening at Lt. Col. James Wilkerson's home in Roveredo in Piano, a small town in northeast Italy with a view of the nearby Dolomite mountains, still dusted in a recent spring snow.

They were friends, all officers and F-16 pilots. Lt. Col. Wilkerson was joined by Major Gerremy Goldsberry, Major Albert Lowe and Col. Dean Ostovich, the vice wing commander, who drove them to Aviano through the south gate.

After the show, the men stopped at the on-base club, and the only single man in the group, Col Ostovich, struck up a conversation there with three women from the Medical Group. He and the women, Captain Dawn Brock, Captain Tanya Manning and Kim Hanks, agreed to go somewhere else, maybe another bar, and everyone piled into his car to make a stop at Lt. Col. Wilkerson's home first to drop off the married men. It was a tight fit, with not enough seatbelts for everyone, but they drove the 1.6 miles without incident.

At Lt. Col. Wilkerson's home, Beth Wilkerson was keeping an eye on their son and two visiting boys who were spending the night. It was the visiting boys' first night away from their mother in the ten months since their father had been killed in a car accident. Their mother had told Beth they were having trouble sleeping and worried they wouldn't want to stay in the house if they woke up.[4]

Still, everyone was awake when the group arrived, and when Col. Ostovich. took it upon himself to invite them all in, Beth welcomed them with, by all accounts, grace and friendship. A "no notice" gathering wasn't unusual in the fighter pilot community. There's always an open invitation to visit, especially when the hosts were as gracious as the Wilkersons. It was assumed the revelers would have a drink and be on their way.

The Wilkersons' six guests stayed for about an hour and a half. They were offered a drink and given a tour of the home. The visiting boys were put to bed, and Lt Col Wilkerson told them a story before they went to sleep. Hanks visited the boys' room and talked with them, discussing an injury one of them had. Her time in the room overlapped with Lt. Col. Wilkerson's as he told them goodnight.

About 11 or 11:30 p.m., after a friendly visit, the guests began to leave. First was Captain Brock, who asked Beth to drive her back to the base. While all three women from the Medical Group resided off base in local communities, this night they each had a room on base at the Temporary Lodging Facility (TLF). They'd made reservations there so they could go to the concert, stay on base and not worry about drinking and driving. Beth agreed to drive Captain Brock back to the base and offered Hanks a ride as well, but she refused. The other guests weren't ready to go, either.

Next to leave were Col. Ostovich and Capt. Manning. They departed together in Col. Ostovich's car before Beth returned from dropping off Captain Brock. About this time, Lt. Col. Wilkerson tried to wrap up the evening by asking the other officers to leave. Beth and the two majors, with Hanks, discussed taking Hanks back to the base, but Hanks again refused the offer, and the other officers left. Shortly before midnight, Lt. Col. Wilkerson went to bed. Beth again offered to drive Hanks back to the base. She again refused. Seeing few other options and tired, Beth said that Hanks could sleep in the guest room on the lower level of the home. Hanks accepted her offer.

Here is where the accounts of the remainder of the evening diverge.

Hanks "was suddenly so tired, she went right to sleep," she wrote in her initial official statement to the Sexual Assault Response Coordinator (SARC). She testified that sometime before 3 a.m., she was "having a dream. It felt like I was floating, and I was being touched over my body. A very bright light came on, I rolled over to cover my eyes, and I heard a man say loudly, 'What the hell is going on?' I woke up and felt a hand that was down the front of my pants being removed. I opened my eyes and saw a man about six inches from my face, squinting with his eyes closed... I heard, 'Get the hell out of my house' and looked up and saw Beth at the light. I looked down and saw that I was still fully clothed, with my belt buckled."

Hanks said she left the house, walked into the center of the village and called her friend Master Sergeant Danielle Dunnivant.[5] MSgt. Dunnivant, another friend and co-worker, had attended the concert and gone to the club with Hanks, but she went home early. She was not at the Wilkersons' house.

The Wilkersons dispute Hanks' version of events. Beth said Hanks was up wandering the main floor of the house twice between 12:30 and 3 a.m. Finally, sometime before 3 a.m., Beth confronted Hanks again and, at that time, asked Hanks to go to bed or leave, at which time Hanks left the Wilkerson home. Both the Wilkersons said Lt. Col. Wilkerson never left his bed after retiring around midnight.

Wilkerson was arrested and, based solely on the testimony of Hanks, taken all the way to court-martial by his commanders. What followed was an unreal nightmare, highlighted by a poor investigation and overly zealous JAG officers and prosecutors tacitly, if not explicitly, egged on by a commander who violated Air Force policy against command influence. The allegation was a case of she said, he said, but the trial was more about fighter pilots and their traditions and culture than about the truth. The judge suppressed evidence, the commanders cherry-picked the Article 32 investigating officer, and the system stacked the jury with officers sympathetic to the defendant and predisposed to be hostile toward all fighter pilots. The outcome rocked the military justice system to its core.

SETTING THE STAGE

The case that developed hinges on what happened inside the Wilkerson home on the night of March 23-24, 2012. To understand the testimony, it is necessary to understand the layout of the Wilkerson home, particularly with regard to the location of bedrooms, kitchen counters and exits.

The Wilkerson house is a private residence off base in a nearby village barely a mile and a half from the Aviano Air Base south gate. The three-level house is surrounded by a concrete wall with extensive landscaping. The wall varies in height from about three to six feet. There is a pedestrian gate at the walkway entrance and a vehicle gate on the other side of the compound. These gates must be opened (buzzed) from inside the house or via a remote opener kept in the Wilkersons' car in order to permit access.

The pedestrian walkway approaches the main floor of the home, while the driveway leads to the garage door on the opposite side of the compound, down one level to the basement. The basement is halfway below grade, with the garage door on the driveway side only. The main floor is at ground level and faces the major street. Outside stairs go from a kitchen exit down to the driveway and garage entrance. No stairs exist on the main street side of the home.

The main floor of the home consists of a living room, dining room, kitchen, and a hallway leading to an office, bathroom and guest bedroom. Two exits are on either end of the kitchen, and the main entrance/exit is in the living room and leads to the front walkway. The hallway intersects the main living area at a stairwell that goes both up and down stairs to the other two levels of the home. There are two bedrooms and two bathrooms on the upper, third floor. The basement consists of a laundry room, bathroom, storage area and a guest bedroom/playroom. There is a boiler room on the outside of the building with an access door but no access to the basement. The only exit from the basement is through the garage.

These rooms and exits would be confusing but critical points in Hanks' testimony as her case unfolded against Lt Col Wilkerson.

WILKERSON HOUSE AND COMPOUND
ROVEREDO IN PIANO, ITALY

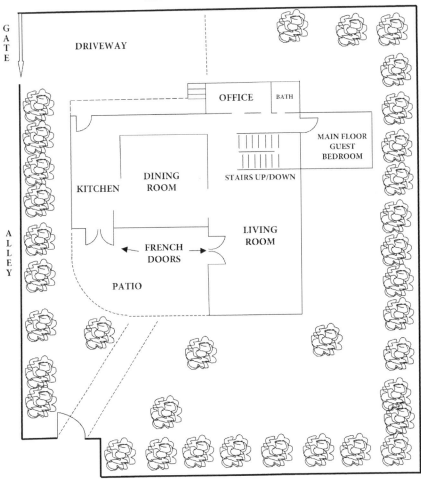

WILKERSON HOUSE, LOWER LEVEL

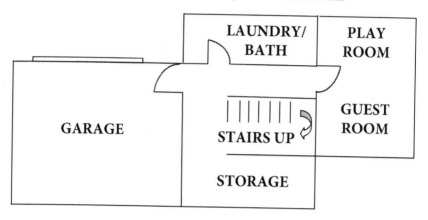

WILKERSON HOUSE, UPPER LEVEL

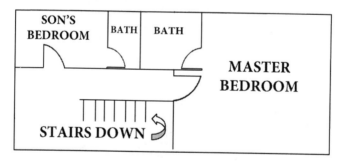

If you would like to see the house on Google Maps, the address is: 2 Vitporio Venetto Roveredo in Piano, Italy. In the photo on Google Maps, the house is on the corner of Via Vitporio Venetto and Via Risorgimento (to the upper right of the "A" when you call it up on Google). It has the three levels of roofline. It is the one with the small parking pad in front of the white concrete wall. You will clearly see the compound wall and vegetation. Remember, the jury had none of these pictures — no diagram, no Google Map photos, no visit.

Location of Wilkerson house and compound, Roveredo in Piano, Italy

Map showing house: Imagery ©2013 DigitalGlobe, European Space Imaging. Map data ©2013 Google
Map of Italy: ©2013 Google — Basarsoft. GeoBasis-DE/BKG (©2009), based on BCN IGN España, TerraMetrics

Wilkerson house from the main street

Note the size and construction of the fence and the personnel gate that must be opened to enter.

Wilkerson house from the side alley

Note the vehicle gate that must be opened to enter the grounds.

2

SHOCK AND AWE

"All concerns of men go wrong when they wish to cure evil with evil."
— *Sophocles*

On November 2, 2012, Lieutenant Colonel James H. Wilkerson was found guilty of all specifications and charges, which included aggravated sexual assault and conduct unbecoming an officer. My immediate thought was, "How?" I was there for the trial. I was a witness for the defense. I was not permitted inside the courtroom until after I had testified, but I had been hearing about the trial each night from people who were there. I knew what the defense team believed — this was a weak case: a "he-said, she-said" with a twist. It was actually Beth Wilkerson's testimony versus that of the accuser, Kimberly Hanks; a "she-said, she-said." Defense attorneys were certain Lt. Col. Wilkerson would be found not guilty, that this was nothing more than a show trial. What happened? I didn't understand, and I wanted to know more. I also didn't like the way the prosecution portrayed pilots and the Air Force fighter pilot culture overall. I felt they used unsubstantiated accusations and hearsay that had nothing to do with sexual assault to gain a kangaroo-court-style conviction. I believed the investigation was a sham and the trial was about a conviction, truth be damned. But was I wrong? Was Lt. Col. Wilkerson guilty? I was going to find out and do whatever I could to help correct the injustice if it was wrong. It was my Air Force that had done this. It was despicable and needed to be fixed.

Granted, I was biased in that I know Lt. Col. James "Jay" Wilkerson. I had known him for about five years prior to the trial, first as a neighbor just down the street in Sumter, South Carolina, while we were both stationed at Shaw Air Force Base. Later, I was attached to the squadron where he was the Operations Officer, and I flew with him once or twice.

I'd been to his house on many occasions, "getting together," as the prosecution would say. He and Beth, his wife of sixteen years, had been to our home many times as well. I've been to their beach house with them, and my wife had been there on several occasions both with and without me. In short, I had been around both Wilkersons long enough and in enough situations with them to believe that what Lt. Col. Wilkerson was accused of was not true. Nonetheless, I was forced to do some serious soul-searching. Had I missed something? Could it be so?

"Make no mistake, the fighter pilot culture was convicted here today." Those are the first words I wrote when the verdict was announced. How could a court-martial panel of five officers have reached a guilty verdict "beyond a reasonable doubt"? I didn't see how it could be true, given everything I knew about the case and what I saw at the trial. I needed to do more research and find out what happened.

The defense team had asked my wife and me to testify as character witnesses for the Wilkersons. As witnesses, we were not permitted to be in the courtroom during the trial until after we had testified and were released. However, I listened each night to others who had been in the courtroom all day as they described each day's events and offered assessments of the trial. I was more incensed each day by the prosecution's tactics. The lead prosecutor, Colonel Don Christensen, was Chief of the Government Trial and Appellate Counsel Division and Chief Prosecutor for the Air Force. His office is at the Air Force Legal Operations Agency at Joint Base Andrews, in Maryland. Col. Christensen said he "detailed himself" to the Wilkerson case because the Aviano JAG asked him to, because "the vice wing commander was expected to testify."[6] Some speculated that he took the job because of the high-profile nature of a case against a colonel fighter pilot.

Col. Christensen's prosecution strategy seemed to be to throw dirt at the wall to see what stuck. Most of that dirt was related to fighter pilot traditions and was not relevant to the issue of sexual assault. Somehow, because some fighter pilots act like college boys, that meant Lt. Col. Wilkerson was guilty of sexual assault. Col. Christensen had what he was overheard calling his "dream jury" because it consisted of three medical colonels (from Kim Hanks' career field) and not a single pilot. In fact, there was not a single pilot in the jury pool; therefore one could not be selected to sit on the jury. So the "bad boy" offense played well to this jury.

The prosecution continuously denigrated fighter pilots in general. Without exception, each time a fighter pilot was called to testify, one of the first questions by the trial counsel or assistant trial counsel was, "And you are a fighter pilot also?" It seemed as if they were trying to lessen the impact of the testimony of the fighter pilots by suggesting to the jury that a fighter pilot's testimony would be less credible. The prosecution was attempting to paint a picture that all fighter pilots are deviant, misbehaving, frat boys gone wild.

Now, don't get me wrong. Some fighter pilots can, at times, behave like that, but what did such behavior have to do with the charges of sexual assault? The prosecution was using a stereotype to make Lt. Col. Wilkerson look like an overall bad guy. His insinuation was, "Hell, he's a fighter pilot; he's guilty of something, so let's just call him guilty." That attitude played an important part in the trial. The Record of Trial shows the prosecution's overall theme was to list multiple fighter pilot transgressions to insinuate guilt in this case.

It bears explaining that Col. Christensen, as an Air Force attorney, is not in an "operational" or "combatant" career field. Personnel in combatant operational specialties are more likely to see combat. Although others can be and are often deployed to combat locations, in the Air Force, pilots, other aircrew members and other combatant career fields traditionally sustain more combat losses. Simply put, combatant career fields are much higher-risk career fields than some of the "professional" career fields in the Air Force, such as the JAG corps and Medical corps. This difference helps foster the cultural divide between fighter pilots and some other career fields. This cultural divide played a significant role in the outcome of this case.

Col. Christensen and his assistant trial counsel, Captain Benjamin Beliles, without fail, consistently introduced colleagues of Lt. Col. Wilkerson and witnesses for the defense as either "fellow pilot" or "also a pilot."[7] Col. Christensen also ensured the jury knew that Beth's father (who died in an aircraft accident), her stepfather and her first husband were all fighter pilots. She was, he said, "ingrained in the fighter pilot culture."[8]

While examining another colonel, who wore a uniform that clearly bore pilot wings, Christensen said: "And you're a pilot, obviously?"[9] Even when it was obvious to all, Col. Christensen emphasized the identification as a pilot. And when talking about the impromptu gathering at the Wilkerson home that evening, Col. Christensen said, "And I would imagine, in the pilot world, that this happens quite frequently — people get together?"[10] This was a telling remark as Col. Christensen was deliberately attempting to separate the pilot world from that of others, in particular the world of the jurors. (The answer the fighter pilot under direct examination gave was: "I believe, in a normal world, people get together.")

Let's take a high-level look at the case as presented against Lt. Col. Wilkerson. There was absolutely no physical evidence of any kind to support an allegation of sexual assault. There were three incidents, and one side issue, none of which were associated with the night in question — or related to sexual assault — that were of particular interest to the prosecution and consumed quite a bit of the testimony over four days of the five-day trial.

The first incident was the burning of a couch. Upon completion of a combat deployment, it is a fighter pilot tradition to burn a piano. The tradition was handed down from our British Allies in World War II and rejuvenated in the U.S. Air Force during Desert Storm. Typically, a squadron gathers in a prescribed area, takes proper precautions to ensure the fire is controlled, then burns the piano (or couch, in this instance). That was the case in August 2011 when the 77th Fighter Squadron from Shaw Air Force Base completed its combat operations in support of the war in Libya. The men didn't have a piano, so they burned a couch.

Lt. Col. Wilkerson was present at the burning and stepped in to intercede with the Security Forces airmen when they responded. One Security Forces airman was called to testify and said basically that Lt. Col. Wilkerson might have had something to drink and was rude to him. The prosecution portrayed the fighter pilot tradition (of burning something) as a crime and made a big deal of it. They repeatedly raised the issue as if Lt. Col. Wilkerson single-handedly burned the couch in a reckless manner, despite having an affidavit from the 77th Fighter Squadron Commander accepting full responsibility.

The second incident, as relayed by several sources, occurred in 2010 while Lt. Col. Wilkerson was the commander of the 80th Fighter Squadron at Kunsan Air Base, South Korea. Kunsan is a remote, unaccompanied assignment, meaning no wives or family members are permitted on a permanent basis. Some family members visit, but none are allowed to remain on base except for brief visits. The alleged incident occurred in Bruni's, the fighter squadron bar, referred to as a "hooch." Each squadron in Kunsan has a hooch where the squadron members unwind, hang out and often drink, hosting various events and parties throughout their one-year unaccompanied assignment. Bruni's has one, unisex restroom with one urinal and one stall and one main door that locks.

One evening, a squadron event took place there. It was a restricted event, meaning only active duty personnel from the 80th Fighter Squadron were supposed to attend. No one outside of squadron personnel were supposed to be in the building. During this event, there was a commotion in the restroom. Lt. Col. Wilkerson went to investigate. The main door was not locked, and he found several men inside waiting to use the stall. No one inside the stall was answering to repeated calls, so Lt. Col. Wilkerson pulled himself up the stall partition to look over the top to see if anyone was inside. Indeed there was. There were two of his pilots' wives visiting from the United States, hiding in the stall. They had been outside waiting for their husbands, but the weather was hot, so they snuck into the building to get cool and took refuge inside the restroom. Lt. Col. Wilkerson had no expectation that someone other than squadron members might be present. He was unaware the two wives were visiting from the states and therefore had no way of knowing they might be inside the bathroom stall. Lt. Col. Wilkerson immediately dropped to the floor and apologized to both of them when they came out of the stall. Nothing further was said or done, and the issue was dropped.

However, the prosecution repeatedly brought up the incident during the October 2012 trial. A member of the Aviano JAG office, knowing Lt. Col. Wilkerson was under investigation, asked a pilot's wife,

"What's the worst thing you've ever heard Lt. Col. Wilkerson do?" The wife, who was also a civilian employee on Aviano, said she had heard he "peeked" over a stall in the bathroom in Korea. The prosecution raised this issue repeatedly during the trial but offered no first-hand witnesses or statements on the incident. They had only the hearsay story relayed to them by this woman, who wasn't in Korea at the time. The prosecution repeatedly mischaracterized the Korea incident, saying Lt. Col. Wilkerson "peeked" at a woman using the toilet. In short, they embellished a hearsay story to suit their agenda.

The third incident focused on the use of seatbelts in Col. Ostovich's car. More accurately, the focus was on the lack of seatbelt use by two individuals. Remember that during the ride from Aviano Air Base to Lt. Col. Wilkerson's house the night of the alleged assault, seven people rode in a car driven by Col. Ostovich that had seatbelts only for five.

The prosecution argued that Lt. Col. Wilkerson was responsible for two people in the car not wearing seatbelts. There were six officers in the vehicle but, according to the prosecution, Lt. Col. Wilkerson was criminally negligent by not enforcing the seatbelt rule on the other passengers. While there is established Air Force policy for the individual (must wear a seatbelt), and the driver (must ensure every passenger has a seatbelt), there is no guidance, written or otherwise, for a passenger who is properly restrained by a seatbelt as to his or her actions toward others who are not wearing seatbelts.

The other side issue used to slander fighter pilots and Lt. Col. Wilkerson was the singing of fighter pilot songs. When I testified as to Lt. Col. Wilkerson's military character, I was asked these three questions:

"Sir, do you know that on 12 August 2011, the accused, after drinking here on Aviano Air Base, burned a couch...?"

"Were you aware that during his time of being at Kunsan Air base, he intentionally peered over a stall at a female urinating?"

"Were you aware that he has sung sexually explicit raps at squadron functions?"[11]

Sexually explicit raps? The prosecution was attacking another fighter pilot tradition. The singing of songs has been a tradition in all of the U.S. flying services since the beginning of military aviation. And, yes, those songs include curse words and sexual content.

This was a new standard of behavior for the Air Force created by Col. Christensen during this court-martial. It led to several questions for Air Force leaders: Are Air Force personnel now prohibited from singing any songs with foul words in them? Does that include rap songs often heard on the radio? Does that mean we cannot play music with curse words on Air Force bases? Would such a policy apply to all Air Force members, or is it only the fighter pilot community that is prohibited from singing songs with questionable lyrics?

If the charges against Lt. Col. Wilkerson had not been so serious, I would have laughed at the absurdity of the line of questioning. The entire issue was ridiculous and just another attack on the fighter pilot culture.

These incidents were used in an effort to impugn Lt. Col. Wilkerson's military character as "conduct unbecoming of an officer." While the two officers not wearing seatbelts were not punished, Lt. Col. Wilkerson was maligned in a court-martial. It is critical to note that none of the specifications of the charges against Lt. Col. Wilkerson mentioned seatbelt wear, singing songs, burning couches or peering over a wall in a bathroom. These allegations were simply used to throw dirt in front of a non-pilot jury in a general attack on the fighter pilot culture to gain a conviction against one fighter pilot. All of these issues were completely irrelevant to the allegation of sexual assault. In hindsight, the defense should have objected each and every time one of these irrelevant red herrings was offered by the prosecution.

Col. Christensen used a strategy of indicting all fighter pilots, insinuating all of them are bad people. He used the term "fighter pilot" as if it were a dirty word in and of itself. Col. Christensen said this in his closing argument: "He's a fighter pilot — a fighter pilot — he — *we can rely on our common sense and knowledge of the ways of the world...*"[12] (Emphasis added.)

There you have the entire case summed up by the prosecution; *"We can rely on our common sense and knowledge of the ways of the world..."* Col. Christensen clearly intended that our common sense would tell us all of the frat-boy fighter pilots were deviants and guilty of misbehaving, so it must be true that Lt. Col. Wilkerson was guilty of sexual assault.

There was no evidence of sexual assault of any kind presented during the five-day court-martial. It was Hanks' testimony versus the testimony of Beth Wilkerson and the videotaped interview of Lt. Col. Wilkerson — a "he-said, she-said." How could there not be reasonable doubt?

3

Why Risk It All?

"The price of success is hard work, dedication to the job at hand,
and the determination that whether we win or lose,
we have applied the best of ourselves to the task at hand."
— *Vince Lombardi*

I wrote this book because what I witnessed at the court martial of Lt. Col. Wilkerson did not make sense. It didn't fit with my vision of our justice system, and it did not fit with what I knew about Lt. Col. Jay Wilkerson. While I interviewed many people and conducted extensive research, this book is my version of what happened. All of the research is mine, and all of the opinions are mine unless stated otherwise. It is my writing, not that of Lt. Col. Wilkerson or anyone else.

What really didn't make sense to me was that Lt. Col. Wilkerson would risk what he had worked so hard to achieve by assaulting someone. Besides not being that type of guy, he simply had too much to lose, and he had worked too hard and too long to risk it all.

I met the Wilkersons five years earlier in Sumter, South Carolina, when both Lt. Col. Wilkerson and I were stationed at Shaw Air Force Base. Lt. Col. Wilkerson is an energetic, conscientious fighter pilot who worked hard to get where he is. He is a world-class swimmer who nearly made the U.S. Olympic swimming team while a student-athlete at Florida State University. He comes from a Southern family in the Columbia, South Carolina, area and was raised with Southern religious values. I had interacted with him on many occasions in social gatherings and some professional settings as well. While at Shaw, we were in separate work centers and did not interact regularly, but I did occasionally fly with the same fighter squadron. On a social level, I had been to his house and family beach house many times and had seen him when he partied and drank. I had never witnessed or heard of any aggressive behavior toward women or any other indication he was capable of what had been alleged. My wife had also been to the Wilkerson home and beach house, both with and without me, and she likewise has never seen or heard anything that would support the allegations against him at this trial.

Before a young officer pilot candidate can get to pilot training, there must be an available training slot. When Lt. Col. Wilkerson first pinned on the rank of second lieutenant, there were not enough pilot training classes available for him to attend training right away. He joined many other officers at that time who became known as "banked" pilots — those officers slotted for pilot training but waiting for a class start date. His dream of being an Air Force fighter pilot was put on hold.

According to his performance reports, Lt. Col. Wilkerson worked hard in his ground duties and became a standout young officer, a pattern over the first three years that held true throughout twenty years' worth of performance reports.[13]

Three years later, Lt. Col. Wilkerson finally got to pilot training. When a pilot candidate nears the end of Air Force pilot training, he or she is ranked against all others in the same class for abilities. Then, the rankings are matched to the available aircraft assignments and preferences of each student. The top student usually gets one of his or her top three choices. Traditionally, unless one wants to fly for the airlines, the top candidates strive for fighter assignments. As you can imagine, the competition is tough.

When Jay Wilkerson graduated from pilot training, there were not enough fighter assignments for him, and he was assigned to the B-52 Bomber, the venerable BUFF as it is called ("Big Ugly Fat F—"). Still undaunted, Lt. Col. Wilkerson again performed at a high level, impressing his commanders to such a high degree they recommended him for a cross-flow assignment to fighters.[14] In June 2000, Lt. Col. Wilkerson finally achieved his dream. He graduated from F-16 training at Luke Air Force Base in Arizona. He'd made it.[15]

Rather than that being an end to how hard Lt. Col. Wilkerson worked, his performance reports continued to document how quickly he excelled. He worked his way up the ranks, now in the highly competitive F-16 community, to become a squadron operations officer and a highly respected squadron commander.

Beth Wilkerson is the daughter of a fighter pilot who was killed in a training accident. Her step-father is also a fighter pilot. She is an Air Force "brat," having been raised around the fighter pilot culture and having been a part of it much of her adult life. Likewise, I have witnessed firsthand her behavior in social settings like the one on the evening of March 23-24, 2012. Beth has always been a gracious hostess, and it is not out of character for her to tell her husband to go to bed while she waited for the others to leave. Additionally, as mentioned, the evening of the Seether concert, Beth was taking care of the two boys whose father had died; again, something typical of her.

Because the boys were visiting, Beth's version of events made even more sense to me. She would have been naturally attuned to listen for noise coming from the main floor, because that's where the two boys were sleeping.

Additionally, given the current political pressure, the awareness of how aggressively the military is pursuing those accused of sexual assault could not go unnoticed by a senior leader in the air wing. It is unlikely Lt. Col. Wilkerson would not have been acutely aware of the penalties and consequences of a sexual assault. All Air Force members have to undergo annual training, and leaders, even more often. Air Force personnel are taught that one drink — just one drink — makes a woman incapable of legally consenting to sex.[16] It is not possible for Lt. Col. Wilkerson not to have known that.

With an otherwise sterling professional background, and my own personal interaction with Lt. Col Wilkerson as evidence of his character, I could not believe the accusation against him. There was no indication of this type of behavior in his past, and I had personally seen him go to bed while others were visiting only to have Beth visit longer. I have seen both the Wilkersons be kind hosts, so the idea that they would offer a room to Hanks after she refused several offers of a ride to the base was not out of character.

Their story, as provided both in and out of court, matched what I had witnessed before and all that I had ever heard about them. On the other hand, Hanks' version of the allegation kept changing.

4

'SHE SAID'

"If falsehood, like truth, had but one face, we would be more on equal terms. For we would consider the contrary of what the liar said to be certain. But the opposite of truth has a hundred thousand faces and an infinite field."
— *Michel Eyquem de Montaigne*

It is important to review the events of the evening from both sides of the courtroom, accuser and accused. This chapter will focus on Kim Hanks' version or, more accurately, versions of the story. Her testimony was the only evidence of any kind submitted to support her accusation. There was no physical evidence to support her story.

Kim Hanks' evening began with her renting a room on base at the Temporary Lodging Facility (TLF), where she met up with her friends to walk to the concert. She met Captains Brock and Manning and MSgt. Dunnivant at either the TLF or at the concert. They all stopped at the club for drinks after the concert.

During the club visit, Hanks, Captain Manning and Captain Brock met Col. Ostovich, Lt. Col. Wilkerson, Major Goldsberry and Major Lowe. The two Captains knew who Col. Ostovich was because he was the vice wing commander. They were familiar with Major Goldsberry, because his wife was a co-worker of theirs at the Medical Group. None of the women knew Lt. Col. Wilkerson or Major Lowe. Hanks did not know any of the men.

After being introduced to one another and socializing a while at the club, Col. Ostovich and the women decided to continue the evening together. All seven people drove to the Wilkerson home in Col. Ostovich's car. The plan was to drop off Wilkerson and the two majors. The women testified they thought they were going to another bar. Once at the Wilkerson home, Col. Ostovich suggested the "no-notice," or impromptu visit.

The Record of Trial shows the six guests began leaving about 11 p.m., but Hanks repeatedly refused offers to drive her back to the base. By midnight, everyone else had left. Because Hanks refused multiple offers of a ride to the base, Beth eventually offered that Hanks could sleep in the guest room on the lower level of the home. By now, only the Wilkersons, the visiting boys and Hanks remained in the Wilkerson home, and it was believed that everyone had retired for the evening. That was just prior to midnight.

Hanks wrote in a report to the Sexual Assault Response Coordinator the week after the alleged assault that she "passed out" about 0045 to 0100 hours (12:45 to 1 a.m.).[17] Hanks' statement to the Office of Special Investigations (OSI) on April 17, 2012, says: "I was so tired; I remember crawling into the bed fully clothed and turning out the light and went to sleep."[18] She reiterated this in her June 2012 Article 32 testimony: "I was suddenly really tired. They walked me part way down to the room. I went straight to bed."[19]

Hanks' statement continued. She wrote that at approximately 3 to 3:20 a.m. she was "having a dream. It felt like I was floating, and I was being touched over my body. A very bright light came on, I rolled over to cover my eyes and I heard a man say loudly, 'What the hell is going on?' I woke up and felt a hand that was down the front of my pants being removed. I opened my eyes and saw a man about 6 inches from my face squinting with his eyes closed... I heard 'Get the hell out of my house' and looked up and saw Beth at the light. I looked down and saw that I was still fully clothed, with my belt buckled."

Hanks would later add that Lt. Col. Wilkerson, whom she said was the man who was in the bed with her, had penetrated her with his finger. "I felt a little pain on the left side of my inner labia near my vagina. I felt a finger go partially in my vagina. The finger felt like it uncurled and curled in my vagina."[20]

Hanks says she left the Wilkerson home through French doors, scaled the concrete wall and walked around the village until finding "five English-speaking men." She called MSgt. Dunnivant and told her, "They threw me out of the house." Hanks asked one of the men to give MSgt.

Dunnivant directions to their location on the phone so that MSgt. Dunnivant could find her.[21] Hanks testified she drank a beer with the five men while waiting for MSgt. Dunnivant to come pick her up and give her a ride back to the base.[22]

Hanks relayed her allegation of sexual assault to MSgt. Dunnivant during the drive back to the base but asked her to not tell anyone: "She made me promise not to say a word to anyone as she was afraid she would get fired. She is a contractor," MSgt. Dunnivant said. "…I told her she should report it."[23]

MSgt. Dunnivant dropped Hanks back at the TLF about 4 a.m., where she said she slept until 7 or 7:30 a.m. Sometime before she left the TLF, Hanks spoke to Suzanne Berrong on the phone and told Berrong her allegation of sexual assault. At 8:30, Suzanne Berrong met Hanks at her home in Sacile, Italy, and drove her to the medical clinic on base. At the clinic, Hanks was interviewed by Major O'Keefe, a friend and co-worker, who was the technician on duty that morning. Hanks asked Major O'Keefe to run tests for date-rape-type drugs but refused a Sexual Assault Forensic Examination, requested by Major O'Keefe. She told Major O'Keefe "she did not want anything on record."[24] Major O'Keefe also encouraged Hanks to report a sexual assault.

Berrong then drove Hanks back to her residence. Sometime late that week, Hanks met with the Sexual Assault Response Coordinator (SARC) to discuss filing a report of sexual assault. Hanks filed a report with the OSI on April 17, 2012, three and a half weeks later.

5

FLIP SIDE

"To be yourself in a world that is constantly trying to make you something else is the greatest accomplishment."
— *Ralph Waldo Emerson*

Lt. Col. Wilkerson did not testify at the trial but gave an approximately four-hour videotaped interrogation to the Office of Special Investigations (OSI) at Aviano Air Base, portions of which the prosecution used in court. During the entire four hours, Lt. Col. Wilkerson maintained his innocence, repeatedly stating he did not assault Hanks.[25] To this day, Lt. Col. Wilkerson maintains he went to bed about midnight and woke up early the next morning to cook breakfast for the visiting boys and his own son. He denies leaving his bed at any time in between, and he consistently and repeatedly denies assaulting Hanks.

As mentioned previously, this was a "he-said, she-said" case, except it had a twist. The "he-said" story is from Beth Wilkerson, so it became a she-said, she-said trial. During the trial, it was Beth who provided much of the testimony for the defense, because her account of the evening's events involved interaction with Hanks. Beth's account is quite different from Hanks'. Beth's statement, Article 32 testimony and trial testimony are remarkably consistent. She claims Hanks was up wandering the house in the middle of the night at least twice. When Beth confronted her the second time, Hanks left the house. According to both Wilkersons, Lt. Col. Wilkerson was never present in the room where Hanks says the alleged assault occurred. Both Lt. Col. Wilkerson and Beth Wilkerson say he never left his bed after he retired for the evening.

Beth states that after she returned from driving Captain Brock back to the base, she realized Col. Ostovich and Captain Manning had left together. Their departure left Kim Hanks there without her friends and without a ride home. At that time, before the two majors left for the evening, both majors and Beth again discussed with Hanks driving her back to the base. Hanks again refused a ride. She said she had misplaced her shoes again and didn't want to walk on base without them. Beth testified she offered Hanks a pair of shoes or sandals to wear to go back, but Hanks refused that offer as well.[26]

The Air Force is strict about drinking and driving. Beth, who never intended to leave her home that evening, had consumed a glass of wine and did not want to drive through the gate to drop Hanks off. Beth said she would drop Hanks at the gate as she had done for Captain Brock. The walk from the gate to Hanks' rented room was a thousand to two thousand feet, less than one third of a mile. Hanks said she didn't want to walk through the gate without shoes and refused to accept shoes Beth offered to loan her, Beth testified. "I decided she could stay the night," she said. "I put her in the playroom in the basement, gave her a bottle of water and said goodnight."[27] This was just before midnight.

Beth testified that, a short time later: "I heard Kim Hanks talking. I don't know who she was talking to." Beth went back downstairs to investigate, and Hanks was talking on her phone and "leaning against the stove in the kitchen. She was upset because her friends left her. I told her to be quiet. She calmed down, told her friend 'the wife' was there and that she ('the wife') was going to make tea or coffee. I made her some tea and some coffee for myself. When we finished, I sent Kim back downstairs."[28] This account was corroborated by Suzanne Berrong, the woman on the other end of the 12:30 a.m. phone call. Berrong was Hanks' best friend at the time and had never met the Wilkersons.

Beth testified that after the tea and talk, she went back upstairs to bed. She thought the time was about 1:40 a.m., which is corroborated by Hanks' phone records. Those records indicate Hanks sent another text at 1:43 a.m.[29] Beth testified further: "Fifteen to 20 minutes later, I heard Kim Hanks back in the kitchen. I went back downstairs. Kim was near the room where the visiting boys were sleeping," on the main floor of the house. "I asked Kim what she was doing. I gave her two choices: Leave or go back downstairs to bed. Kim opened the back door, grabbed her purse and glasses and left."[30]

Beth said she didn't think Kim Hanks would leave, but when she did, Beth put on a coat and drove around the village looking for her. She intended to, once again, offer Hanks a ride to the base, but she did not find Hanks. Beth testified she returned home and went back to bed. The next day, she found Hanks' shoes in the bedroom where the visiting boys slept and noticed the bed in the basement was never slept in.[31]

6

THE CHARGES

"Whatever is begun in anger ends in shame."
— *Benjamin Franklin*

Here listed are the charges filed against Lt. Col. Wilkerson on June 14, 2012:

II. CHARGES AND SPECIFICATIONS

CHARGE I: Violation of the UCMJ, Article 120

Specification 1: Abusive Sexual Contact. In that LIEUTENANT COLONEL JAMES H. WILKERSON, United States Air Force, 31st Operations Group, Aviano Air Base, Italy, did, at or near Roveredo in Piano, Italy, on or about 24 March 2012, engage in sexual contact with Ms. Kimberly Hanks, to wit: fondling her breasts with his hands, doing so when Ms. Kimberly Hanks was substantially incapable of appraising the nature of the sexual contact.

Specification 2: Aggravated Sexual Assault. In that LIEUTENANT COLONEL JAMES H. WILKERSON, United States Air Force, 31st Operations Group, Aviano Air Base, Italy, did, at or near Roveredo in Piano, Italy, on or about 24 March 2012, engage in a sexual act with Ms. Kimberly Hanks, to wit: digital penetration of her vagina, doing so when Ms. Kimberly Hanks was substantially incapable of appraising the nature of the sexual act.

CHARGE II: Violation of the UCMJ, Article 133

Specification 1: Conduct Unbecoming of an Officer and a Gentleman. In that LIEUTENANT COLONEL JAMES H. WILKERSON, United States Air Force, 31st Operations Group, Aviano Air Base, Italy, a married man, did, at or near Roveredo in Piano, Italy, on or about 24 March 2012, wrongfully enter a bed occupied by Ms. Kimberly Hanks, a woman not his wife, which act, under the circumstances, constituted conduct unbecoming an officer and a gentleman.

Specification 2: Conduct Unbecoming of an Officer and a Gentleman. In that LIEUTENANT COLONEL JAMES H. WILKERSON, United States Air Force, 31st Operations Group, Aviano Air Base, Italy, a married man, did, at or near Roveredo in Piano, Italy, on or about 24 March 20 12, wrongfully engage in sexual contact with Ms. Kimberly Hanks, a woman not his wife, to wit: fondling her breasts with his hands, which act, under the circumstances, constituted conduct unbecoming an officer and a gentleman.

Specification 3: Conduct Unbecoming of an Officer and a Gentleman. In that LIEUTENANT COLONEL JAMES H. WILKERSON, United States Air Force, 31st Operations Group, Aviano Air Base, Italy, a married man, did, at or near Roveredo in Piano, Italy, on or about 24 March 2012, wrongfully engage in a sexual act with Ms. Kimberly Hanks, a woman not his wife, to wit: digital penetration of her vagina, which act, under the circumstances, constituted conduct unbecoming an officer and a gentleman.

Note that each of the specifications in charge No. 1 includes the words "substantially incapable." "Substantially incapable" is a legal term meaning the alleged victim was asleep, drunk, or drugged and not substantially capable of understanding the sexual nature of the actions of the alleged attacker. As explained by Lindsay L. Rodman in *Joint Forces Quarterly*, April, 2013:

The Uniform Code of Military Justice (UCMJ) 14 defines *aggravated sexual assault* as a sexual act committed against the victim by placing the victim in fear, causing bodily harm, or committing the act while the victim was "substantially incapacitated." Anecdotally, substantial incapacitation is the most frequently charged type of aggravated sexual assault. *Rape*, by contrast, is defined in most cases as a sexual act by force. But it can also be charged for rendering the victim unconscious, personally administering a drug or intoxicant causing substantial incapacitation, causing grievous bodily harm, or placing the victim in fear of death, grievous bodily harm, or kidnapping.[32]

Sexual assault is covered under Article 120 of the Uniform Code of Military Justice (UCMJ):

Punitive Articles of the UCMJ Article 120:
Rape, sexual assault, and other sexual misconduct

Upon a person substantially incapacitated or substantially incapable of appraising the act, declining participation, or communicating unwillingness:

(i) That the accused engaged in a sexual act with another person, who is of any age; and (Note: add one of the following elements)

(ii) That the other person was substantially incapacitated;

(iii) That the other person was substantially incapable of appraising the nature of the sexual act;

(iv) That the other person was substantially incapable of declining participation in the sexual act; or

(v) That the other person was substantially incapable of communicating unwillingness to engage in the sexual act.[33]

Substantial incapacitation requires either sleep, alcohol or drugs to a level where the victim is substantially incapable of appraising the nature of the act or substantially incapable of saying no. By definition, Kim Hanks could not have been substantially incapacitated without one of those three requisites. The defense intended to show Hanks had none of these.

Charge No. 2 addresses "Conduct unbecoming of an Officer and a Gentleman," covered under Article 133 of the UCMJ.

Punitive Articles of the UCMJ Article 133: Conduct unbecoming an officer and gentleman

(2) *Nature of offense.* Conduct violative of this article is action or behavior in an official capacity which, in dishonoring or disgracing the person as an officer, seriously compromises the officer's character as a gentleman, or action or behavior in an unofficial or private capacity which, in dishonoring or disgracing the officer personally, seriously compromises the person's standing as an officer. There are certain moral attributes common to the ideal officer and the perfect gentleman, a lack of which is indicated by acts of dishonesty, unfair dealing, indecency, indecorum, lawlessness, injustice, or cruelty. Not everyone is or can be expected to meet unrealistically high moral standards, but there is a limit of tolerance based on customs of the service and military necessity below which the personal standards of an officer, cadet, or midshipman cannot fall without seriously compromising the person's standing as an officer, cadet, or midshipman or the person's character as a gentleman. This article prohibits conduct by a commissioned officer, cadet or midshipman which, taking all the circumstances into consideration, is thus compromising. This article includes acts made punishable by any other article, provided these acts amount to conduct unbecoming an officer and a

gentleman. Thus, a commissioned officer who steals property violates both this article and **Article 121**. Whenever the offense charged is the same as a specific offense set forth in this Manual, the elements of proof are the same as those set forth in the paragraph which treats that specific offense, with the additional requirement that the act or omission constitutes conduct unbecoming an officer and gentleman.[34]

Conduct unbecoming is not normally prosecuted on its own. It usually accompanies other charges. In this case, the alleged sexual assault was what constituted the "conduct unbecoming." It is important to understand that while the prosecutor spent a great deal of time on the burning of a couch, the Korea incident and the seatbelts, none of those were the bases for any charges. None of those were specified in the charges or specifications, nor was singing sexually explicit rap or Air Force heritage songs. Those issues were not part of the charges and therefore were frivolous and irrelevant to the case. I asked the defense attorney why he did not object to this information being admitted. He stated these were small issues and not important. It would slow things down and might upset the court if he kept objecting. In hindsight, it is my firm belief that the defense should have objected to them each and every time they were raised. A great deal of time and testimony focused on issues outside of the charges, issues that were obviously used to insinuate Lt. Col. Wilkerson was an overall bad guy, so he must be guilty. Evidently, that tactic did help convict a fighter pilot of sexual assault.

7

THE RECORD

"The truth is more important than the facts."
— *Frank Lloyd Wright*

"Reasonable doubt" is the standard of proof required to convict a defendant in criminal proceedings. This premise is the same inside the military justice system. It is the highest standard of proof and is required in criminal cases because our criminal justice system is based on the "value determination of our society that it is far worse to convict an innocent man than to let a guilty man go free."[35] The prosecution *must prove* guilt *beyond a reasonable doubt.* When jurors have reasonable doubt whether the defendant is guilty, they should reach a not-guilty verdict. If jurors have *no doubt* or their doubts are *unreasonable,* they may find the defendant guilty.

So, what really happened? Based on all I know, I believed Jay Wilkerson was innocent. So how did these five jurors conclude otherwise beyond a reasonable doubt? What went wrong with the trial? If he was innocent, as I suspected he was, I wanted to do my utmost to correct this wrongful conviction. I was embarrassed and angry at what I perceived was an unprofessional investigation and a railroad job in court. I wanted to know the truth.

About six weeks after the trial concluded, in accordance with law, the Air Force provided Lt. Col. Wilkerson and the defense a written transcript known as the "Record of Trial." Two weeks after receiving the Record of Trial, any comments or additional information the defense felt relevant to the trial and sentencing was due to the convening authority; in this case, Lieutenant General Craig Franklin, 3rd Air Force Commander. This is known as the clemency review phase. "Clemency is a highly discretionary command function of a convening authority."[36] It is that phase of the military court-martial process where the Convening

Authority reviews the trial evidence, verdict, and punishment — to add another set of eyes on the process. The purpose of this clemency review by the Convening Authority is to seek agreement with the verdict and sentence. Under the Uniform Code of Military Justice (UCMJ), the Convening Authority may modify (reduce) a sentence or, in rare circumstances, set aside a finding of guilty.

During clemency, the defense may submit additional information on the defendant's behalf that the Convening Authority may, or may not, consider. It is normal procedure for family and friends of the defendant to submit letters to the Convening Authority during this clemency phase. The Convening Authority then approves or disapproves the verdict and the sentencing. The clemency phase of the Wilkerson trial lasted four months — a significantly longer than normal amount of time.

The defense had two weeks to write and submit clemency information. During that time, I dedicated myself to researching the Record of Trial. This was an opportunity to really understand what happened that night from the reports, statements and testimony of everyone involved. It wasn't hearing someone else's recounting of what happened during a trial; this opportunity to research the entire record provided a full view from all of the players as the events unfolded.

During my research, it became obvious to me that to understand what may or may not have happened was critically dependent on determining and understanding the timeline. As I researched the Record of Trial, I attempted to put a timeline together to follow the story as it developed (not in hindsight but as it unfolded). I planned to go where the facts led as if I were an investigator. Unfortunately, there are multiple versions of the evening's events.

With the goal of finding the truth, I read every word of the Record of Trial from the first witness statement to the final sentencing. I read the first person's statement and, within ten minutes, I knew something wasn't right.

What follows is as faithful to the facts and the Record of Trial as I can determine, with references cited extensively for each document.

THE TIMELINE

The alleged incident occurred on the night of March 23-24, 2012. This timeline lists only the facts as agreed to by testimony. The missing middle of the timeline, where the stories differ, is discussed in detail later. This establishes the facts.

12 a.m. (midnight): Everyone in the Wilkerson home was in bed or had been shown to a bedroom.

12:23 to 12:38 a.m.: Hanks was in the kitchen on the main floor of the Wilkerson home on the phone with Suzanne Berrong as Beth Wilkerson entered the room.

Between 12:38 and 1:43 a.m.: Beth Wilkerson and Hanks had tea and then retired again, Beth to the top level and Hanks to the basement guestroom.

1:43 a.m.: Hanks sent a text to another friend, Master Sergeant (MSgt) Dunnivant. The text is lucid and correctly spelled.

3:02 a.m.: Hanks reached MSgt. Dunnivant on her cell phone and asked her to come pick her up.

3 to 3:20 a.m.: Hanks says she drank a beer with five English-speaking men on the street corner while waiting for MSgt. Dunnivant.

3:20 a.m.: MSgt. Dunnivant drove Hanks to the air base.

4:06 a.m.: Hanks sent another text to Berrong.

6:33 a.m.: Hanks began another thirty-minute phone call with Berrong.

8:30 a.m.: Berrong picked Hanks up from her home in Sacile.

9 a.m.: Hanks and Berrong enter the Aviano Medical Clinic through the back entrance, and Hanks begins her interview with Major O'Keefe.

Hanks went to the Sexual Assault Response Coordinator on March 29.[37]

The Office of Special Investigations (OSI) interviews were conducted on the following days:

Kim Hanks: April 17, 2012
Captain Tanya Manning: April 18, 2012
Captain Dawn Brock: April 18, 2012
Suzanne Berrong: April 19, 2012

Lt. Col. James Wilkerson: April 19, 2012
Mrs. Beth Wilkerson: April 19, 2012
MSgt. Danielle Dunnivant: April 20, 2012
Colonel Dean Ostovich: April 23, 2012
Major Gerremy Goldsberry: April 24, 2012
Major Michael O'Keefe: April 25, 2012

These are the hard facts agreed to (eventually) by all relevant parties. It is a simple timeline, with the central question being, what happened between 1:43 and 3:02? Let's assume it took a minimum of fifteen minutes for Hanks to find her way out of the yard and to the center of the small village. What happened in the hour between 1:43 and 2:45 a.m.?

INCONSISTENCIES

My intense research and scrutiny of the timeline uncovered a number of readily available and easily recognizable inconsistencies and unusual aspects of Hanks' story.

When did Hanks go to sleep, if at all?

Central to the case is that Kim Hanks claims she was asleep in the bed about 12:45 a.m.: "I was suddenly so tired ... I went straight to sleep ..." and that she awoke at "approximately 0300 to 0320" with a man in bed with her and Beth Wilkerson telling her to get out of the house. In her initial statement submitted to the OSI on April 17, 2012, Hanks wrote that as she was leaving the house: "I checked my phone and it was I think 0320."[38] During Oct. 29 testimony at the trial, Hanks testified that she tried to reach MSgt. Dunnivant between 3 and 3:30 a.m., adjusting her timing in this version of her story to an earlier time in the night.[39] No longer did she say it was 3:20 when she left the Wilkerson home. In fact, her phone records prove she attempted to contact Suzanne Berrong twice just prior to 3 a.m. and reached MSgt. Dunnivant at 3:02 a.m. Hanks changed her timeline after she had access to her phone records. She now understood it could not have been 3:20 when she checked her phone, as she had spoken with MSgt. Dunnivant at 3:02.

There are two major issues with the timeline Hanks provided. First, in trial testimony, she admits her first written account of the alleged assault — the fact sheet she filled out for the Sexual Assault Response Coordinator (SARC) — says, "I passed out in the bed with my clothes on at about 12:45 to 1 a.m."[40] Phone records prove she was on the phone from 12:23 to 12:38 and did not go to bed right away as she stated. Hanks changed her version of the story during her Article 32 hearing testimony: "I talked to Suzanne Berrong on the phone but didn't initially remember until she reminded me the next day."[41] This is important, because when Berrong picked Hanks up at her home the next morning, Hanks told Berrong she had tea with Beth after their phone call. Berrong verified this again by testifying that she heard Hanks say during the 12:23-12:38 a.m. phone call that "the wife was going to make her some tea."[42]

Berrong's statement corroborates Beth's version of the timeline. Beth says that after she found Hanks up, talking loudly on the phone shortly after midnight, they had tea and coffee and talked for about forty minutes before going off to bed again. In this version of the timeline, Hanks was not asleep between 12:45 and 1 a.m., as she had written in her statement, but rather was awake at least until 1:30.

The next major discrepancy with Hanks' version of the timeline comes less than ten minutes after saying a second time that she was in bed asleep. During Hanks' trial testimony, she testified that after drinking tea and talking, she "fell right asleep." "I still had all of my clothes on and crawled in under the covers and turned off the light and ... fell asleep."[43] However, phone records again prove Hanks was not asleep as she said a second time. These records show Hanks sent another text from her phone at 1:43 a.m. The text was clear and understandable and had no typographical errors. When pressed by defense counsel during cross-examination at the court-martial, Hanks admitted, "No, I said I was probably not asleep yet."[44] In fact, phone records prove Hanks was not asleep— as she twice testified. With regard to this timeline, to this point, Hanks has been proven to have inaccurately described the truth, twice.

There are more inconsistencies between the reported timeline and actual events. MSgt. Dunnivant received a phone call from Hanks at exactly 3:02 a.m. The defense had a screen shot of the incoming call on MSgt. Dunnivant's phone with the date and time stamp. The timing of this call is inconsistent with Hanks' original statement saying she was in the house until approximately 3 to 3:20 a.m. before anything happened.[45] Remember, Hanks wrote that she "checked my phone and it was I think 3:20" when she left the Wilkerson home.[46] We now know this is not accurate.

The Wilkerson home is about a ten-minute walk from the village downtown area if one is familiar with how to get out of the walled yard and knows the route to the village center. There is no way of knowing how long it actually took Hanks to walk to the village center or which path she took. Assuming Hanks immediately found a place to scale the wall and that she walked directly to the village center, she had to have been out of the house no later than 2:45 a.m. Phone records prove she sent a text at 1:43 and called MSgt. Dunnivant at 3:02. That leaves, at the outside, only one hour for her to have fallen asleep and the alleged incident to take place — enough time, if you assume that after her 1:43 text, she immediately went to sleep.

The morning timeline Hanks testifies to is also confusing. She states MSgt. Dunnivant took her back to the room she had at the Temporary Lodging Facility (TLF) on base. In her April 17 statement, she wrote "back at the TLF I slept."[47] In her Article 32 testimony she expands this to: "When I got to the TLF, I set my alarm for 07:30 hours" and added: "The next morning, I was really out of it. I went online, I was concerned about how I had been feeling because I was so out of it. I looked up my symptoms online."[48]

During the trial, Hanks testified in greater detail, saying once she returned to the TLF about 4 to 4:15 a.m.: "I went right to sleep, initially. And then, and then I woke up about I think 7-7:30. And I was concerned about how I was feeling because I didn't feel like really, really drunk. And there was a part of me that was concerned that I might have been drugged... So I looked up what the date rape drugs were, and what the symptoms were. And they were pretty — they were pretty vague; covered a lot of things."[49]

Hanks claims she "went right to sleep" (again) after she returned to her lodging room on base. She is explicit that she set her alarm for "07:30 hours." However, her phone records and physical location again prove otherwise. MSgt. Dunnivant picked her up in the village between 3:20 and 3:30 and drove her back to base, a trip that took about fifteen minutes. Hanks' statement about being back in her room about 4 a.m. is probably accurate. At 4:06, Hanks sent a text to Suzanne Berrong saying she wanted to talk. At 06:33, Berrong called Hanks. They talked for more than thirty minutes.

Berrong picked up Kim Hanks at her home in Sacile sometime around 8:30 a.m. Sometime between 4 a.m. and 8:30 a.m., when Berrong arrived at Hanks' home in Sacile, Hanks had checked out of her room on base and driven home — a drive of at least 20 minutes. There would have been a record of Hanks checking out of the TLF, but it appears the OSI did not check this. There is no mention of any investigator verifying, or even asking, if her statement is accurate. Also between 4 and 8:30 a.m., Hanks claims to have conducted an Internet research on date rape drugs. When Berrong arrived at her home, Hanks told her a version of the assault slightly different than what she told MSgt. Dunnivant and then said she thought maybe she had been drugged.[50] Berrong drove Hanks to the medical clinic back on base. According to Major O'Keefe, a friend and co-worker, and the medical technician on duty that morning, Hanks arrived at the clinic at "approximately 9 a.m."[51]

Piecing together a timeline from the facts, it is easy to see Hanks is again not accurate (truthful?) in her story. She could not have been asleep until 7 or 7:30 a.m. as she said, because she was, once again, on the phone with Berrong. If she checked out of her room and drove home immediately after her phone call with Berrong, there wasn't much time to conduct an Internet search that, as she testified, "covered a lot of things" before Berrong arrived at her home. At most, Hanks may have slept from about 4:15 to 6:33 a.m. Phone records once again prove she is not telling the truth when she testified she slept until 7 or 7:30.

Beth Wilkerson maintained throughout the entire process, from initial interview to trial testimony, that Kim Hanks was up and walking about the house a second time prior to 3 a.m. Beth stated she found Hanks at the entrance to the bedroom where the two visiting boys were sleeping on the main floor and that she found Hanks' shoes in that room, next to the bed, late the next day.[52] Everyone agreed Hanks had been in the bedroom visiting with the boys at some time during the evening, and

Hanks' own testimony is that she "normally" takes her shoes off when she enters a house and that she often does so at home as well as at work. [53]

Finally, Beth Wilkerson testified that after Hanks left, Beth got in her car and drove around looking for her to offer her another ride home. Beth testified she returned home from driving to see the clock in the kitchen as she came in indicating "a little before 3 o'clock in the morning."[54] If it were still prior to 3 a.m. when Beth returned, then Hanks departed the house even earlier than 2:45. Did Hanks sleep at all? She texted MSgt. Dunnivant at 1:43 a.m. and called MSgt. Dunnivant at 3:02. Beth said it was about fifteen to twenty minutes after they finished tea that she heard Hanks up and about again. Perhaps she actually left the house closer to 2:20 a.m. (Hanks' statement said she looked at her cell phone and it said 3:20 — maybe she did look at her cell phone as she left, and it said 2:20.) That would make sense and fit a logical timeline if it took her a while to find a place to scale the concrete wall. Hanks would have been very lucky to find a low spot to climb over immediately. Perhaps she wandered in a roundabout route to the village center. She would also have been lucky to find the shortest path to the village center on the first attempt. Perhaps more time passed than she testified before calling MSgt. Dunnivant.

The timeline presented by other testimony does not support Hanks' version of what happened. Hanks' version is loaded with inconsistencies. On the other hand, the timeline supported by testimony of multiple other witnesses closely aligns with the testimony and statements of Beth Wilkerson.

In addition to the timeline issues, another question seems obvious: Why didn't Hanks leave the Wilkerson home when given multiple opportunities?

One of the most puzzling oddities of the evening is that Hanks did not accept any of multiple offers of a ride back to the base. Why did Kim Hanks stay at the Wilkerson home? She didn't know the Wilkersons — she only just met them both that evening, Lt. Col. Wilkerson at the club and Beth Wilkerson when the group arrived at the Wilkerson house. Why did Kim Hanks refuse multiple offers of rides back to the base but instead choose to stay in a house where she knew no one? Or, for that matter, why didn't she ask for a ride to her own home in Sacile or accept the ride offered by her best friend, Suzanne Berrong?

Why didn't Hanks take a ride when Beth drove Captain Brock back to the base? Her Article 32 testimony says she told Captain Brock she was ready to leave. "I saw Captain Brock and we both said we were ready to go. I told Captain Manning I was ready to go. I was not aware of others leaving. They took Captain Brock home and left her outside the gate."[55]

Captain Manning testified at the trial: "At some point ... each of them (Brock and Hanks) came out ... to let me know they were leaving. ... At the time I left, I had — I had assumed that they both left together ... they both had indicated they had a ride."[56]

Captain Dawn Brock testified: Beth "said to ask the other individuals — that she could (drive me back to base) — but ask the other individuals if they also wanted to go back to base. ... I'm pretty sure I had mentioned it to Kim. I can't recall for sure now. I know that I went out to Manning and told her that I was leaving, and find out if she wanted to go, and she was fine. I just — I don't remember the conversation exactly with Kim like I do walking outside to Manning. ... I did float through everybody. I just — I don't remember what the individual conversations were."

Hanks' trial testimony elaborates further:

> Q. At some point was there some discussion about people leaving for the evening?
> A. Yes. There was — I saw both Tanya and Dawn. Dawn, I remember distinctly because we're — she was coming down and I was going up the staircase, and we met at the landing. And I asked her if, you know, if she was ready to go, and she said, "yes," and I said, "Yeah, me too." And we talked briefly about let's see who we can let know that we'd like to go home.[57]

This testimony raises questions about how Hanks was left behind. Did Captain Brock, whom Kim Hanks said she told she was ready to go, just blow off her friend and take the ride from Beth without saying, "Hey,

Kim wants to leave, too"? Would Captain Brock have left her friend there after Beth asked her specifically to check with the others and, according to Captain Brock's testimony, she was "pretty sure I had mentioned it to Kim"? Why would Captain Brock leave without Kim if Kim had told her she was "ready to go"? Why wouldn't Captain Brock have waited for and taken Kim with her?

Hanks' trial testimony is contradictory with respect to another offer of a ride home, that by Major Goldsberry and Major Lowe. After Beth returned from dropping Captain Brock at the gate, she, Major Goldsberry and Major Lowe again discussed who would drive Hanks home."[58] In her Article 32 testimony and under direct examination by the prosecutor, Hanks said she did not remember this conversation. However, under cross-examination, she admitted that one of them did say they would figure out a way to get her home. She declined this ride also. Testimony indicates she refused this time because she couldn't find her shoes again.[59]

Here is her testimony under direct examination:

> Q. Did Major Goldsberry or Major Lowe ever offer you a ride home?
> A. No. I don't know how they got home.

But when cross-examined, Hanks changed her story:

> Q. Do you recall Major Goldsberry or Major Lowe saying that they'd figure out how to get you home?
> A. They said, "Yeah, we'll figure out a way." I don't know if they were specifically directing it towards me, but I think, in general, they were saying, "Yeah, we'll figure out a way."[60]

This is also an interesting answer: "In general, they were saying" but "I don't know if they were specifically directing it towards me." Interesting, because there was no one else left at that time who might need a ride. Each of the Majors had his own car outside, so they could not have been talking about each other. The Wilkersons lived there. Who else could they have been talking about? So, evidence shows Hanks did have another offer for a ride home, which she also refused.

The lead defense attorney for Lt. Col. Wilkerson, Frank Spinner, asked Hanks during cross-examination: "Do you recall at your Article 32 testimony, when you were asked about things that you don't remember, you said you don't remember whether Major Goldsberry or Major Lowe said that they'd figure out how to get you home?"[61]

Hanks offered a confusing answer that seemed to deflect the question but did admit that she had testified she did not remember whether Major Goldsberry or Major Lowe said that they'd figure out how to get her home.[62] She confuses her answer, stating she didn't remember which one of the two officers had said it, not whether they had discussed it with her. At this point in her trial cross-examination, it is clear Hanks was either terribly confused or was being purposefully evasive. Earlier, her answers to the prosecutor were clear.[63]

Hanks said in her Article 32 testimony: "I never talked to Major Goldsberry or Major Albert Lowe after we arrived at the party."[64] In the trial, several months later, she admits that statement wasn't true.

There was one more offer of a ride from Beth, and one more refusal. In her Article 32 testimony, Hanks said: "Beth Wilkerson offered me a ride to base after she said everyone had gone. I said I couldn't stay at the house. I was freaking out that I had been left at the house. I didn't take Beth up on the offer to get a ride."[65]

At the trial, Hanks said: "She offered me to stay there, and I said: 'I don't want to stay. I really need to go back. I've got a room at the TLF.' So she offered to take me back..." But Hanks was concerned about being dropped off outside the gate and having to pass through security after she had been drinking, so she refused this ride also.[66]

If I were "freaking out" about being left, and "I couldn't stay," and I told the woman of the house, "I don't want to stay. I really need to go back," why would I stay? Why refuse yet again? Hanks didn't tell Beth at the time, but during testimony, she admitted she was concerned about walking through the Air Force base gate and its security after she had been drinking: "I was worried about going past the gate people intoxicated." Hanks also testified she heard others say, "if you go through and you have alcohol on your breath and you're going through the gate, it's a big deal. I didn't know — I didn't really want to be dropped off. I didn't know how far I'd have to walk to the TLF. And you know, I had been drinking, so I was concerned about getting in trouble."[67]

The distance between the gate and her TLF room was not far. Depending on which building her room was in, the walk from the gate is a thousand to two thousand feet. Accepting a ride and being dropped at the gate appears to be a semi-normal event because of the Air Force's policies on drinking and driving. Earlier, Captain Brock took the ride back to the gate from Beth and didn't raise an issue with walking through the gate to the TLF. Hanks' concern was that she did not want to appear to the gate security to have been drinking, rather than concern over the distance she might have to walk. If passing security personnel was such a concern and she really didn't want to stay at the Wilkersons, there was another option. Why didn't she ask for a ride to her home in Sacile? That village — Sacile itself — was only fifteen minutes away, nearly as close as the base.

Shortly after saying "I don't want to stay" but deciding not to leave, Hanks called Suzanne Berrong. Berrong testified at the Article 32 hearing: "Around midnight, I spoke to Kim Hanks on the phone for about fifteen minutes. She said she had been left at a house. She didn't know where she was or who she was with. She sounded drunk. I offered her a ride multiple times. I asked her if there was someone there who could tell me where she was. I heard a woman's voice in the background and told Kim to put her on the phone to give me directions so I could come get her. Kim was talking about tea. I heard Kim tell the woman it was too far for me to come get Kim. She told me multiple times she didn't know where she was or who she was with."[68] Here was another offer of a ride, this time one without the restriction of being dropped at the gate. Why not accept this offer of a ride from a best friend who repeatedly said she would come get her?

Berrong testified that she offered multiple times to come give Hanks a ride home and asked Hanks to let her talk to "the wife," as Hanks had called Beth Wilkerson.[69] Berrong said Hanks refused to let them talk to each other and refused repeated offers by Berrong to come get her. Why?

Hanks' written statement for the OSI on April 17 said that at approximately 12:45 a.m., "I called my girlfriend. I didn't remember calling her until she told me — she said, 'you were slurring your words — you were making sense and sort of not making sense; it didn't sound like you.' I remember telling her I didn't know where I was but that it is too late and too far to drive and I will stay there."[70]

The obvious question is, if Hanks didn't know where she was, how could she think it was too far for her friend to come get her? It could have been very close, maybe even in the same village. It was actually about a fifteen-minute drive from Berrong's home to the Wilkerson home. But no one knew that at the time. Kim Hanks did not allow Beth Wilkerson to tell Suzanne Berrong where they were.

Hanks' trial testimony about the phone call to Berrong was unconvincing. In this testimony, she attempted to explain why she refused Berrong's repeated offers. "Ah, I was pretty upset, and she — I told her, you know, that everyone left me and she offered — she said, 'Where are you?' And I said, 'I don't know.' And she said, 'Well, I can come pick you up.' And I said, 'You know it's probably too far.' And at this point I was embarrassed. I was, you know, I was crying and the Wilkersons were hearing, and I didn't know them. It was late, late, late, and I just — so I said: 'Just forget it. I will stay here, I, it's okay. I'm just going to stay here tonight.' "[71]

So Hanks testified she did not want to stay at the Wilkersons, was "freaking out," did not know where she was or how long a drive it might be, but she refused to let her best friend find out where she was.

Now, let's analyze Beth Wilkerson's account of what happened. Beth's statement to the OSI says: "There was one girl left that I tried to either take to the base or offered her a place to sleep."[72] Beth's Article 32 testimony said: "Within thirty minutes after I returned from dropping off Captain Brock, everyone left ... There was some talk of Kim Hanks leaving with Major Gerremy Goldsberry and Major Albert Lowe, but she had lost her shoes again and didn't want to walk on base without shoes. I decided she could stay the night."[73]

During the trial, Beth testified:

Q. What — did you offer anyone else a ride at that point? Since you were going to that trouble to take her (Captain Brock) back to the base, did you offer a ride to anyone else?

A. I offered a ride to Kim Hanks. She was standing — when I went back in, I told Jay that I was going to take her (Captain Brock) back to the base, and Kim Hanks was standing there, and I asked her if she wanted to ride back to the base.

Q. What did she say?

A. "No. No, I'll just stay here." Or "No." It was definite she wasn't going with me.

Beth's account of the evening, including the details of offering Hanks multiple opportunities for a ride to the base, is consistent from her first statement to the OSI on April 19, 2012, through her Article 32 testimony in June and the court-martial in late October.

Why did Kim Hanks refuse multiple opportunities of a ride back to Aviano and refuse to leave a stranger's house? Only Kim Hanks knows that. The bottom line is that she had multiple offers to leave the Wilkerson home, to be dropped off outside the gate and even to be picked up by her best friend and driven on the base proper. She refused them all.

THE PANTS QUESTION

Another inconsistency in statements and testimony is whether or not Kim Hanks' belt and or pants were undone. She claims her assailant's hand was in her pants, so this point is relevant.

MSgt. Dunnivant testified in the Article 32 hearing: "Kim said her pants were undone."[74] And again in trial testimony, MSgt. Dunnivant said: Kim "told me... 'and you know my pants were unbuttoned.' "[75] Hanks, however, testified her pants were not undone.[76]

According to MSgt. Dunnivant — the first person Hanks relayed her story to — Hanks said her pants were undone. But Hanks did not say anything about her pants being undone or not undone to Suzanne

Berrong during the 6:33 a.m. phone call or during the 8:30 a.m. drive to the base. When Major O'Keefe interviewed her in the medical clinic and asked to do an examination, she made no mention of whether her pants or belt had been undone as she refused the exam. This seems like a relevant detail for an allegation of sexual assault. Hanks is a physician's assistant and clearly knows the possibility of DNA or bruising evidence.

Later, in testimony under oath, Hanks denied telling MSgt. Dunnivant that her pants were undone. But why would MSgt. Dunnivant make that up? Col. Christensen, the lead prosecutor, throughout the trial kept saying of Hanks: "She has no reason to lie." To apply his logic, then, what reason would MSgt. Dunnivant have to lie with respect to Hanks telling her that her pants were undone?

Was a hand inside Hanks' pants?

The story of a hand being inside Hanks' pants also has inconsistencies. First, it appears to be a physical challenge to perform the act as Hanks describes it. She told Major O'Keefe at the Medical Group that the man was "lying on her with his hand down her pants."[77] She testified during the trial: "I was on my back ... it got really bright. I rolled over on my left side and felt a hand come out of my pants. I heard a guy yell loudly, 'What the hell is going on?' I sat up. My belt was still buckled, and my clothes were still on."[78]

This description of events drew skepticism from women who've read it. One clemency letter asked: "How could a grown man get his hand down her pants, which were still buttoned / zipped / buckled? Moreover, even if he could do this, how could he do this without waking her up?"[79]

The story, as relayed to Berrong — the second person with whom Kim Hanks discussed the alleged assault — is different than the testimony of MSgt. Dunnivant. In Berrong's April 19 statement, she wrote: Kim "saw his face and his hand starting to go down her pants."[80]

Was his hand "starting to go down her pants" as Hanks told Berrong, or was it "being removed" as she said in her own statement? Were her pants undone or still buckled? According to the official record, Hanks had relayed the events to only two people by 9 a.m., and there were two differing versions.

Finally, Hanks is not a large person: five feet six inches and 140 pounds.[81] How could she roll over with a man under the covers on top of her with his hand down her pants?

Hanks' story evolved further with later statements and testimony.

Hanks' OSI statement on April 17, twenty-four days after the alleged incident, is the first mention of "digital penetration." She wrote: "I felt pain initially being touch on the left inner labia, then it stopped hurting and I felt being touched just inside my vagina. … His finger was in my vagina, and he pulled his hand out. It didn't feel like his entire finger, it was curled / flexed and felt like perhaps to middle interphalangeal joint."[82]

She had not made reference to digital penetration when telling the story to anyone she spoke to during the three and a half weeks between the alleged incident and submitting her OSI statement. In her OSI statement, written twenty-four days after the night in question, she made this allegation for the first time.

In addition to the added detail and the discrepancies in timing, even the format of her statement was odd. The first two pages of her statement are written on plain white paper, and the bottom of the second page is "Z'd" out, which commonly indicates the witness is finished writing. It is written as if she completed it somewhere else before meeting with the OSI. However, there are additional pages, and these extra pages are formatted differently — this time on standard OSI forms. Digital penetration is mentioned only on a third page of her statement, a page that appears to have been added later, on paper that is formatted differently from the first two pages.

Hanks expanded the details of the digital penetration portion of her story during her Article 32 testimony: "I felt like I was having a dream. I was on my back, floating. It was very quiet. I felt being touched over my clothes on my torso area, breasts and stomach. After that, my next memory was, I felt a little pain on the left side of my inner labia near my vagina. I felt a finger go partially in my vagina. The finger felt like it uncurled and curled in my vagina. My underwear was on. After I felt the finger, it got really bright. I rolled over on my left side and felt a hand come out of my pants. I heard a guy yell loudly, 'What the hell is going on?' I sat up. My belt was still buckled, and my clothes were still on."[83]

Of note, Hanks provided greater detail over time. According to Los Angeles Police Department detective Toni Wolf, "It has been proven that memory of a traumatic event lapses with the first twenty-four to forty-eight hours."[84] Yet Hanks' retelling of this story actually increases in detail over time, and the more time that passes, the greater the detail in her story, contrary to proven psychology for real traumatic events.

According to MSgt. Dunnivant's testimony, Hanks "did not specify what part of her body was touched."[85] MSgt. Dunnivant did not mention digital penetration in any of her statements or testimony. Neither did Berrong. [86] Neither did Major O'Keefe, who interviewed Hanks at the clinic. It only came up as Hanks was meeting with the OSI; and only on a third page, on different paper.

This is an important point, because Charge 1, Specification 2 is: Aggravated Sexual Assault. According to the judge's instructions, to find Lt. Col. Wilkerson guilty of Aggravated Sexual Assault, the jury must be convinced beyond a reasonable doubt that he digitally penetrated Hanks while she was substantially incapable of appraising the nature of the act."[87] This clearly means, if not for the alleged digital penetration, the charges would not have included aggravated sexual assault. Rather, they would have been, at the most severe, Wrongful Sexual Contact — groping. The overall seriousness of the charges is significantly increased by the digital penetration statement. Some say, without this allegation, the charges might not have risen to the level of court-martial. Regardless, the Wilkersons remain adamant that Lt. Col. Wilkerson never left his own bed that night and did not assault Hanks in any manner at any level. The point is that digital penetration, added as an afterthought, increased the level of seriousness of the allegation.

The next inconsistency is why couldn't Hanks identify a man only six inches from her eyes?

"I opened my eyes and saw a man about six inches from my face squinting with his eyes closed."[88] That was Hanks' initial statement, written three and a half weeks after the alleged event. Her Article 32 testimony was: "I saw the man's face about six inches away from mine. He was facing me. We were both under the covers."[89] Yet, also in her Article 32 testimony, Hanks said she could not remember "whether the man in the bed had facial hair. I don't recall any facial hair."[90] She said, even though she was six inches from his face and, according to her, a bright light came on, she "could not see the man clearly." She "cannot remember if he had a moustache." It is important to note Hanks offers only a vague description of her alleged attacker.

It is interesting such a vague description of the alleged attacker is provided while descriptions of other parts of the crime are more detailed, some minutely detailed. Hanks had just spent several hours with Lt. Col. Wilkerson, yet she did not "recall any facial hair." In trial testimony, Hanks admitted she knew all the men had moustaches because they were commenting on them in the bar.[91] However, in her Article 32 testimony, she did not know whether the alleged attacker had a moustache.[92]

In the fighter pilot culture, March is known as "moustache March." Many fighter pilots grow moustaches throughout the month, and all of the men at the house that evening had moustaches. Hanks spent more than three hours talking to and near Lt. Col. Wilkerson, yet, she said, when she awoke with his face six inches away, she could not remember if the man she said she saw had a moustache and could not recall any facial hair. She knew Lt. Col. Wilkerson had a moustache, but she could not recall any facial hair on the alleged attacker.

One observant clemency letter writer said "she has vivid details of exactly what was alleged to have occurred in her pants, an event that would have occurred in less than one second, but fails to know whether or not the man six inches from her eyes had a moustache."[93]

WHY HAVE A BEER?

Why would Hanks drink a beer with five strange men on the street?

Hanks' testimony about having a beer with five guys in the village is baffling and inconsistent with her story of being sexually assaulted just moments earlier. As mentioned, Hanks said she met five English-speaking men in the small village after leaving the Wilkerson home. One of the men gave directions to MSgt. Dunnivant so she could drive to pick up her friend. The oddity was highlighted in a clemency letter: "If (Hanks) had been assaulted by a 'stranger,' why in the world would she have consumed a beer with five new male strangers in the town once she left the Wilkerson home? If you had just been assaulted by a strange male after having drinks with him, why would you put yourself in the situation to have a drink with five additional unknown males?"[94]

Another inconsistency is the identification of these five strange men Hanks met before 3 a.m. on the street in Roveredo. In Hanks' April 17 OSI statement, she first refers to them as "English-speaking young men." Then, on an added page, while discussing what she had to drink, she is identifies them as "Airmen" — U.S. Air Force enlisted personnel.[95] In her Article 32 testimony, they were again "English-speaking men."[96] In her trial testimony six months later, these were "Americans" "walking down the street on the opposite side, coming towards me."[97] Her original statement clearly indicates she thought they were in the Air Force and in all likelihood stationed at Aviano Air Base, but she continuously attempts to downplay that fact by calling them "English-speaking young men."

Why was Hanks vague about the identity of these Airmen in the first portion of her April 17 statement and after? It appears to be a slip-up when she identifies them as Airmen in the added section of her statement where she is discussing what she had to drink. That begs the question: Why did they become "English-speaking men" and not "Airmen"? If they were Airmen, is it likely they could have been located and questioned. There is only one air base near Roveredo. It would have been easy for the Wing Commander to order all Airmen to notify the OSI if they had been one of these young men. I can find no evidence or testimony that the OSI or anyone else made any attempt to find these five Airmen.

There is another inconsistency concerning these five strangers. MSgt. Dunnivant testified at the Article 32 hearing when Hanks called her at 3:02 a.m.: "I heard some guys in the background as I was talking to Kim. I asked to speak to one of them."[98]

Hanks, however, testified: "I told her (MSgt. Dunnivant) I wasn't sure where I was, and there were these guys that were walking down the street on the opposite side, coming towards me — four or five young men — and they were Americans. So I said, 'Hang on,' and I walked across the street and … asked them if they could tell her where we were so she could come pick me up."[99]

MSgt. Dunnivant could not have heard the men talking in the background if, as Hanks said, they were still on the other side of the street coming toward her. According to MSgt. Dunnivant, Hanks was already with (or near enough for MSgt. Dunnivant to hear) the five strangers, and it was MSgt. Dunnivant who asked to talk to one of them.

Does the contradiction in these stories matter? Yes. It is relevant, because if Hanks had been talking to these five Americans for, say, ten additional minutes, and if it took perhaps ten extra minutes to find a suitable location to climb the wall at the Wilkerson home, the combined timing would mean it was highly unlikely Hanks went to bed at all at the Wilkerson home. She sent a text at 1:43 a.m. and called Dunnivant at 3:02. If it took Hanks fifteen to twenty minutes to walk to the village and she had been talking with them for an additional ten minutes, it would mean she left the Wilkerson house no later than 2:35 a.m. What if she left even earlier? You recall, Hanks' OSI statement said, "I checked my phone and it was I think 3:20."[100] We know now that she called MSgt. Dunnivant at 3:02. Perhaps it was really 2:20 when she left the Wilkerson house.

The difference between Hanks and MSgt. Dunnivant's versions of that phone call at 3:02 a.m. may be small, but it is telling. MSgt. Dunnivant's testimony is a direct contradiction of Hanks' testimony. Remember, MSgt. Dunnivant is the first person Hanks told her story to. According to MSgt. Dunnivant, the story had changed. Again, to paraphrase Col. Christensen, MSgt. Dunnivant "has no reason to lie."

Beth Wilkerson testified that after the first episode of finding Hanks up and about and talking with Berrong, and after talking and drinking tea for about forty-five minutes, it was only fifteen to twenty minutes more before she heard Hanks again and went to investigate a second time.[101] According to Beth, this is the time Hanks left. This would have been sometime after 2 a.m. Perhaps 2:20? Could Hanks have misread her phone when she testified it was 3:20, and it was really 2:20? Could Hanks have taken thirty to forty minutes to find a way out of the walled compound and down to the village center to meet the five English-speaking men? Could Hanks have chatted with and drunk a beer with the five men for a few extra minutes before she called MSgt. Dunnivant?

Imagine what these five English speaking men could have contributed to this case. They would have been able to testify to Hanks' demeanor and state of intoxication. They may have been able to testify to how much time passed from when they first met her to the phone call with MSgt. Dunnivant. But the OSI never found the five men. In fact, there is no evidence of any effort to search for them at all. What the five Airmen might have had to say could have been a game changer. But more importantly, what they might have had to say could have helped find the truth.

Next, why didn't Hanks notice her friend arrive?

Testimony shows Hanks did not notice MSgt. Dunnivant drive up. MSgt. Dunnivant had to get out of the car and approach Hanks before Hanks recognized that her friend had arrived. Someone who had just been assaulted and now was in the company of five totally unknown men, one might think, would be anxiously looking for the safe haven of a trusted friend.

In trial testimony, MSgt. Dunnivant said: "I pull up, and I get out. And she didn't recognize my car. She had thought I had — I used to have a BMW, but I totaled that. And so she was looking — she was expecting a BMW and told the guys to look for a BMW. And ah, but I got out, and she was like, 'Oh.' And she said, 'What happened to the BMW?' And I told her what happened, and I said, 'This is what I have now.' And so I said, 'Are you ready to go?' And she said, 'Yeah.' And so we got in the car and started driving back to billeting."[102]

Hanks told MSgt. Dunnivant on the phone that her reason for needing a ride was that the Wilkersons "kicked me out." According to MSgt. Dunnivant, Hanks "seemed okay" when she arrived to pick her up and started to cry after MSgt. Dunnivant and Hanks were in the car driving back to base, and only after MSgt. Dunnivant asked "what happened, how did you end up here, because she didn't have her shoes."[103]

Hanks didn't notice her friend until MSgt. Dunnivant got out of the car and approached her. She didn't get in the car and say something like, "I am so glad you came to get me." Instead, she asked about the new car.[104] MSgt. Dunnivant testified that only after she asked Hanks what happened, Hanks started to "tear up."

What was Hanks' demeanor when MSgt. Dunnivant arrived?

In her Article 32 testimony in June, MSgt. Dunnivant said: "When I first saw Kim as I got there, she seemed okay. She was talking to the guys who had stayed with her."[105] However, according to the OSI report, MSgt. Dunnivant told the investigators in her first verbal interview with them on April 20: Hanks appeared to be "tipsy, somewhat intoxicated."[106] That description of Hanks appearing intoxicated was omitted from MSgt. Dunnivant's statement and her testimony at both the Article 32 hearing and trial. It was never mentioned except in the OSI report.

MSgt. Dunnivant's testimony changed dramatically at the trial. No longer did Hanks "seem okay." The Master Sergeant testified: "She seemed upset, disoriented. She was kind of — I don't know. She — I could tell she'd been drinking just a little, but she was coherent. You know, she was making complete sentences. I didn't think, you know, she was drunk or anything."[107]

MSgt. Dunnivant's account went from her first interview with the OSI when she said Hanks "seemed okay" and was "tipsy, somewhat intoxicated" to her testimony during the court-martial, when she said Hanks "seemed upset and disoriented, and I don't think she was drunk or anything."

Wow, what a difference between her story to the OSI and her testimony. These vastly different versions by MSgt. Dunnivant are disturbing. Which was it? Was Hanks "tipsy and somewhat intoxicated" and "seemed okay"? Or was she "upset and disoriented?" The defense failed to explore this contradiction.

REFUSING THE EXAM

Why did Hanks refuse an exam and rape kit?

At 6:33 a.m., Suzanne Berrong called Hanks. Hanks told Berrong her allegation of sexual assault but did not remember their phone conversation the night before, until Berrong reminded her. At 8:30 a.m., Berrong arrived at Hanks' home in Sacile, Italy. Hanks again began relaying her allegation, and Berrong again had to remind her that they had just talked on the phone two hours earlier. "When I went to pick Kim up at Sacile," Berrong said, "she did not look herself, little messy and I could still smell alcohol."[108]

Hanks told Berrong she felt as if she had been drugged.[109] Berrong encouraged Hanks to go to the medical clinic on base where they both worked. Berrong drove her to the clinic, where Major Michael O'Keefe, a friend and co-worker, was the attending technician on duty. Major O'Keefe asked for a Sexual Assault Forensic Examination, but Hanks refused. According to Major O'Keefe, Hanks "declined examination and did not want anything on record."[110] Hanks said she would only get a drug test (date-rape-type drugs). She said she would file a report of sexual assault only if the tests came back positive.[111]

Why did Hanks refuse a Sexual Assault Forensic Examination? She is a medical professional — a physicians' assistant. She would understand that if a man had his hand forcibly in her pants, some DNA might have remained. She would understand that if a man had had his finger inside her and it hurt as she described, there might have been evidence of bruising. Standard sexual assault protocols require the sexual assault examination. Major O'Keefe should have conducted one. It may have revealed evidence to potentially corroborate her story. So, why did Hanks refuse an examination after being convinced to go to the clinic?

Suzanne Berrong arrived at Hanks' home at 8:30 a.m. She wrote in her OSI statement: "When I went to pick Kim up at Sacile, she did not look herself, little messy and I could still smell alcohol, which I told her."[112]

Major O'Keefe from the clinic wrote in his statement: Hanks "was really shaken up. Her eyes were very puffy, like she had been crying. She wasn't her normal, bubbly self."[113]

Could it be Hanks didn't look like "her normal, bubbly self" to Major O'Keefe because she had been awake most, if not all, of the night and still smelled of alcohol? The Record of Trial proves Hanks had more to drink than she admitted and she had not slept as she claimed. Major O'Keefe, not knowing Hanks had been up all or most of the night, could easily have assumed her unkempt appearance might have been from something else. On the stand, Major O'Keefe admitted he had not been aware of Hanks' lack of sleep or that she had drunk a beer with the five men as late as 3:20 a.m.[114]

THE MISSING SHOES

During the trial proceedings, the prosecution made a big deal of the fact that Hanks left the Wilkerson house without her shoes. She walked to the village in only her socks. The prosecution used the fact that Hanks did not have her shoes to bolster the idea that she left in a hurry. Otherwise, the significant amount of testimony concerning these shoes is irrelevant.

Beth testified she thought Hanks was looking for her shoes when Beth found her near the room where the visiting boys were sleeping. Testimony shows Hanks took off her shoes upon entering the Wilkerson home and misplaced them multiple times during the evening.[115] Just prior to taking Captain Brock back to the base, Beth Wilkerson testified she found Hanks' shoes and gave them to her. Upon returning from dropping Captain Brock at the base, Beth discovered Hanks had lost her shoes again.[116]

Hanks' testimony:

> Q. Do you remember that people were trying to look for your shoes that night, to help you find your shoes?
> A. Ah, I think — did I ask Beth were my shoes were? I may have asked her that night.

This is another elusive non-answer.

> Q. Do you have any recollection that people were actually looking all around for your shoes that night?
> A. No. [117]

Finally, a direct answer, but it did not match the statements and testimony of at least four other people.

Lt. Col. Wilkerson's statement on April 19 to the OSI also included two references to the missing shoes. Speaking of the time just after Beth returned from dropping Captain Brock at the gate, Lt. Col. Wilkerson wrote: "At this point I believe we learned that Kim was missing her shoes," and "We attempted to locate the missing shoes and had no luck. I think an attempt at loaning shoes was made."[118]

Beth Wilkerson's Article 32 testimony: "Kim said she lost her purse and shoes. I found her shoes in the bathroom, showed her that I found them, and put them on the rug in the hallway. Captain Brock came up to me and said she wanted to go home and wanted to go home now. I drove Captain Brock to the south gate, dropping her at the gate. When I returned, Kim Hanks had lost her shoes again. Kim was in the kitchen and had 'rallied.' She was being playful and putting her arm around me and my husband."[119]

Major Lowe testified: "I remember Kim Hanks couldn't find her shoes. I was asked to help look for them. I looked for about twenty seconds and then stopped."[120]

Major Goldsberry said, "I helped Kim Hanks look for her shoes for about ten minutes."[121]

Hanks was attempting to hide that she repeatedly misplaced her shoes throughout the evening in an effort to provide some reason, other than Beth's version of events, for not having them when she left the house. The fact that Hanks repeatedly misplaced her shoes and that others repeatedly searched for them supports Beth Wilkerson's testimony that Hanks was just outside the visiting boy's room looking for her shoes and was about to leave anyway when Beth found her up and about the second time. Beth said she discovered the shoes in the visiting boys' room the next day.

Hanks said she had no recollection of others looking for her shoes.[122] So, when Major Lowe, Major Goldsberry, and both Wilkersons said they were helping look for her shoes, were they making that up? The prosecution certainly wanted the jury to believe they were. But if someone was going to make up a story about Kim Hanks having misplaced her shoes and everyone looking for them, would Major Lowe then admit he stopped looking after only twenty seconds? Why would the subject of looking for shoes ever come up in testimony if it was not an issue at the house? If people were going to make up a story, would they come up with "she lost her shoes"? To what purpose?

Subsequent letters from co-workers and friends indicate Hanks often goes without her shoes, even at work. One letter-writer indicated she had filed several complaints with Medical Group leadership about Hanks' behavior at work, including that she "sees patients without her shoes." This co-worker wrote to Lt. Gen. Franklin: "When I heard Ms. Hanks had lost her shoes" the night of the alleged incident, "I was not surprised."[123] Additionally, Hanks herself admitted in her testimony that she would take her shoes off at work: "I take them off. I do."[124]

So, it appears that it was not unusual for Hanks to remove her shoes wherever she was. But still, it was a big deal to the prosecution that she did not have them when she left the Wilkerson home. It makes a good story and probably influenced the jury. But isn't it just as likely, if not more so, given the effort to hide the fact that she misplaced them several times during the night, that she just misplaced them again and couldn't find them?

Hanks' other recollections also raise questions about where she was in the house. Hanks said her purse, cell phone and glasses were not in the bedroom with her. They were on a counter near a door. "I walked out the door, and I realized that I didn't have my purse with me … and I turned around and I started to walk back in, and on the counter was my purse and my glasses, and my phone was inside my purse. So I walked in and I picked it up off the counter."[125]

Hanks had her phone with her at 1:43 a.m. when she texted MSgt. Dunnivant. This is during a time she said she was asleep in the guestroom. But now she testified her purse was on the counter by the exit on the main floor of the house. How could she text someone from the downstairs bedroom she claims to have been in when her phone was on the counter by the exit? If she had it in the bedroom to send a text at 1:43, when did she put it on the counter? She clearly remembers the purse, with the cell phone in it, being on the counter when she left. So she could not have had it in the bedroom to send a text. It could not be in two places at once. She had to have been up again, by the counter, and not asleep (in any bed), as she testified. Once again, her own testimony contradicted her story.

Hanks also seemed confused about the bedroom light. She described the room she said she slept in during her trial testimony. She testified there was a table lamp "right at the head of the bed" and she "had no recollection of any other light in the room."[126] Just a few minutes later, she testified the light she said came on "was an overhead light."[127] This is a direct contradiction of her previous testimony. Which was it — a lamp or an overhead light? In the photos of the Wilkerson home, there is no table or lamp in the only bedroom "a few steps down" which Hanks testified is the room where she slept.

Hanks' perception of the house was also relevant to her memory of leaving it.

During the trial, Hanks' description of the room she said she was in was not accurate, nor was the path leaving the house, as she described it. The defense petitioned the judge to allow the jurors to visit the Wilkerson home, but the judge denied the request in deference to a prosecution objection.[128] Photographs presented into evidence by the defense demonstrate that the way Hanks testified she departed the Wilkerson home was not possible given the physical layout of the house. In particular, Hanks described how she exited the house: "So I stood up and I walked past her and walked down the hallway, and there was a door open leading to the outside. ... So I walked out the door, and I realized that I didn't have my purse with me ... and I turned around and I started to walk back in, and on the counter was my purse and my glasses, and my phone was inside my purse. So I walked in and I picked it up off the counter."[129]

The inconsistency was in Hanks' trial testimony. She testified the room she was offered was "a few steps down": "There was this room that had like an Italian-style twin bed in this little room a few steps down."[130] She also said Beth "went down to make up the bed," and "I don't remember ever going down to that bedroom until I went down to go to sleep," and when she was going to bed (the second time) the Wilkersons "walked me partway down," obviously referring to some stairs to go down in order to get to the guest room. In fact, Hanks repeatedly and numerously referred to having to go "down" to the guest room where she claimed the alleged assault occurred.[131] Yet, her testimony about leaving is that she walked past Beth straight out a door. That is not physically possible in the Wilkerson house.

A video of the house was provided by the defense. It clearly showed a flight of stairs between where Hanks said she slept and the exits to the house. This was the only unoccupied room available, and it was the only room in the house that was down any stairs at all. The video showed there was no exit as described by Hanks on the floor where she said she slept — straight down a hallway through French doors. Had she been in the bedroom she claimed to have been in, it would have been impossible to walk straight down the hallway and out through a French door leading to the outside.

Beth Wilkerson testified she heard Hanks up walking around a second time and found her at the entrance to the room where the visiting boys were staying, on the main level of the home with the kitchen and the exits.[132] Beth testified at the trial that she "waved her toward me, towards the kitchen, where we ended up" and that Hanks left from the kitchen. The kitchen has an exit to the outside at each end. Both exits are near counters.

Hanks' statement said: "The room with the French doors is a straight shot from the room I slept in. The doors lead to the yard, not the driveway."[133] The French doors are in the kitchen on the side of the house that leads to the yard. If Hanks exited French doors, she was on the main floor and not in the basement guestroom where she claims to have been assaulted.

According to her own testimony, Hanks exited the house through the kitchen on the main floor of the home. Had the jury been given the opportunity to visit the home, it might have seen this significant discrepancy in Hanks' testimony.

Another odd piece of testimony is that Hanks said the door was open: "There was a door open leading to the outside … So I walked out the door."[134] Testimony from the Record of Trial indicated the low temperature that night was 45 degrees Fahrenheit.[135] Who leaves a door "open leading to the outside" when they go to bed at night when it is 45 degrees outside? Especially when the master bedroom is on the second floor and two visiting children are sleeping on the main floor?

At the trial, Hanks could not identify the bed she allegedly slept in or the room where the alleged assault occurred. When shown pictures of each of the bedrooms in the Wilkerson home, she stated, "I know I did not sleep in any of these beds."[136] When specifically shown the guest room in the basement and asked by the judge, "Does that look like the bed you slept in that night?" she answered, "Oh, no, definitely not."[137] The photo was of an Italian-style daybed. This was the room Hanks previously described in her testimony. It is the only room in the house "a few steps down." It is the only room she described in her testimony, yet she failed to identify it in the photos.

At this point, the defense thought the case was won. Hanks didn't identify any room in the Wilkerson home, not the one downstairs and not the one on the main level where the boys were sleeping. But while Hanks couldn't say which room she was supposedly in, Col. Christensen did. Col. Christensen presented a creative proposal in his closing arguments. Sticking with the theme that everyone on the Wilkerson side of the case lied, Col. Christensen said, "Only Beth, and nobody else, only Beth says Kim Hanks slept in that daybed; nobody else."[138] Col. Christensen claimed Hanks was in the bed the visiting boys were in.[139] He completely disregarded Hanks' own testimony of a room a "few steps down with an Italian-style twin bed." Rather, he simply changed her testimony by telling the jury she slept in the bedroom on the main level where everyone testified the visiting boys were. Col. Christensen changed Hanks' story, again.

The room with an "Italian-style twin bed" that was "a few steps down" was in the basement. It is the only room in the house to fit Hanks' description. The guest room on the main level had a queen-size bed. According to Kim Hanks' own testimony, she was not in the guest room on the main floor. In a case with zero evidence, where the only thing that could convict a man and send him to prison was the testimony of one woman, the jurors disregarded her own testimony. Instead of listening to the words of Hanks, the jury went along with Col. Christensen's creative solution. They chose to believe something contrary to the accuser's own testimony, to convict a man, a fighter pilot, beyond a reasonable doubt.

One last note: In the OSI record, Hanks told investigators Beth Wilkerson "made a twin bed in a downstairs room." What other room in the Wilkerson house is downstairs?[140] None.

WHAT SHE DIDN'T REMEMBER

During her Article 32 testimony, Hanks testified to a number of things she said she could not remember. The following list is from her sworn testimony:

> Things I don't remember:
> How long I was at the club.
> How long it took to get to the accused's house.
> Whether Major Goldsberry or Major Lowe said they'd
>   figure out how to get me home.
> Going through a gate to the house.
> Whether there was a path or stairs to the house.
> How the yard at the house was landscaped.
> I didn't immediately recall Beth Wilkerson's name.
> That people went outside that night.
> The oldest visiting child's name.
> Talking to the younger visiting child, his name, age, or
>   hair color.
> Why Beth Wilkerson's son was sick.
> Beth's son's name.
> The name of the woman with dark hair.
> The specifics of my conversation with Beth Wilkerson.
> How long I talked to Beth or how many times we talked.
> Texting Suzanne Berrong after the concert.
> Whether there was an overhead light in the room I slept in.
> Where my shoes or black sweater were.
> Whether I was touched over or under my clothes.
> What the accused was wearing.
> Whether the accused was unclothed.
> Whether the man in the bed had facial hair. I don't recall
>   any facial hair.

How long I walked after I left the house.

Calling Suzanne Berrong after I left the house.

Texting anyone that it was my fault.

Hanks readily admitted she was "pretty out of it."[141] She claimed memory losses in many details, but then she claimed significant detail in other events. She also seemed to "remember" more and in greater detail as time passed.

Some of these twenty-five things Hanks admitted she didn't remember might be understandable, e.g., item six: "How the yard at the house was landscaped." But others seem far more significant. Note item thirteen: "The name of the woman with dark hair." All witnesses (except Hanks) agree, there was no other woman at the house with dark hair or otherwise. Why did Hanks believe there was?

Note item No. 3: "Whether Major Goldsberry or Major Lowe said they'd figure out how to get me home." Hanks also testified at the Article 32 hearing: "As we were walking to the house, I asked how I was going to get home. Either Major Goldsberry or his friend said they'd figure out a way."[142] But she said that neither major offered her a ride home. Was she sparring with the defense counsel, parsing words? And why would she have asked this question when she first arrived? Wasn't she with two of her friends? If anything, wouldn't she have said, "How are 'we' going to get home?"

Hanks also said at the hearing, "I never talked to Major Goldsberry or Major Lowe after we arrived at the party."[143] We've seen testimony from both Major Goldsberry and Beth Wilkerson that they had a conversation with Hanks about getting her home after Captains Brock and Manning had left.[144]

As mentioned previously, in her testimony, Hanks said the two majors would "find a way" to get her home, but also said she never talked to them after arriving. Both majors and Beth Wilkerson testified differently. So again, who do we believe — a woman who admitted she didn't remember much about the night — "*She describes herself as 'out of it'* "[145] — or three witnesses who all said the same thing? Col. Christensen convinced the jurors the other three must be lying, again.

At least one trial observer thought without a doubt Hanks had been coached to intentionally confuse the issue as a way to avoid the answer. "I attended both the Article 32 hearing and the entire seven days in court," and Hanks' "demeanor during the Courts Martial was 180-out and rather focused and much more serious and direct. I can only assume that she was coached by someone on the legal team, as they are the only individuals who could have pointed out the inaccuracies between her signed statement and the Article 32 hearing testimony and the statements, testimony, and phone records of the other witnesses." [146]

Note item No. 17 in the list of things Hanks said she didn't remember: "Whether there was an overhead light in the room I slept in." At trial, Hanks testified there was a lamp "right at the head of the bed" and she "had no recollection of any other light in that room."[147] But only a few minutes later in her same testimony during the October trial, she contradicted herself and stated the bright light that came on "was an overhead light."[148] There were no bright lights in the basement room of the Wilkerson home. From the video presented by the defense, there was only an energy-saving overhead light that initially came on very dim and brightened over the first minute.[149] And, there is no table or lamp.

Note item No. 22: "Whether the man in the bed had facial hair. I don't recall any facial hair." A man was supposedly only six inches from her face with a bright light on, and she could not remember if he had any facial hair. As a reminder, it was Moustache March. Lt. Col. Wilkerson had not shaved since February 28. It was March 23.

The bottom line is Hanks freely admitted she was "pretty out of it" and had memory losses in many details. It is left for us to wonder how the jurors felt her story was true "beyond a reasonable doubt" despite those many inconsistencies, her memory loss, and her "being out of it."

CROSS-EXAMINATION

These following examples are intended to show the manner in which testimony was solicited (led) by the prosecution and how Hanks evaded questioning under cross-examination.

In her testimony during cross-examination, Hanks seemed confused, and during direct examination, she was often led by the prosecution. For example, when questioning Hanks about how much she drank, Captain Beliles asked: "Did you have any sips of anything else at the concert?"[150] — "*sips.*" Captain Manning testified she and Hanks shared the entire bottle: "I would actually (say) that she shared that with me throughout walking to the ... concert and a little bit inside the concert." Captain Manning also admitted they drank the entire water bottle of grape juice and vodka between them. "It was gone. It was completed."[151] Captain Beliles was well aware of Captain Manning's statements and testimony and chose to say "sips" to lead Hanks to the more conservative answer.

Captain Beliles again leading the witness:

> Question: Not a significant amount?
> Answer: No, no. I just tasted it to taste it.[152]

Oddly, when Hanks wandered off from the prosecutor's lead at the October trial, her testimony became more detailed (embellished?) over her previous versions. For example, at no time prior to her trial testimony did she mention Lt. Col. Wilkerson was awake or present when she drank tea with Beth Wilkerson. It is not in her statement, or her Article 32 testimony, nor is it mentioned by Berrong, who was on the phone during that time, in any of her statements or testimony. Yet, when Hanks testified under cross examination, her story changed to: "We" got ahold of Suzanne Berrong to "talk to her about possibly picking me up" and included Lt. Col. Wilkerson for the first time in any version of her story.[153] But Berrong testified Hanks said, while on the phone: "Here comes the wife." It is not possible that Beth and Lt. Col. Wilkerson were there already, and came walking in later as Berrong testified Hanks' said. Berrong also testified at the trial that she never heard a man in the room and was never given the impression a man was in the room during that phone call.[154] The inconsistency is between Kim Hanks and her best friend, Suzanne Berrong. Beth testified Hanks was alone in the kitchen until Beth walked in while Hanks was on the phone. Who is correct — Berrong, or this new version of the story by Hanks at the trial? What is the truth? Kim Hanks said she was "out of it." Suzanne Berrong was sober at home. Hanks was embellishing her story even as she testified.

Another question: Would visiting children hear a man and woman yelling?

As previously explained, there were two young boys, ages 8 and 13, staying at the Wilkersons' home that evening. This was the first night these two boys had spent away from their mother since the death of their father in a car accident ten months prior to that evening, and their mother stated they were having difficulty sleeping and might wake in the middle of the night.

MSgt. Dunnivant's statement on April 20, 2012, said Hanks told her "the man's wife was yelling at her to get out of her house" and, according to her testimony, that would have happened on the same floor as the boys were sleeping.[155] The OSI interviewed both children, and neither reported anything unusual. The boy's mother also testified the children did not report being awakened by yelling or screaming, nor did they report that they noticed anything wrong with the Wilkersons the next day. In fact, the boys wanted to spend the night again Saturday night, and did.[156]

What about Beth's version of events? Col. Christensen said she made it up. But if Beth Wilkerson had caught Lt. Col. Wilkerson as Hanks said, would she make up a story about the "victim" being up walking around? If Beth had just caught her husband in bed with another woman, would Beth fabricate a story about asking Hanks to leave? Isn't it more likely she would react as a woman scorned? Perhaps it is simply that Beth Wilkerson was upset with Kim Hanks for walking around the house before 3 a.m., thinking she might wake the visiting boys.

Finally, there's one last inconsistency, or really another oddity in the story worth pondering: Would a man yell, "What the hell is going on?" if his wife just caught him with another woman? It seems to me that he would be the only one in the room who knew what was going on.

There were so many inconsistencies in Hanks' story. To review, they included: a confusing timeline; her claim of being asleep three times when she was actually texting someone or talking on the phone; her denial that others searched for her shoes; a description of the room she said she slept in that does not fit the physical layout of the house; her inability to identify the bedroom where the assault was alleged to have occurred; the fact that how she claimed to have exited the house was not possible; her purse and phone being on the counter by the exit while she said she sent a text from the guest room; the contradiction in testimony regarding a lamp versus an overhead light; testimony that said her pants were done and undone; conflicting descriptions of the hand starting to go down her pants, as she told Berrong, and or coming out of her pants as she wrote in her statement; and her admission that she was "out of it" and could not remember twenty-five things, including whether a man six inches from her face had any facial hair.

How did this jury not have any reasonable doubt?

8

ASLEEP, DRUNK OR DRUGGED?

"Good people do not need laws to tell them to act responsibly,
while bad people will find a way around the laws."
— *Plato*

The charges in this case were based on Hanks being substantially incapacitated and not able to appraise the nature of the sexual contact. Legally speaking, "substantial incapacitation" requires the victim to be either: 1) asleep, 2) drunk, or 3) drugged and not substantially capable of understanding the sexual nature of the actions of the alleged attacker. The defense strategy was to prove Hanks was not substantially incapacitated — not asleep, drunk, or drugged. We will discuss these in reverse order.

All drug test results were negative.[157] Major O'Keefe, who interviewed Hanks at the medical clinic at about 9 a.m., wrote in his OSI statement that Hanks had said "she did drink alcohol the night before but felt very different. Hanks reported after arriving at the house and drinking she began to feel out of sorts." She said "she is familiar with the effects of alcohol in her and last night was above and beyond any reaction felt before and not equal to what she consumed."[158]

Hanks asked Major O'Keefe to run a full scan of drug tests. "I ran a standard drug screen, which tests for a variety of narcotics, illegal substances, cocaine, heroin, prescription medicines like Benzodiazepines, Demurral, morphine. And then I also went ahead and ordered a GHB screen and a Rohyponol screen."[159] These are date-rape drugs. "All drug testing came back negative."[160]

A toxicology expert testified, based on what Hanks said she drank, her blood-alcohol content would not have been high enough for her to have been drunk. The expert said Hanks' blood alcohol levels would have been: 0.06 at midnight, 0.04 at 1 a.m., 0.02 at 2 a.m. and 0.00 at 3 a.m.[161] These levels were based on what Hanks testified she had had to drink. As with other parts of Hanks' story, there was discrepancy about what she actually drank.

The defense strategy was also to show Hanks was never asleep. In her very first written statement on March 29, 2012 — the report to the Sexual Assault Response Coordinator (SARC) — Hanks wrote: I "passed out."[162] However, when confronted with the 12:23-12:38 phone call to Suzanne Berrong, Hanks changed her story to "I must have been drugged" and claimed she "went right to bed" after the phone call.[163] That claim was also proven not true by her phone records when she texted MSgt. Dunnivant at 1:43.[164] The next morning, when she told Berrong she must have been drugged, Hanks admitted she had stayed up and drank tea with Beth after the midnight call.[165] And, when pressed under cross-examination, Hanks admitted she had not been asleep before the 1:43 a.m. text. [166]

We know Hanks was downtown in the village by 3:02 a.m., but we do not know exactly when she left the house. She claimed to have been asleep sometime between 1:43 and leaving the house before 3 a.m. But was she? Beth said that after sending Hanks to bed a second time, it was only about "fifteen to twenty minutes later, I heard Kim Hanks back in the kitchen, I went back downstairs. Kim was near the room where the visiting boys were sleeping" on the main floor of the house. "I asked Kim what she was doing. I gave her two choices: Leave or go back downstairs to bed. Kim opened the back door, grabbed her purse and glasses and left."[167] Hanks said she looked at her phone and it said 3:20 when she left the house.[168] But she called MSgt. Dunnivant at 3:02 a.m., so we know that was not accurate. Beth testified when Hanks left, Beth went to look for her in the car, and when Beth returned to the house, it was just before 3 a.m. [169]

From this information combined from both Hanks and Beth Wilkerson, it is probable that Hanks left the house at 2:20, not 3:20. That time fits with both Beth's account and Hanks' 3:02 phone call from the village.

It took extensive research for me to determine this was a far more probable timeline than Hanks' story. This likely timeline means Hanks was never asleep. She was not drugged, and she was not asleep. Was she intoxicated? The defense chose to show, based on what Hanks said she drank, that she was not intoxicated. I believe this to be an error. I believe Hanks had more to drink than she admitted. I believe Hanks never went to bed and was up and about causing a disturbance, precisely because she had been drinking Red Bull and alcohol.

9

Eat, Drink and Be Merry

"Responsible drinking? Now that's an oxymoron."
— *Aaron Howard*

From Kim Hanks' original OSI statement on April 17, 2012, here is what she says she had to eat on March 23, 2012: "breakfast burrito, lunch? Sandwich, no dinner." [170]

On an empty stomach, the following is what Kim Hanks wrote she had to drink for the 24 hours from the time she went to the concert until she was back in the room at the TLF.

> Alcohol:
> 5:30-7 p.m.: Half bottle of mulled wine
> 9 p.m.: One and a half plastic cups draft beer
> 10 p.m. One small glass white wine
> Midnight: One glass — unsure if Prosecco or non-alcoholic
> 3:15 a.m. Part of a cheap light beer
> No water[171]

Prosecco is an Italian sparkling wine. Hanks said she was unsure if she drank it when it was offered to her at the Wilkerson home.

There were multiple discrepancies with this story as well. Here is a description of what Hanks had to drink according to others who testified, throughout the statements, Article 32 hearing, and trial.

Temporary Lodging Facility (TLF): At the beginning of the evening, while waiting at the TLF to meet the other women who went to the concert, Hanks said she drank a half of a bottle of wine she purchased on the way over to the TLF. "I had my — I had the wine, so I was using a mug from the room. ... I had a half a bottle" of wine before leaving billeting.[172]

MSgt. Danielle Dunnivant, who attended the concert and club with Hanks but went home early, testified that Hanks "had one beer or something like that" at the TLF.[173] However, the OSI report indicates another, unnamed witness who saw that MSgt. Dunnivant and Hanks both had "about two glasses of hot wine while waiting in the lobby" before the concert.[174] (The Air Force redacted this witness' name in the OSI report, therefore it is unknown.) The OSI report seems to indicate these two glasses of wine were drunk in the lobby in addition to the half bottle of wine Hanks said she drank in her room.

Drinks at the TLF not reported by Hanks: two additional glasses of wine.

Concert: According to the OSI report, while at the concert, another unnamed witness recalled running into Captain Manning and corroborated Captain Manning's testimony that she had a "20-ounce water bottle of grape juice and vodka" and that she "shared it" with Kim Hanks. Manning said it was completely empty before the concert ended: "I would actually (say) that she shared that with me throughout walking to the ... concert and a little bit inside the concert. It was gone. It was completed."[175] The unnamed witness recalled drinking a Gatorade and vodka mixed drink and passing it around the group, which included Hanks.[176] Hanks herself said, "I started to feel buzzed at the concert."[177]

Drinks at the concert not reported by Hanks: half a bottle (about 10 ounces) of grape juice and vodka and some Gatorade and vodka.

Club: Kim Hanks claims all she had to drink at the club was a beer and a half, and she bought it herself.[178] But Captain Manning said she (Manning) bought vodka drinks and gave one to Hanks when Hanks first arrived: "Dawn and I bought a few drinks (four), and when Kim and MSgt. Dunnivant arrived, we gave two drinks to them."[179]

MSgt. Dunnivant testified these were Red Bull and vodka. "Captain Manning bought four drinks of Red Bull and vodka and gave one to Kim Hanks.[180] ... I saw Kim Hanks drink one drink."[181] MSgt. Dunnivant again changed her testimony during the trial. She changed it to say she saw Hanks take the drink but was not sure she drank it. This detail is important, because this is the version of MSgt. Dunnivant's story the jury heard. The defense counsel did not challenge her during cross-examination.[182]

At the Article 32 hearing and during trial testimony, Kim Hanks denied that she drank any vodka: "Captain Manning offered me a drink, but I didn't want to mix."[183] But both Captain Manning and MSgt. Dunnivant said Hanks took it and drank it.

The OSI report completed on October 12, 2012, states:

Suzanne Berrong said, by the time they were at the club, Hanks "had consumed some liquor and wine."[184] In her April 19 written statement, Suzanne Berrong wrote about her conversation with Hanks the next morning: "We talked about everything she had drunk, and the vodka was from an outside source and the tea the wife made."[185] Also, in her Article 32 testimony, Berrong said: "We talked about what she (Hanks) drank: tea, vodka and wine" and "she said she had been drinking vodka and wine."[186] So, according to Berrong, Hanks admitted drinking vodka, a statement corroborated by two other witnesses, including MSgt. Dunnivant.

Later, Hanks denied to Berrong drinking *any* vodka that night: "In early May, Kim and I had dinner. She told me she didn't drink any vodka the night of March 23, 2012."[187] But Berrong's statement was already part of the record and she, unlike MSgt. Dunnivant, did not change her story during the trial.

Drinks at the club not reported by Hanks: at least one Red Bull and vodka.

Wilkersons' house: According to the OSI report, Hanks said she drank a glass of white wine soon after arriving at the Wilkerson house as part of a toast.[188] Hanks says she turned down a glass of Prosecco, but Captain Manning told the OSI that Hanks did, in fact, drink the Prosecco.[189] In the Article 32 hearing, Captain Manning confirmed what she told the OSI: She saw Kim Hanks drink the Prosecco.[190]

Drinks at the Wilkersons' not reported by Hanks: at least one additional glass of wine (or Prosecco).

In total, what did Hanks really have to drink on 23 March, 2012?

Here is a list of the drinks Hanks admits to and the additional drinks others testified Hanks had.

TLF, 5:30 to 7 p.m.:
Half bottle of mulled wine
Two glasses of white wine
Concert, 5:30 to 7 p.m.:
Shared two water bottles with Gatorade and vodka and grape juice and vodka
Club, 9 p.m.:
At least one Red Bull and vodka drink
1½ plastic cups of draft beer
Wilkerson home, 10 p.m.:
1 small glass of white wine
1 glass of Prosecco
Possibly another Prosecco, around midnight
Part of a cheap light beer, 3:15 a.m.
No water

These are the *additional* drinks beyond what Hanks admitted to under oath but that other witnesses testified that she drank:

Two glasses of mulled wine
Half a water bottle of vodka and grape juice
Several sips of Gatorade and vodka
At least one Red Bull and vodka drink
1 glass of Prosecco

Testimony and statements prove Kim Hanks had more to drink than she admits. Once again, her story has multiple inconsistencies or outright falsehoods. The real question is why — why does she want to hide what she has had to drink?

According to MSgt. Dunnivant, Hanks was "tipsy" and "somewhat intoxicated" at 3:20 in the morning after Hanks swore she hadn't had anything to drink since midnight and that she was asleep at some point in between.[191] How could Hanks be tipsy and somewhat intoxicated at

3:20 a.m. if she only drank what she claimed and stopped drinking altogether by midnight?

Berrong said Hanks smelled of alcohol at 8:30 the next morning. This is after Hanks claims she slept three hours. How could that be?

Hanks admitted repeatedly that she didn't remember. She testified at the Article 32 hearing, "I started to feel buzzed at the concert," saying I was "out of it," and she admittedly didn't remember many details of the evening.[192] Captain Manning wrote in her OSI statement on April 18, 2012: Kim "told me she does not remember much after going to the house. I asked how she got home, and she told me she did not remember."[193]

Suzanne Berrong, in her April 19 OSI statement, wrote: "Speaking with (Hanks) during the first phone call, she was slurring in speech and did not seem herself. I have gone out with her before, and she usually drinks ale/cider, not a mix of alcohol, wine, etc."[194]

These statements from MSgt. Dunnivant, Captain Manning and Suzanne Berrong are from three of Hanks' friends who spoke with her, met with her and transported her. All three statements are remarkably the same — the effects of alcohol were readily apparent. So, if Hanks didn't remember how she got home the next day, how much of her story are we supposed to believe? And isn't that reasonable doubt?

TEA

Hanks did not mention having tea with Beth Wilkerson in her original statement to the OSI on April 17, 2012. She did not mention it to Major O'Keefe when she asked for the drug test.[195] Nor did she mention it during her Article 32 testimony. However, the prosecution did bring it up first during the trial. The fact that Hanks sat up with Beth and drank tea, in direct contradiction to her statement and Article 32 testimony, is telling. Hanks claimed to be asleep but, in truth, she sat up for about forty minutes talking with Beth. The prosecution had to address that untruth. It was going to come out in the defense case anyway, and it looked better if they, the prosecution, brought it up first. Hanks made no mention of drinking tea in any of her statements or previous testimony, but she told

Berrong about it, and Berrong had mentioned it in her OSI statement. The defense was going to bring it up because it validated Beth's account that she found Hanks up on the main floor in the kitchen talking loudly on the phone, and to calm her, Beth made tea, and the two talked for about forty minutes.[196] This testimony also disputed Hanks' version that she went right to bed.

The defense walked through the timeline and the variations in Hanks' story — the "passed out" comment; the "I was suddenly so tired" and "went straight to bed comments," the tea, and the text at 1:43 a.m.[197] The defense thought those changes in Hanks' story provided reasonable doubt. Hanks had offered three versions of the same story, and all three were full of conflicts.

'I DIDN'T WANT TO MIX'

Hanks testified, under oath, during the Article 32 hearing that "I didn't want to mix" my alcohol types. By her own testimony, Hanks drank wine, beer, more wine, and more beer. Witnesses said she drank vodka and grape juice, vodka and Gatorade, Red Bull and vodka, and Prosecco. All on an empty stomach in an eight-hour span. If she "didn't want to mix," she failed.

Hanks consumed far more alcohol the night in question than she admitted. In all probability, she was intoxicated more than the toxicology expert testified. His testimony was based on what Hanks said she drank. We now know she had at least seven more drinks than she admitted, at least one of which was a Red Bull and vodka. In fact, at least three of those drinks included vodka in some mixture. We also know now that Hanks, at 140 pounds, had very little to eat — a sandwich for lunch and no dinner — prior to consuming this amount of alcohol. We also know that MSgt. Dunnivant said Hanks was "tipsy, somewhat intoxicated" at 3:20 a.m., and Berrong said Hanks still smelled of alcohol at 8:30 in the morning.

Hanks drank more than she admitted and freely admitted not remembering much. She even confided to her friend she did not remember how she got home. If she was not truthful about when she went to bed (if ever) or what she had to drink, why did the jury believe the rest of her story — beyond a reasonable doubt?

1 0

RED BULL AND VODKA

*"Nothing in the world is more dangerous than sincere ignorance
and conscientious stupidity."*
— *Martin Luther King Jr.*

During testimony about what Hanks drank the evening of March
23, 2012, one of the jurors asked MSgt Dunnivant the following question:

> Q. Could you please explain what is in the drinks
> purchased — "red" and "something"? What goes in
> those drinks?
> A. Red Bull and vodka.[198]

Depending on whose testimony you believe, Hanks had at least one
and maybe two Red Bull and vodka drinks while at the club just prior to
going to the Wilkerson home. During the trial, expert testimony as to
Hanks' level of intoxication by 3 a.m. was based on what Hanks said she
drank. A review of what others say Hanks drank revealed the Red Bull
and vodka at the club and Gatorade and vodka at the concert. Red Bull is
a caffeine drink, and one might assume it would counteract the effects of
alcohol … or would it? Research has revealed interesting side effects of
Red Bull and vodka.

Two articles, by Joy Collymore at Examiner.com and by Christine
Hsu at Medicaldaily.com, were helpful in understanding the effects of
combining Red Bull with vodka.[199] Among the effects is that "caffeine
intoxication causes nervousness, anxiety, restlessness, and insomnia."[200]
This seems in line with Hanks' behavior as described by Beth Wilkerson
— restlessness and insomnia. Perhaps that restlessness and insomnia
manifested itself in Hanks walking around the house (pacing) and being
unable (unwilling) to sleep.

According to Hsu, "researchers found that this combination of uppers and downers can lead to a range of serious health problems like heart palpitations, sleeping difficulties and jolt and crash episodes."[201] People who drink this mixture are "four times more likely to have trouble sleeping and were more likely to suffer tremors, irritability and so-called 'jolt and crash episodes' or sudden bouts of energy followed by long periods of exhaustion," often "leading people to do things they might not do otherwise. These symptoms are similar to those produced by caffeine, one of the main ingredients in popular energy drinks like Red Bull."[202]

Beth testified Hanks had "rallied" when Beth returned from dropping off Captain Brock. Beth said Hanks was up walking around, restless and talking on the phone in a loud, animated voice.[203] Berrong corroborated this account with her testimony, saying Hanks was very upset and cursing loudly.[204] Beth then said Hanks did not go to sleep but was up, yet again, walking around the house, making noise just prior to Beth asking her to leave.

Hsu's article says people who drink this mixture of caffeine and alcohol also have a "greater chance of experiencing several side-effects related to over-stimulation, including increased speech speed, sleeping difficulties, agitation, irritability, and tension."[205] Remember, when MSgt. Dunnivant picked up Hanks, Dunnivant said she "appeared to be tipsy, somewhat intoxicated."[206] Berrong stated Hanks "did not look herself" and "I could still smell alcohol."[207] And finally, Major O'Keefe said, "Ms. Hanks appeared very distressed ... She did not appear to be her usual self at all."[208] All of these symptoms are consistent with those symptoms research found in people who drank Red Bull and vodka.

11

SEXUAL ASSAULT RESPONSE COORDINATOR

"Hell is paved with good intentions, not with bad ones.
All men mean well."
— *George Bernard Shaw*

The Sexual Assault Response Coordinator (SARC) helps victims of sexual assault, provides awareness training and files reports. These reports can be "restricted" — meaning no law enforcement or military chain of command is notified — or "unrestricted," meaning both law enforcement and the military chain of command are notified immediately. "Restricted reporting allows a victim to report a sexual assault without triggering an investigation." It is intended to provide treatment and counseling for the victim without notifying command or law enforcement officials and to give the victim time and control over the release of information. Further, a restricted report also "empowers the survivor to make an informed decision about participating in the criminal process."[209] Hanks attempted to file a "restricted" report and, indeed, thought she had.[210]

One of the best explanations of the sexual assault reporting system in the military was published in the National Defense University Review in the April 2013 issue of *Joint Forces Quarterly*, written by Captain Lindsay Rodman, USMC.[211] As mentioned, the military "restricted report" provides the opportunity for a victim to avail himself or herself of resources without prompting an investigation or prosecution of the accused. According to Rodman: "It is difficult for a Service member to submit a restricted report without making a mistake that would convert the submission to an 'unrestricted report,'" which prompts an investigation. "Restricted reporting can only be communicated to a chaplain, medical professional, or victim advocate or counselor. Consequently, when a (Service member) confides in his or her best friend about a sexual encounter, that friend is obligated under military order to disclose the communication to the command."[212] Rodman wrote that many investigations actually begin when a roommate or friend reports the incident on behalf of the Service member. She says that while such reporting can be "beneficial in some cases, in other cases it forces the victim into a role he or she has not chosen — that of an accuser."[213]

On March 24, at the encouragement of Suzanne Berrong, who drove her, Hanks went to the Aviano clinic and requested a drug test. At that time, she asked Major O'Keefe "to keep it quiet, because I didn't know what I wanted to do. I was inclined not to report it if the drug test came back negative, but to report it if it came back positive."[214]

Major O'Keefe verified this request in his own statement on April 25: "No, she did not want anything reported. She did not want anything documented. There was some concern on her part — she was worried about what would happen to her because she was new to the military, as being a contractor working on a military base."[215]

Late in the week after the alleged incident, Hanks visited with the SARC and attempted to file a restricted report — no notification of law enforcement or the chain of command. However, the person (a new employee) who took the report made a mistake. Civilians cannot file restricted reports. If a civilian employee files any report at all, it is an unrestricted report. Therefore, Hanks, because she was a civilian, inadvertently filed an unrestricted report. There is some confusion as to what happened next, but in any event, the report was forwarded up the chain of command, and law enforcement was notified. By many accounts prior to the Article 32 hearing, this was without Kim Hanks' intent or knowledge. As Captain Rodman wrote in her *Joint Forces Quarterly* research, this reporting happens often by mistake.[216] It appears in this case, Hanks did not intend for this report to be unrestricted.

During the Article 32 hearing, Hanks provided a story to explain the confusion with the reporting process. She said "The SARC described restricted/unrestricted reporting. I initially decided to go restricted. The SARC called me the following week. (The SARC) told me because I was a civilian; a restricted report was not an option. I either had to file an unrestricted report or drop it."[217]

The defense attorneys were told a slightly different version. The story they were told is that the new person made a mistake, but since she had already revealed the information to the military chain of command via the SARC committee, the report must go forward as unrestricted and, in fact, already had gone forward by the time a supervisor called Hanks. The supervisor explained that now, since the report went forward, Hanks' only remaining option was to not cooperate with authorities — not to testify. It was too late to drop it. Once again, similar to when Suzanne Berrong convinced her to go to the clinic, outside pressure pushed Hanks forward in the process.

Most of this information came out in an investigation by the defense counsel, but the defense did not feel it was relevant to the case and did not pursue it.[218]

Hanks also refused a medical examination. According to Department of Defense instructions, a Sexual Assault Forensic Examination shall be offered to the victim. The instruction states even for a restricted report, the results of this examination will be kept on file for five years (to be used if the case ever goes unrestricted).[219] So, had any evidence been collected from Hanks during an examination, it could have been used or not, depending on the decision she made. However, despite Major O'Keefe requesting an examination to collect and preserve evidence, Hanks, a physician's assistant and fully cognizant of what the results might reveal, refused an examination."[220]

Hanks went to the clinic at the urging of Berrong, but she only wanted a drug test and refused a Sexual Assault Forensic Examination. She stated she only wanted to provide a restricted report — no notification of law enforcement or military chain of command. One has to wonder why.

12

A R T I C L E   3 2   H E A R I N G
A N D   T H E
I N V E S T I G A T I N G
O F F I C E R

"Never ascribe to malice that which
can adequately be explained by incompetence."
— *Napoleon Bonaparte*

An Investigating Officer (IO), Lt. Col. Paula McCarron, was assigned to conduct the Article 32 investigation, which is similar to a preliminary hearing in civilian court. No case may proceed to a court-martial without an Article 32 Investigation first. During this investigation, the prosecution is required to show "probable cause" to support the charges.[221] The Uniform Code of Military Justice (UCMJ) "requires a thorough and impartial investigation of charges and specifications before they may be referred to a general court-martial. The hearing is normally attended by the investigating officer, the accused and the defense counsel."[222] The Investigating Officer is required to complete a report on her findings and make a recommendation to the Convening Authority whether to proceed to court-martial.

The Article 32 hearing, and the report Lt. Col. McCarron provided, also had many inconsistencies and oddities, including the final recommendation. Lt. Col. McCarron wrote: "This case all comes down to what happened between midnight and 3 a.m. on 24 March. ... Unless the accused testifies, this case will essentially boil down to the testimony of two witnesses: Hanks and Beth Wilkerson."[223]

Here is how Lt. Col. McCarron described Kim Hanks as a witness: "Ms. Hanks' demeanor when testifying was fairly straightforward. She freely admits she does not recall many of the details of the night after she got to the Wilkersons'. She became teary on a few occasions, but was otherwise composed. She did, oddly, doodle when she was being questioned by defense counsel, but she was able to answer defense counsel's questions. Her recollection of the alleged assault, in contrast to other details of the night, is very detailed to include describing the finger uncurling and curling inside her. She told MSgt. Dunnivant, Ms. Berrong, and Major O'Keefe almost immediately some of the details of her account."[224]

Yes, in fact, Hanks did tell each MSgt. Dunnivant, Berrong, and Major O'Keefe *some* of the details. But these three versions of her story are different, and Hanks did *not* mention digital penetration in *any* of the three versions or in her report to the SARC. She did not talk about penetration of any sort. Didn't that seem an odd omission in these three statements to the IO? Lt. Col. McCarron also commented on how Hanks "oddly doodled" during questioning — an odd enough event for Lt. Col. McCarron to write it in her report.

Lt. Col. McCarron described Beth Wilkerson: "Beth Wilkerson makes a good witness. She had little to drink that night, and her recollection of her account of the evening was clear. I did find it odd that she buzzed the gate open for Ms. Hanks when she didn't think Ms. Hanks would leave."

Let's ask just one more question: "Why did Beth do that?" In order to leave the walled compound surrounding the Wilkerson home; the gates have to be remotely opened, or "buzzed." So why would that be odd? If a person is leaving, someone has to disarm the lock to allow the gate to open; otherwise they have to climb over the wall. Why did Lt. Col. McCarron think this was odd? Why didn't she ask why Beth buzzed the gate? It was the only issue in Beth Wilkerson's testimony that Lt. Col. McCarron thought worthy of mention, so why not ask?

Lt. Col. McCarron wrote: "Mrs. Wilkerson did not go to sleep, but the accused did." [225] If Beth did not go to sleep, where was she when her husband supposedly got up from his bed and went down two flights of stairs? And really, would he do that if his wife was awake?

Lt. Col. McCarron continued: "Ms. Hanks suddenly became very tired." She "went straight to bed in her clothes (IO Ex 24)."[226] Lt. Col. McCarron takes this as fact. She does not say "Ms. Hanks' version is" or that "Ms. Hanks said" she suddenly became very tired but rather states it as fact. Whereas, when writing about Beth Wilkerson's version of the evening, Lt. Col. McCarron writes: "Mrs. Wilkerson *says* she put Ms. Hanks in the basement playroom" (emphasis added).[227] Notice how Lt. Col. McCarron does not add the qualifier when she writes Hanks' version. Here is the acceptance as fact that a sexual assault has occurred. Unconsciously or otherwise, Lt. Col. McCarron has assumed the allegation is true and communicated that in her report.

When I dug deeper into the Record of Trial, I discovered some things that really should have caused concern. Some of those twenty-five things Lt. Col. McCarron documented should have raised suspicion, but an even bigger clue to a possible false allegation perhaps comes from Hanks' discussion with Suzanne Berrong. Berrong testified during the Article 32 hearing: "During the thirty minutes I spoke to her on the phone that morning … she didn't want anyone to know … She was concerned about people finding out. She was concerned about 'them saying something happened before she could.' "[228]

Hanks "was concerned about *them saying something happened before she could.*" Did that statement not give the OSI or Lt. Col. McCarron reason to check into a possible false allegation? Hanks also told MSgt. Dunnivant something similar, which MSgt. Dunnivant reported to the OSI but left out of her statement and testimony. MSgt. Dunnivant said Hanks told her she was "concerned that she (Hanks) could be fired because she was a civilian contractor or that (Wilkerson's) wife would try to get her (Hanks) in trouble."[229] What was it that could get Hanks fired? Also, notice it says *Wilkerson's wife*, not Wilkerson. Why say wife? What could "the wife" do or say that might get Hanks in trouble?

Suzanne Berrong also testified at the Article 32 hearing: "In early May, Kim and I had dinner. She told me she didn't drink any vodka the night of 23 March 2012 … At this point, I started to think her story didn't add up."[230] By this time, you had two of Hanks' friends indicating she had something to hide and one of them, her best friend, indicating she did not believe the story.

These statements have obvious connotations that will be explored in detail in a later chapter but, even on the surface, they offer some doubt as to the motivation for Hanks' story. Why didn't Lt. Col. McCarron ask some questions? Did she not see these statements? Why didn't she think this testimony by Hanks' best friend might warrant investigation to dig deeper into the possibility of a false allegation? Why didn't the Air Force, someone, anyone, look into this prospect? The clues were there. The questions should have been asked. Why didn't the IO, or the jury, see that?

Lt. Col. McCarron described Beth Wilkerson as a "credible witness." She also documented that Beth's Article 32 testimony on June 19 was consistent with her April 19 OSI statement.

"Mrs. Wilkerson testified that everyone had gone to bed, she and the accused upstairs on the third floor of the house and Hanks in the basement. Sometime after midnight, Mrs. Wilkerson heard Hanks downstairs talking. When she went to investigate, she discovered Hanks talking on the phone in the kitchen ... She asked to her to be quiet (the boys who were spending the night were asleep in a guest room off the kitchen) and ended up making Hanks tea and herself coffee. Mrs. Wilkerson testified she and Hanks both went back to bed after their tea and coffee."[231]

Lt. Col. McCarron said the case would boil down to the credibility of two witnesses: Hanks, who admitted she had been drinking, was "buzzed," and "freely admits she does not recall many of the details of the night," and Beth Wilkerson, who "makes a good witness. She had little to drink that night and her recollection of her account of the evening was clear."[232]

Lt. Col. McCarron went on to write: "Most who observed or talked to Ms. Hanks during the evening of 23-24 March, described her as drunk, slurring her words and stumbling. She describes herself as 'out of it,' and admittedly does not remember many details of the evening."[233] What, then, influenced Lt. Col. McCarron to find there was sufficient evidence or reason to proceed to trial? What was it that made her give more credibility to Hanks, who had been drinking and cannot remember things, than Mrs. Wilkerson, who "makes a good witness," whose "recollection of her account of the evening was clear"?

"In the end, what compels my recommendation that there are reasonable grounds ... to believe that the accused committed the offenses alleged (RCM 405 U)(2)(H)) is the absence of any apparent motive on the part of Ms. Hanks to fabricate the allegations. She had never met the accused prior to that night, was not in a relationship she felt she needed to protect, does not display any malice about being told to leave the house, has not told anyone she was mad at the Wilkersons, or have any other apparent reason to make up her allegations."[234]

Lt. Col. McCarron said the absence of any apparent motive for a false allegation was sufficient and that Hanks had not told anyone any apparent reason to make up a story. But Hanks had. There was plenty of documentation to suggest Hanks was hiding something. Lt. Col. McCarron did not investigate these statements. She did not investigate whether Hanks had motivation to cover up being told to leave the house. She did not question why Hanks would say "I need to get my story out before they do" or how "the wife might get (Hanks) in trouble." She did not question if Hanks was concerned about an alcohol-related incident, such as being asked to leave a house in the middle of the night. Lt. Col. McCarron did not investigate, in any way, the possibility that Hanks fabricated this story. No one did.

Was it the defense team's responsibility to find "apparent motive" prior to or during the Article 32 hearing? Is that the new standard in the Air Force — the defense must prove the accuser lied, or the defendant goes to prison? What happened to the standard of reasonable doubt and preponderance of evidence? Many attorneys I have interviewed said this case would never have gone to trial in the civilian court system.[235] There was a complete lack of evidence, a "she-said, she-said" with nothing to support Hanks' story. But the Air Force is under a lot of political pressure to "do something" about sexual assault, and it has an unlimited budget for prosecutions. Perhaps these points were factors?

Finally, Hanks refused the Sexual Assault Forensic Examination. Didn't it seem strange to Lt. Col. McCarron that a physician's assistant, fully aware of what the examination might show, should refuse?

Shouldn't that have caused some doubt for Lt. Col. McCarron and a jury that perhaps something wasn't quite right with the story?

At the conclusion of the Article 32 hearing, Lt. Col. McCarron told Beth Wilkerson in confidence: "There's no way this is going anywhere." But then, three days later, she reversed herself and recommended proceeding to court-martial based on the conclusion that Hanks "has no apparent reason to lie."[236] Might this change of heart have had something to do with the visiting colonel from Washington, D.C.? Lt. Col. McCarron is a JAG officer from North Carolina. Colonel Christensen, a senior JAG officer from Washington, came all the way to Aviano to be present for the hearing. This was a highly unusual visit. Why was he there? "She-said, she-said" became "she has no (obvious) reason to lie," so let's go to trial. That is an interesting recommendation, particularly given Lt. Col. McCarron did not investigate possible motives for a lie.

Perhaps this decision by Lt. Col. McCarron had something to do with the August 2013 emails released by the Air Force in response to our FOIA request. In these emails, the wing commander, Brig. Gen. Zobrist, said: "We have a list of several senior lawyers that could run the 32, but are pushing for a reserve Lt. Col. who has the right credentials and experience, and is a known commodity. We hope she is available so I can appoint her as the Article 32 hearing lead."[237] According to these emails, Brig. Gen. Zobrist chose the investigating officer personally because she was "a known commodity." That is an interesting comment, and perhaps it has something to do with why Brig. Gen. Zobrist personally hand-picked her out of the list of available senior officers.

Why was Col. Christensen at the Article 32 hearing, and why did Lt. Col. McCarron change her mind about proceeding to a full court-martial? Could it have had something to do with her being hand-picked for this case? That statement by Lt. Col. McCarron — "she has no reason to lie" — would become Col. Christensen's central theme during the trial. I wonder who came up with it first.

13

TRUTH OR CONSEQUENCES

"Truth is generally the best vindication against slander."
— *Abraham Lincoln*

The prosecution's case was based on the premise that the Wilkersons were lying. Prosecutors said both the Wilkersons were liars because they had so much to lose — Lt. Col. Wilkerson was lying to protect his career, and Beth was lying to protect her son.[238] The standard of guilt, the prosecution successfully conveyed to the jury, was that the Wilkersons had something to lose, therefore they were lying. Whereas, according to the prosecution, Hanks had no reason to lie, therefore she was not lying.

Prosecutors said the Wilkersons made up or concocted their story about asking Hanks to leave between 2 and 3 a.m. Col. Ostovich visited the Wilkersons at 10:30 the next morning — Saturday, March 24. This was before any report on the allegation. During that visit, the Wilkersons told Col. Ostovich that Hanks had been drunk and up walking around the house during the night and that Beth had asked her to leave. On Sunday, Suzanne Berrong and Col. Ostovich, who knew each other, spoke on the phone. During that Sunday phone call, Col. Ostovich relayed Beth's account to Berrong.[239] In Berrong's original OSI statement on April 19, she said Col. Ostovich "mentioned that Roscoe/Beth mentioned that Kim was up walking around through the house. I think something about she was found in the bed with one child or more than one child … I don't remember exactly what was said — but that Beth was asking her to leave the house, that she was being a little belligerent and Beth asked her to be quiet, not wake the kids."[240]

Testimony proves this account of the night — Beth's story — never changed throughout the entire process from her interview with the OSI at her home through the completion of the trial. Think about it. The prosecution claimed the Wilkersons and Col. Ostovich made up this story on Saturday morning, that Col. Ostovich then accurately relayed this account to Berrong as early as Sunday, March 25, long before any allegations surfaced. The account, Col. Ostovich told Berrong only one day later, never changed. This would mean the Wilkersons told the story immediately to Colonel Ostovich, and he told it to Berrong before he knew of an allegation. Berrong said she mentioned that something happened to Hanks but did not give Col. Ostovich any details during that call.[241] Col. Ostovich telling Berrong what happened according to Beth corroborated Beth's statement and testimony in detail, including how Hanks was found outside the bedroom where the visiting children were sleeping and that Beth asked her to leave. In short, Col. Ostovich's testimony supported Beth's account.

The prosecution's theory was that by 10:30 the following morning, not only had the Wilkersons created this story, but they had communicated it so effectively between themselves and Col. Ostovich that by the next afternoon, he was able to relay it to Suzanne Berrong, Hanks' best friend, so that there were no inconsistencies or changes from that point forward through all the statements, interrogations, interviews, Article 32 hearing, and trial. Is that plausible? Beyond a reasonable doubt?

If the Wilkersons made up this story, they would have had to work pretty quickly that morning before Col. Ostovich arrived and convinced Col. Ostovich to go along with their story, making him a liar. In fact, Col. Christensen accused Col. Ostovich of being just that. Referring to Col. Ostovich when addressing the jury, Col. Christensen said: "You're supposed to believe him? He's a poor officer."[242]

There is much more to know about Col. Ostovich. For reasons that have never been explained, the prosecution offered testimonial immunity to Colonel Dean Ostovich and Captain Tanya Manning. Neither of these officers was present during the timeframe of the alleged assault. They both admitted to having a consensual relationship that evening at the Colonel's residence. This is a violation of the UCMJ.

Article 92 of the UCMJ lists "unprofessional relationships" that are considered a violation. "Unprofessional relationships are those that compromise military authority or create an appearance of impropriety. The definition of unprofessional relationship is a bit fluid, but it essentially covers relationships that adversely affect or have the reasonable *potential* to adversely affect the military by eroding morale, good order, discipline, respect for authority, unit cohesion, or by compromising the military mission itself."[243]

Article 92 of the UCMJ addresses sexual or romantic relations. Article 134 of the UCMJ describes adultery. There is no information available on what specific transgression by Col. Ostovich might have required immunity from prosecution. However, testimonial immunity does protect both officers from ever being prosecuted for anything covered in their statements or testimony.

Col. Christensen, immediately upon Col. Ostovich taking the stand, asked Col. Ostovich about testimonial immunity and an unprofessional relationship.[244] Col. Ostovich had left the Wilkerson home earlier in the evening and had nothing to offer as testimony concerning an alleged assault but only possible information on a cover-up. However, Col. Ostovich didn't testify to a cover-up but rather corroborated Lt. Col. and Beth Wilkerson's versions of events.[245] That may explain why, even though Col. Ostovich was a prosecution witness, Col. Christensen impeached his credibility during the trial, saying: "Colonel Ostovich. You've got a guy who was fired for unprofessional misconduct; who was a poor officer; and we're supposed to believe him? You're supposed to believe him? He's a poor officer."[246] (Brig. Gen. Zobrist removed Col. Ostovich from his position as Vice Wing Commander sometime between the alleged incident and the trial.)

Col. Christensen went on to say about Col. Ostovich: "are we supposed to believe that he didn't pass on to Lt. Col. Wilkerson, 'Hey, by the way, she's saying you did something, too, dude,' to his best friend?"[247] But Col. Christensen has covered up the timeline here. He is saying Col. Ostovich warned Lt. Col. Wilkerson at 10:30 a.m. Saturday. In reality, and truth, there is no way possible for Col. Ostovich to have known that Hanks was "saying you did something" by 10:30 a.m. She arrived at the clinic at 9 a.m., no report was filed that day, and Berrong did not speak to Col. Ostovich until the next day. Col. Christensen was caught disparaging a senior officer for a fantasy scenario, again with no evidence.

The prosecution went out of its way to provide Col. Ostovich testimonial immunity, only to call him to the stand and impeach his credibility immediately. He was a prosecution witness! In his closing argument, Col. Christensen called Col. Ostovich a poor officer and insinuated he was a liar. But why would Col. Ostovich lie? What did he have to gain? He was granted testimonial immunity, so anything he said was without repercussion. It appears Col. Christensen was saying Col. Ostovich was lying to protect Lt. Col. Wilkerson. Would Col. Ostovich really do that? He'd only known Lt. Col. Wilkerson for a short time — less than ten months. Would he lie under oath just to protect Lt. Col. Wilkerson? Col. Christensen said so, and the jury evidently believed so.

What other testimony might offer support that this story was not made up, as Col. Christensen said? Besides the conversation with Col. Ostovich and the statement by Berrong, the fact that the visiting boys reported no disturbance might offer some insight. The OSI interviewed both the boys.[248] Neither reported any unusual activities that night or the next day.[249]

The statements from Col. Ostovich, Berrong, the boys and their mother, in addition to the following points (scattered throughout the trial testimony and interviews with the author), paint a picture of a normal relationship between Lt. Col. and Beth Wilkerson after the alleged event.

The next-door neighbor arrived around 12:30 p.m. on March 24 (the next day) and visited with Beth on the porch until approximately 3 p.m., when Lt. Col. Wilkerson returned from playing baseball. The neighbor testified Beth was happy and normal and that Lt. Col. Wilkerson kissed her when he returned — that there appeared to be no difference in their relationship.[250]

The mother of the visiting boys arrived around 6:30 p.m. She also testified Beth was in good spirits. Beth offered to keep her children again the following day, to which all agreed.[251]

The following week, Monday-Friday, was normal. The Wilkersons' son was in school, and Beth spent the time exercising with the next-door neighbor, as was their routine. Lt. Col. Wilkerson worked and flew a normal schedule all week.[252]

On Easter Sunday, the Wilkersons shared Easter Brunch at the Club on Aviano Air Base with four other couples, all of whom testified that there was nothing out of the ordinary with the Wilkersons.[253]

The Wilkersons went on a trip to Greece on Monday, April 9, for a vacation. A co-worker's wife and daughter accompanied them to the airport. The daughter noticed Beth and Lt. Col. Wilkerson holding hands and commented about it. Neither noticed anything out of the ordinary about the Wilkersons.[254]

The Wilkersons enjoyed a vacation in Greece with three other couples who testified there was nothing out of the ordinary with the Wilkersons.[255]

On April 19, both Wilkersons were questioned by the OSI independent of each other. Both statements and interviews are simultaneous, and their stories and statements, although not identical in detail, match. Both Wilkersons willingly cooperated with the investigators.

By all testimony, the Wilkersons' demeanor and behavior as a couple and as members of the leadership team at Aviano had not changed between the night of the alleged incident and their interviews with the OSI. Those who knew them best testified there was no difference in their relationship. Could they have been the same couple with the same relationship if Beth had caught Lt. Col. Wilkerson in a bed with a strange woman in their own home? Those people closest to the Wilkersons do not believe they could.

14

The Truth, The Whole Truth

"A lie gets halfway around the world
before the truth has a chance to get its pants on."
— *Sir Winston Churchill*

As Lt. Col. McCarron, the Article 32 Investigating Officer, wrote, "this case comes down to the credibility of two witnesses, Hanks and Beth Wilkerson."[256] Beth Wilkerson's statement, Article 32 and trial testimony are remarkably consistent, and the investigating officer called her a "credible witness." The prosecution, however, insisted, and evidently convinced the jurors, that Beth Wilkerson was lying.

Beth admitted she cancelled a small planned get-together at her home that was scheduled for Saturday afternoon. She testified she had slept late, until about 9 a.m. Saturday, after being up past 3 a.m. She admitted she told a white lie to her friend — that she (Beth) was not feeling well and wanted to cancel the get-together.[257] Col. Christensen, the lead prosecutor, referred to this admitted lie often, saying since she lied about that, she was lying about everything else.[258]

Col. Christensen claimed the Wilkersons were actually up early and spent the morning creating a cover story.[259] He said Beth lied because she had so much to lose. She was "lying to protect her son," Col. Christensen repeated, "… in order to believe Beth Wilkerson is lying, all you have to do is believe she's protecting her son. That's all you have to believe."[260] *That's all you have to believe.* Simple case: Beth is protecting her son, so she is a liar.

As we discussed, the prosecution needed to discredit Col. Ostovich telling Berrong Beth's version of the night. Remember, if by noon Saturday, the Wilkersons and Col. Ostovich so meticulously planned and rehearsed a fictional account that it held up throughout months of investigation, statements, Article 32 hearing and a trial without variation, they had to have time to work on it. Therefore, they must have been up early creating the story. But Beth and Lt. Col. Wilkerson both claim Beth slept until about 9 a.m.[261] Lt. Col. Wilkerson and Beth Wilkerson were simultaneously interrogated/interviewed in different locations — Lt. Col. Wilkerson on base at the OSI office and Beth Wilkerson at her home by other agents. Their stories matched.[262] Col. Christensen claimed this was because they had done such a thorough job fabricating the story that morning.[263]

In any event, Col. Christensen needed to discredit Beth's version of the night in question, because if Beth actually slept until 9 a.m., there was not enough time to make up a story. Col. Christensen attacked Beth's account by claiming Beth was not sleeping until 9 a.m. because there were phone calls and texts on her phone. There was a seven-minute phone call at 6:59, a text to the same number at 7:11, and other received texts and another incoming call at 7:31.[264] The prosecution contended these calls proved Beth was awake and talking on her phone. However, according to Lt. Col. Wilkerson, these texts and phone calls were from, and then to, the visiting boys' mother. Lt. Col. Wilkerson said he was replying via text that his wife was still asleep, and he also allowed the boys to talk with their mother.

Col. Christensen waited until his summation to bring up the phone records and ascribe a reason to these texts and calls. He offered no witnesses to say who was on Beth's phone or what the texts said. This was shrewd but obviously effective. The defense had rested. They could not call a new witness to rebut this accusation. All they could do was cast (reasonable) doubt during their own summation. It is not unusual for a husband to answer a wife's phone while she is sleeping. Spinner, the lead defense attorney, alluded to Lt. Col. Wilkerson answering his wife's phone during closing arguments but otherwise put no effort toward disproving the prosecution theory on that issue. In hindsight, the defense attorneys should have challenged every single statement by the prosecution. There were no "little things" too small to sweat.

Lt. Col. Wilkerson's recollection of who was on the phone is actually corroborated by the visiting boys' mother in her clemency letter to Lt. Gen. Franklin; unfortunately, it was too late for the trial. In her letter to

Lt. Gen. Franklin, the boys' mother vehemently disputed Col. Christensen's mischaracterization of the calls on Beth Wilkerson's phone. She wrote:

> ...the prosecution made mention that Beth's phone was being utilized at 7:00 a.m. on the morning of March 24th, an attempt to correlate this in contradiction to Beth's direct testimony that she slept till 9:00 a.m. on March 24th. The lead prosecutor presented this with dramatic flair in his closing argument which prevented any defense counter. It is true Beth's phone was utilized. I personally called her cell phone and Jay answered it because he said Beth was asleep, just as she testified in court. The prosecutor used this in closing as proof she had lied, when in fact, she was completely truthful. I spoke with Jay and my children and even went as far as to stop by and say hello prior to 8:00 a.m. on Saturday March 24th. I saw Jay, my boys and their son that morning and I did not see Beth because the boys told me she was sleeping. How this was bent into a lie by the lead prosecutor is unforgivable.[265]

The jury did not hear testimony from the boys' mother concerning these phone calls. She was not able to testify to this issue because it was not raised until Col. Christensen's summation, after the defense had given closing arguments. It simply had not come up during the trial until Col. Christensen used it in summation.

Despite building his case on the Wilkersons making up a story and agreeing on it, Col. Christensen, when it suited him, also said their story didn't agree. He made a big deal in the closing argument that Beth said one of the boys wanted to talk to Lt. Col. Wilkerson before going to sleep so "she goes and gets her husband." Col. Christensen is animated as he points out Lt. Col. Wilkerson's statement that says "I went to the room on my own because I heard the boys wanted a story."[266] That seemed like a smoking gun the way the Col. Christensen told it — proof that they had concocted their story. Col. Christensen said "they can't even get that right": "And the sad thing is these two are married, and even when they are telling a story, they can't agree with each other."[267] On the other hand, Col. Christensen adamantly states, with regard to where Beth said she found the shoes, "there is no doubt her (Hanks') shoes were found under that bed with a lamp, the next day."[268] He used Beth's testimony about finding the shoes under that bed so that he could say Beth lied when she said Hanks slept in a different bed. But if Beth was telling the truth about where the shoes were found, a truth Col. Christensen needed to use in order to prove she was lying about which bed Hanks was in, then how was he so sure she was telling the truth about where the shoes were found? Which is it, Colonel? Was Beth "no doubt" telling the truth or lying to protect her son? Do the Wilkersons' stories match or not?

Col. Christensen also said Beth lied about a conversation with Captain Brock. Captain Dawn Brock, the third woman from the club, was distraught that evening. She had been notified earlier that day that she had a serious, life-changing medical issue.[269] Shortly after discovering Col. Ostovich and Captain Manning had hooked up, Captain Brock told Beth she "wanted to go, now!"[270]

Beth drove Captain Brock back to the base and dropped her off just outside the security checkpoint. Captain Brock testified that Beth did not tell her ahead of time that she would be dropped off outside the gate and would have to walk the last couple of hundred yards to her TLF room. Captain Brock said Beth only told her after they were on the way to the base that she would not drive her through the gate.[271] Beth testified she explained this to Captain Brock at the time Captain Brock asked for the ride, before they left the house.[272]

Captain Brock testified that during the drive to the base, Beth asked her, "Did *my husband* do something to you?" (Emphasis added.)[273] Beth said she was concerned about Captain Brock, as she seemed upset. Beth said she asked if Captain Brock "was all right" and asked if Osto (Col. Ostovich) had done something to her.[274]

The defense asked if Captain Brock may have misinterpreted the word Osto for that of "Bosco," which Captain Brock had testified she thought was Lt. Col. Wilkerson's call sign, basically asking if Captain Brock mistook "Bosco" for "Osto." Captain Brock claimed she did not confuse the names and said she heard Beth say, "Did my husband do something?"[275]

Defense counsel did not question Captain Brock about her mental or emotional state as a result of her medical issue or ask how much she had drunk during the evening.[276] Perhaps Spinner should have asked more questions to explore the emotional stress Captain Brock was under as a result of her diagnosis, how much she had to drink and whether those issues may have led to her misunderstanding what Beth Wilkerson asked. It is clear by both testimonies that Beth was concerned about Captain Brock's state of well-being, and it is equally clear Captain Brock was upset.

Might Captain Brock have been upset with Beth about being dropped outside the gate? Might she have been stressed and focused on her medical diagnosis? Might she have felt rejected? Perhaps because of one or more of these factors, Captain Brock simply didn't remember being told in advance that Beth would drop her at the gate. Perhaps because of one or more of these factors, she thought Beth asked if her "husband" had done anything. Perhaps.

Other testimony by Captain Brock supported Hanks but was questionable. During questioning about drinking Prosecco at the Wilkerson home, Captain Brock evaded the defense question. Hanks testified she did not drink the Prosecco given to her by Lt. Col. Wilkerson; she said she only drank a glass of white wine. That testimony was contradicted twice.[277]

Here is Captain Brock's testimony:

> Q. Do you remember if Ms. Hanks took a glass at that point?
> A. I remember her taking a glass. I don't know if she drank it because that's when the conversation started, and I said: "Oh, no, I don't want any. I don't drink Prosecco."[278]

Captain Manning's testimony disputes both Hanks and Brock:

Q. And when you got to the Wilkerson house, she (Hanks) was the one who approached you about Prosecco?

A. Yes.

Q. And she even said to you, specifically, "You have to try this?"

A. Yes.[279]

In her trial testimony, Captain Manning said: "Once I got in the house, I was offered a drink, I believe by Colonel Wilkerson. Ah, and Kim had mentioned that she was drinking Prosecco and said I should have a glass of Prosecco, so I had a glass of Prosecco."[280] *Kim had mentioned that she was drinking Prosecco.*

Why is all this testimony by Captain Brock important? The prosecution thought it was important, and incriminating, when Captain Brock said Beth asked if her *husband* had done anything to upset Captain Brock. Col. Christensen clearly wanted the jury to believe Lt. Col. Wilkerson might have tried something inappropriate with her "also," as he was accused of with Hanks. Why else would this even be a subject of discussion? It sounded damning, but when examining all of the testimony by Captain Brock, and understanding her medical and emotional state of mind that evening, was she really a credible witness? Captain Brock's testimony was disputed twice by others besides Beth Wilkerson. So is someone not telling the truth here, or could it simply be Captain Brock was confused about the events of that evening? She, more than any of the others because of the emotional stress of her medical diagnosis, had reason not to remember the events clearly. Was Captain Brock simply mistaken or perhaps trying to help her friend, Hanks? Spinner did not challenge Captain Brock's testimony, but perhaps he should have.

Col. Christensen insinuated the two majors — fighter pilots — in the Wilkerson home that evening also lied. Lt. Col. Wilkerson stated during his interrogation that, at some point, he had asked the visitors to leave.[281] Prosecutors said this was a lie; that he did not ask anyone to leave. The prosecution asked Captain Brock and Hanks if Lt. Col. Wilkerson had asked everyone to leave that evening, as in, "Hey, it's time for you to go," and they both testified, no, he did not ask them to leave.[282] But Majors Lowe and Goldsberry both testified that yes, Lt. Col. Wilkerson did tell them it was time for everyone to go. "The accused told me the party needed to end."[283] "At some point, the accused wanted everyone to leave."[284] So, basically, Col. Christensen insinuated they must be lying to help their friend.

So far, according to the prosecution, Lt. Col. and Beth Wilkerson, Col. Ostovich and both majors were either lying or covering up for Lt. Col. Wilkerson. It didn't stop there. When referring to Colonel Walker, the Operations Group Commander and Wilkerson's superior officer, Col. Christensen said "obviously, Colonel Walker has blinders."[285] Even more startling was when Col. Christensen was speaking about Berrong's testimony that Hanks was slurring her speech while on the phone. During his closing argument, he said: "There's absolutely no evidence that Kim was slurring her speech other than Suzanne Berrong. Again, maybe that was intentional on Suzanne's part."[286] Now, Col. Christensen accused Hanks' best friend of lying, too?

Continuing to disparage others, the prosecutor made this remark about a retired four-star general: "The imfamous General Ashy," who had written an affidavit on behalf of Lt. Col. Wilkerson.[287] The remark was intended to tell the jurors, none of whom were pilots, that they should believe the current fighter pilot on trial was lying because, of course, they all do, including "the infamous General Ashy." Col. Christensen said about Lt. Col. Wilkerson: "He's a fighter pilot — a fighter pilot — he — we can rely on our common sense and knowledge of the ways of the world."[288] There was no mistaking the intent of the closing argument and that comment. All fighter pilots lie, so this one is no different. Colonel Ostovich lied, Colonel Walker lied, the majors lied, and of course both Lt. Col. and Beth Wilkerson lied. According to Col. Christensen, three senior officers, one senior officer's wife, two majors and even Kim Hanks' best friend, Suzanne Berrong, lied — everyone who supported Lt. Col. Wilkerson was lying.

15

A New Standard of Justice

"Human reason can excuse any evil."
— *Veronica Roth, "Divergent"*

Col. Christensen set a new standard of guilt during his closing argument. One, evidently the jurors agreed with — if someone has something to lose, they must be lying. Col. Christensen summed up the case this way: Kim Hanks had no reason to lie, but Lt. Col. and Beth Wilkerson had plenty of reasons to lie. Therefore Lt. Col. Wilkerson is guilty.

> Mr. President, members of the court. I'm going to say something that's uncomfortable, and it may be uncomfortable for you to hear. Somebody came into this courtroom and lied to you. Somebody lied...[289]
>
> What does Beth Wilkerson have to gain by lying? She protects her lifestyle; she protects her son; and she doesn't have to have the embarrassment of being married to a sex offender.[290]
>
> Kim Hanks has absolutely zero motive to falsely accuse this man ... absolutely no reason to falsely accuse that officer of sexual assault.[291]
>
> But in order to believe Beth Wilkerson is lying, all you have to do is believe she's protecting her son. That's all you have to believe. And when you go back and look at that evidence, and you look at the motives to lie and you look at the fact that you have definitive proof that Beth Wilkerson lied, there's only one conclusion you can come to, only one, that's he is guilty.[292]

If you subscribe to Col. Christensen's reasoning, all you have to believe in order to find Lt. Col. Wilkerson guilty of sexual assault is that he has something to lose. All you have to believe, in order for Beth Wilkerson to be lying, is that she is protecting her son. Col. Christensen said those motives made her a liar and made her husband guilty. It follows then, under Col. Christensen's logic, that all men accused of sexual assault must be de facto guilty (innocent or otherwise). They all have their freedom and careers to lose. If one accepts Col. Christensen's argument, that makes them all liars and therefore guilty. Is this the new Air Force standard — because the defendant has something to lose, he is guilty? And because the accuser has no *obvious* reason to lie, that therefore means she is telling the truth? More accurately, is the accused guilty simply because no one bothered to investigate the possibility of a false allegation? That seems an unconscionable reason for a conviction based on zero physical evidence to support Hanks' story. Unfortunately, there are many similar cases discussed later in this book. Sadly, pushed by political elitists and condoned by ignorance and apathy, this is becoming the standard of proof in the military.

What is, or was, the standard for a guilty verdict? It was, and should be under our system of justice, including military justice, beyond a reasonable doubt. Why, then, was there not enough reasonable doubt in the jurors' minds? What was so convincing to those five men that is not obvious in a review of the Record of Trial? Post-trial, through the grapevine, these panel members indicated they thought Beth Wilkerson's story was "all over the map" and that Hanks' story "never changed." I wonder what trial they attended and how they could have believed that.

When Hanks confirmed she could not remember those twenty-five things, and when she could not identify the room where she says the alleged attack took place, what was it that the jury thought "never changed"? Why did these jurors not see the inconsistencies in Hanks' various versions? One can assume these jurors believed they were right. I can only hope they read the rest of the evidence referenced here and come to understand they actually got it wrong. As the Record of Trial proves, it is Hanks who was "all over the map" and Beth Wilkerson whose story "never changed."

16

THERE ARE
NO WORDS

"In the end, we will remember not the words of our enemies,
but the silence of our friends."
— *Martin Luther King Jr.*

Eight individuals flew to Italy to support Lt. Col. Wilkerson during the court-martial, including one family member, two friends he had grown up with, two people who have known him most of his adult life, and one woman who had come to know the Wilkersons as a neighbor in Italy but who had been reassigned to the United States. My wife and I, who had known the Wilkersons for seven years, also flew to Italy. All eight testified on behalf of both Wilkersons' character and truthfulness. (Testimony as to our knowledge of Beth's truthfulness became relevant when the prosecution decided to build a case that she was lying.) A significant number of people were willing to step up and say that Lt. Col. Wilkerson was not of the type of character who would have committed an assault, and that Beth Wilkerson was truthful and not the type of woman who would stand by any man who had committed an assault. These individuals came from all over the world and all over the Air Force to defend Lt. Col. Wilkerson. Thirteen others wrote affidavits of support prior to the trial, including four general officers.

Those who knew the Wilkersons thought he was innocent, and it seems even the Aviano Judge Advocate General office expected Lt. Col. Wilkerson to be exonerated as well.

It is standard protocol for the JAG office on a base where a trial is located to call ahead to the nearest military prison to notify them of a potential prisoner should there be a conviction. When Lt. Col. Wilkerson's court-martial began, as is required, the Aviano JAG office called the military prison in Mannheim, Germany. They were required to notify Mannheim that they were trying a case to give them notice of a potential new inmate at the conclusion of the trial. During this phone call, the JAG office in Aviano told the Mannheim prison authorities, they were trying this lieutenant colonel, but *"don't expect him."* That's correct, *don't expect him.* Even the Aviano JAG office did not expect a conviction.[293]

The prosecution, too, seemed to know its case was weak.

Prior to the conclusion of the Wilkerson trial, the prosecution moved to include all lesser charges. Judge Brown agreed and instructed the jury that they had the ability to find Lt. Col. Wilkerson guilty of lesser included offenses if they did not find him guilty of the charges as written. This gave the jury the option to find Lt. Col. Wilkerson guilty of Wrongful Sexual Contact in place of either Abusive Sexual Contact (charge 1, specification 1) and/or Aggravated Sexual Assault (charge 1, specification 2).[294]

Although this is a relatively often used tactic, at the time it appeared the request for lesser included offenses was a sign that the prosecution thought they had a better chance of a conviction on the lesser included offense over that of the aggravated assault. The belief is the prosecution again demonstrated that they thought their case was not strong.

Despite strong support of Lt. Col. Wilkerson and a weak case, on November 1, 2012, the jury returned a verdict of guilty on all counts and sentenced Lt. Col. Wilkerson to complete dismissal from the Air Force and one year in prison. "Dismissal" means Lt. Col. Wilkerson was stripped of all benefits he had earned in twenty-plus years of service to his country, including medical and pension benefits.

Nancy Montgomery of the *Stars and Stripes* wrote that Lt. Col. Wilkerson "showed no emotion as the verdict was read, nor did his wife, Beth."[295] Her opinion was not shared by others in the courtroom. I was there, and I saw Lt. Col. Wilkerson flush white. His legs were shaking, and he almost had to sit down to keep from falling down. He and his wife, Beth, were in tears as they hugged each other after the jury was excused.

Nancy Montgomery did point out that one observer was visibly upset with the verdict: "As the verdict was read, several women in the gallery, who were supporters of the Wilkersons, wept, including a lieutenant colonel with the wing maintenance group."[296] Montgomery mischaracterized the reaction in the courtroom and the relationship between the weeping officer and the Wilkersons. She was not a "supporter of the Wilkersons." In fact, she didn't know the Wilkersons. She only knew of Lt. Col. Wilkerson as another officer on in the wing; she was not a supporter or a friend. She did not know Beth. She did not know Hanks, either. She was simply an impartial observer who wanted to observe the trial out of curiosity and for the experience. Upon hearing the verdict, she said she was visibly upset because of the miscarriage of justice.[297]

That emotional response was shared by many both inside and outside of the courtroom. The testimony and lack of evidence just didn't prove guilt at all, let alone beyond a reasonable doubt. In particular, Lt. Col. Wilkerson's friends and family were devastated and angry. I was shocked and angry at the verdict because of the lack of evidence and because of the testimony by Hanks, which I did not find credible in any way. In my opinion, Hanks did not portray herself as a woman who had been assaulted. As I mentioned, I have been a part of four previous sexual assault cases inside the Air Force. Hanks' testimony, during the sentencing phase in particular, was far from convincing. I thought she lacked conviction and actually attempted to fake tears. I was also deeply disappointed and troubled that my Air Force could do such a disgraceful thing. I was there throughout the trial, most often in the lobby area just outside the courtroom, and I heard the daily rundown of the events each evening from those who were present through every minute of the trial. I met with others each evening to review the day's events from top to bottom, and I read the daily reports by Nancy Montgomery. Many felt, and still feel, the fact that there was nothing to support Hanks' story should have been reasonable doubt enough. It seemed to me that if we only needed one person's story to convict someone, we had returned to the days of the Salem Witch Trials. Certainly, the jury needed more than that. I was absolutely shocked that to the jurors, evidently, the complete lack of evidence and the many versions of Hanks' story were not a problem.

I could not, in good conscience, allow a wrongful conviction to stand. Immediately, I sincerely felt that with my understanding of the legal system, Lt. Col. Wilkerson had a substantial possibility of having the conviction overturned during the appeal process. It was just so wrong. I vowed to get involved and help if there was anything I could do, and I was not alone. Immediately after the sentencing, a group of Lt. Col. Wilkerson's friends met to discuss what they might be able to do to help. The first concern was for Beth and their 9-year-old son. The Air Force immediately told Beth she had thirty days to "get out," to leave Aviano and the house the base had procured for them.

We established a support group for Beth and her son and began to organize her move and return to the United States. I established an email list of anyone interested in supporting the Wilkersons and provided regular updates to the group. I provided Lt. Col. Wilkerson's mailing address and visitation availability to all. We needed him to understand we believed in him and that, as a fighter pilot community, we would take care of his family. In the fighter pilot community, we take care of one another's families during tough times. It didn't seem like much, but it was a start.

17

FALSE ALLEGATIONS

"I know there's evil in the world, and there always has been. But you don't need to believe in Satan or demons to explain it. Human beings are perfectly capable of evil all by themselves."
— *Tess Gerristen, "The Mephisto Club"*

False allegations happen. To think otherwise is naive and foolish or to be so blinded by an agenda as to deny the truth.

The issue of false allegations is complex and disturbing. Why would a woman falsely accuse a man of sexual assault? Research shows that false allegations in rape cases occur in somewhere between 2 and 45 percent of all cases.[298] Unfortunately, the statistics vary greatly depending upon the political position of the group reporting. According to Wendy McElroy, author and editor of ifeminists.com and a research fellow for The Independent Institute in Oakland, Calif., while men's groups sometime cite statistics much higher: "Politically correct feminists claim false rape accusations are rare and account for only 2 percent of all reports. Men's rights sites point to research that places the rate as high as 41 percent. These are wildly disparate figures that cannot be reconciled."[299]

Just as McElroy said, groups like Protect Our Defenders say false allegations occur in 2 to 8 percent of cases:

"As an organization that works with victims of rape and assault, we have done extensive research on this matter and can assure you that the generally accepted studies on this indicate the percentage of rape allegations that are false runs between approximately 2 and 8 percent."[300] (Author note: protectourdefenders.com does not cite any studies to support this claim.)

McElroy is correct in that these widely differing numbers may not be able to be reconciled. But there is evidence the rate is far higher than 2 to 8 percent. However low Protect Our Defenders would like people to believe the false allegation rate is, actual statistics point to a rate significantly higher than 8 percent — maybe even as high as 45 percent.

According to the *Los Angeles Daily Journal*, research shows almost half of rape allegations are false: "A *Washington Post* investigation of rape reports in seven Virginia and Maryland counties in 1990 and 1991 found that nearly one in four were unfounded. When contacted by the *Post*, many of the alleged victims admitted that they had lied."[301]

Former Colorado prosecutor Craig Silverman said: "For sixteen years, I was a kick-ass prosecutor who made most of my reputation vigorously prosecuting rapists. ... I was amazed to see all the false rape allegations that were made to the Denver Police Department. ... A command officer in the Denver Police sex assaults unit recently told me he placed the false rape numbers at approximately 45 percent."[302]

The Air Force itself conducted a study of 1,218 reported rape cases between 1980 and 1984 in which the conclusion stated, "approximately 45 percent of the total rape allegations were false."[303]

Of the total reports, 212 were found to be "disproved" as the alleged victim convincingly admitted the complaint was a "hoax" at some point during the initial investigation. The researchers then investigated the 546 remaining or "unresolved" rape allegations, including having the accusers submit to a polygraph. Twenty-seven percent of these complainants admitted they had fabricated their accusation just before taking the polygraph or right after they failed the test. (It should be noted that whenever there was any doubt, the unresolved case was re-classified as a "proven" rape.) Combining this 27 percent with the initial 212 "disproved" cases, it was determined that approximately 45 percent of the total rape allegations were false.[304]

A 1996 study published by the U.S. Department of Justice, "Convicted by Juries, Exonerated by Science: Case Studies in the Use of DNA Evidence to Establish Innocence After Trial," documented twenty-eight cases of individuals who were convicted by juries and, then, later exonerated by DNA tests. The study states: "Every year since 1989, in about 25 percent of the sexual assault cases referred to the FBI where results could be obtained, the primary suspect has been excluded by forensic DNA testing. Specifically, FBI officials report that out of roughly 10,000 sexual assault cases since 1989, about 2,000 tests have excluded the primary suspect…"[305] *Twenty-five percent!* Twenty-five percent of those sent to prison for rape where DNA was later matched were proven to have been falsely convicted.

Numbers can be misleading. This finding does not mean 25 percent of all rape allegations are false, but it certainly does prove innocent men do sometimes get convicted.

The FBI study continued, "These percentages have remained constant for seven years, and the National Institute of Justice's informal survey of private laboratories reveals a strikingly similar 26 percent exclusion rate."[306] Wendy McElroy said "the FBI data is as close to hard statistics that I've found on the rate of false accusations of sexual assault."[307]

To clarify, this study, conducted after the discovery of an ability to analyze DNA, went back to cases where evidence was available to test DNA evidence to determine if the correct person had been convicted. The FBI states 26 percent of the men in prison for rape were innocent. This was in cases in which they had evidence so DNA tests could prove guilt or innocence. Twenty-six percent of men *in prison* were innocent. What could the wrongful conviction rate be for cases without DNA evidence? Protect our Defenders offers no evidence to support their assertions or to dispute the FBI study conclusions.

Finally, the Department of Defense conducted a study in 2012 that found that 17 percent of sexual assault investigations (allegations) were "unfounded," i.e., false allegations.[308] Two percent to 45 percent is a wide range, but these studies do bound the estimates of false allegations. Documentation appears to indicate 17 to 26 percent is more accurate, meaning approximately 17 to 26 percent of allegations and convictions of sexual assault are false.

Does the exact percentage of false allegations matter? If one in ten accusations of rape is false, is that a dangerously high rate or an acceptably low one? Is it more likely a false allegation was filed if the rate is 40 percent? Or is it less likely if the rate is only 8 percent? Neither. The actual statistic is not as important as the fact that false allegations do happen. To put this in perspective, if we use the Bureau of Justice Statistics that show about 200,000 rapes in 2008, at only 10 percent, we could be looking at as many as 20,000 false accusations; at 26 percent, that number could be 52,000.[309] The point is these studies prove that sometimes women lie. It is undeniable that there is a possibility of a false allegation (and therefore wrongful conviction) in this case.

It is not worth arguing a specific percentage of allegations that are false. That is not my purpose. My purpose is simply to show that false allegations do happen. These studies, with facts and evidence to support them, prove that some women do make false allegations. Investigators, JAG officers and military commanders owe a duty to all military members to investigate the possibility of a false allegation just as vigorously as the possibility of guilt, and nothing less.[310]

Our system of justice is designed to err on the side of innocence, thus the standard of "reasonable doubt." It is intended that our society let a guilty man go free rather than incarcerate an innocent man. We should at least investigate the possibility of innocence.

Two more quick points before moving on: It is not just the accuser who lies that contributes to false convictions. Prosecutors and investigators have also been a part of the problem. In 2008 in Simi Valley, California, Tracy West staged a sexual assault on herself and accused her former boyfriend and father of her five-year-old son of rape. West and her new husband reported the alleged attack to the police. The former boyfriend was immediately arrested and spent 83 days in maximum security jail awaiting trial. His defense team, with the help of a forensic investigator and an honest cop, proved that West was lying. They found witnesses, security cameras, phone records and bank withdrawals that fully accounted for his whereabouts on both the morning and afternoon of the alleged rape. This compelling evidence notwithstanding, *prosecutors pushed ahead* with the rape charge based solely on West's accusation. Fortunately, in April 2008 — just one day before a preliminary hearing in the case — prosecutors dropped the charge because their only witness, Tracy West, had been admitted to a local hospital following a "suicide attempt." She didn't want to face the defense team, which had put together clear and convincing evidence that she had lied about being raped by her boyfriend.[311] The point is, despite proof of innocence, these civilian prosecutors pushed forward with the prosecution. This type of overzealous behavior is not limited to attorneys, accusers or investigators or the civilian courts.

There is also the case of Ron Williamson of Pontotoc County, Oklahoma, made famous by John Grisham's book *The Innocent Man*. Williamson was convicted, some say railroaded, by bad cops of the rape and murder of Debra Sue Carter. "On the flimsiest evidence, Williamson was charged, tried, and sentenced to death — in a trial littered with lying witnesses and tainted evidence." [312] *The Innocent Man* is a fascinating story of bad cops, incompetent public defenders, and a justice system that put an innocent man within days of execution.

Just as in our civilian society, for whatever reason, military investigators, prosecutors, judges, etc., sometimes bend the rules, rationalize bad behavior and wrongfully convict innocent men.

18

THE ACCUSER'S MOTIVES

"When one person makes an accusation, check to be sure he himself is not the guilty one. Sometimes it is those whose case is weak who make the most clamour."
— *Piers Anthony*

However large or small the number of false allegations, the fact remains that sometimes women do make false allegations. Whether you believe there are only 2 to 8 percent false allegations or up to 45 percent, the fact is people do lie, and people do bear false witness against others. The question on everyone's mind in the Wilkerson case is specific: Why would Kim Hanks lie? Only Kim Hanks knows the answer, but there is ample evidence to suggest several possible motivations; one in particular appears probable.

Lt. Col. McCarron, the Investigating Officer in U.S. vs. Wilkerson, recommended a trial "in the absence of any apparent motive on the part of Hanks to fabricate the allegations."[313] The prosecution got a conviction partially by saying, "Ms. Hanks has no reason to lie."[314] Many involved with the investigation, particularly the prosecution, appeared to want to believe Hanks. Why didn't they want to believe Lt. Col. and Beth Wilkerson? Why didn't they want to believe the seven other people the prosecution insinuates or said outright were lying? These are interesting questions. In any event, people want to know: Why would Kim Hanks lie?

The Department of Defense Report says its false allegation rate last year was 17 percent. Could this case also be a false allegation? I went back to the Record of Trial to research this question. In my research, I discovered several clues Hanks herself provided. What follows in this chapter is my analysis and thoughts as to why Kim Hanks would make a false allegation about this particular night. What did Hanks have to gain, if anything, by creating this story? Or perhaps it is more appropriate to ask, what did Hanks have to lose in the absence of this story?

CLUES

In the statement provided by MSgt. Dunnivant — the first person Hanks told her story to — there were a couple of clues. First, Hanks said, "They kicked me out of the house."[315] She didn't say, "I was assaulted" or "he attacked me." She said "they kicked me out of the house." Also, MSgt. Dunnivant said Hanks seemed okay when she drove up and did not notice her drive up.[316] Hanks didn't show signs of anxiety. She was drinking a beer with five men — strangers — on the street corner at 3:20 in the morning and didn't notice a car pull up to the curb. It is natural to question these actions. If a woman has just been assaulted and is out in a strange village at 3:20 in the morning, "upset," wouldn't she be little anxious for her friend to arrive? Wouldn't she be looking for a car to pull up? It is a very small town. Not many cars are driving by at 3:20 in the morning.

There are other clues. MSgt. Dunnivant told OSI investigators Hanks was "tipsy, somewhat intoxicated."[317] If Hanks had stopped drinking before midnight as she testified, how could she be intoxicated at 3:20 a.m.? The toxicologist testified that if what Hanks claimed to have drunk was accurate, her blood-alcohol content at that time would have been zero.[318] MSgt. Dunnivant's other observations don't seem to fit with the behavior of a woman who had been assaulted, either. Hanks wasn't upset until she began relaying her story to MSgt. Dunnivant and then insisted MSgt. Dunnivant not tell anyone.

Suzanne Berrong said Hanks smelled alcohol at 8:30 the following morning when she picked her up.[319] Berrong, Hanks' best friend, didn't believe the story: "Her story just doesn't add up."[320] Captain Manning didn't believe Hanks' story either. Captain Manning said: "In my opinion, Ms. Hanks' initial reaction did not seem consistent with someone that had been sexually assaulted."[321] So, both Berrong and Captain Manning, her best friend and one of the two women out partying with Hanks that night, didn't believe her story.

Two significant clues were offered when Hanks told MSgt. Dunnivant she was "concerned that (Wilkerson's) wife would try to get her (Hanks) in trouble" and when she told Berrong she "was concerned about them saying something before she could."[322] These two statements stand out in all the Record of Trial as something that should have been investigated. Notice Hanks said Wilkerson's wife, not Wilkerson. Why say wife? What could Beth say that might get Hanks in trouble? It seems quite possible Hanks was creating a story because she was concerned the Wilkersons would talk about something she did — something that she was afraid would come out. There was only one reason for Hanks to say this. Beth Wilkerson asked her to leave the house because she was drunk and disorderly in the middle of the night.

Hanks was nearing the end of a one-year probation in her job on base. Her renewal was up for consideration at the time of this allegation. An alcohol-related incident could cause Hanks' job not to be renewed, or at least Hanks could have thought it might. She repeatedly voiced concern. So Hanks needed to "get her story out before they do theirs." These comments are big clues. They don't fit with anything associated with Hanks' version of the story.

Also remember that Hanks commented to a co-worker friend of the Wilkersons just two days after the verdict: "I'm sorry. I never meant for him to lose his retirement or go to jail."[323] Again, a sentiment like that does not fit with the story of a woman who has been assaulted.

What would motivate a woman to falsely accuse someone of sexual assault? In an August 2012 article, Houston criminal defense attorney John Floyd and paralegal Billy Sinclair provided some reasons for false allegations:[324]

- A nasty break-up
- The need to deny a consensual tryst (or something else?)
- Big age differential
- Alcohol-fueled encounter
- A mentally unstable accuser
- A compulsive liar[325]

Analyzing these reasons with regard to the Wilkerson case, we can rule out several areas right away. There was no nasty break-up or consensual tryst, as Hanks and Lt. Col. Wilkerson did not know each other prior to that evening, and their age difference is less than ten years. Alcohol was a factor. As we discussed, some of Hanks' behavior was typical of a person who had been drinking Red Bull and vodka. There are the possibilities of a mentally unstable accuser or a compulsive liar, but most interesting is the "need to deny a consensual tryst or something else." Perhaps there is more to the possibility that Hanks was motivated to cover up something else?

According to Floyd and Sinclair, if a person is a compulsive liar, her reason for a false allegation may "overlap with the others. If a woman is sufficiently selfish that she has no difficulty lying — to extricate herself from trouble or for other reasons, she may not even need one of the reasons noted above to tell a rape lie. Some women will tell rape lies to avoid getting into trouble for being late for work."[326]

Some women tell rape lies to avoid getting into trouble ... Hanks offered enough statements to prove she was concerned, if not afraid, of an alcohol-related incident. Perhaps she was afraid of such an incident because she thought she would get in trouble or it might endanger her job. That's what she said; she was afraid she might get fired.

Dr. Charles P. McDowell, a researcher in the United States Air Force Special Studies Division, in 1985 published research that "revealed there were certain characteristics or indicators that were found with greater frequency in baseless reports than in proven reports." For example, while true victims tend to report immediately and directly to authorities, false accusers are more likely to tell family members or close friends. These friends often then push or convince the "victim" into reporting the alleged assault.[327] This case is classic. Hanks told everyone she spoke with — MSgt. Dunnivant, Berrong, Major O'Keefe, her male co-worker, and a Croatia tour traveling companion — that she did not want to report an assault. Berrong convinced Hanks to go to the clinic. Major O'Keefe convinced her to fill out the initial SARC report and, according to Hanks, her male friend traveling in Croatia convinced her to go forward with the unrestricted report.[328]

Dr. McDowell continued: "In discussing the alleged rape, false accusers may be unable to provide detailed descriptions of the rape or may provide too much detail."[329]

Hanks' account was odd from the beginning. Hanks cannot remember many details about most of the evening (think back to the twenty-five things the Investigating Officer listed in her Article 32 hearing report), but she recounts the one second when the light comes on and a man yells "what the hell is going on" in stark, vivid detail.

In true rape cases, the assault often includes numerous sexual acts. Cases where the accuser is fabricating allegations of rape tend to focus their descriptions on very limited and narrow sexual activity.[330] Hanks went into minute detail about feeling the digital penetration as she is awakened by the light. She vaguely remembers "touching" and cannot say if it was over or under her clothes, but she details a finger curling and uncurling.

"McDowell's research leads to the conclusion that because the false accuser may have never actually suffered a rape, the allegations may be physically improbable (if not impossible) or bizarre."[331] Again, Hanks is relating a story of how a man who was on top of her, facing her, under the covers with his hand down her pants was able to penetrate her with his finger, despite her belt and pants remaining buckled, all without waking her prior to a light coming on.[332] Certainly Hanks' detailed description of penetration may be considered "bizarre."

According to Dr. McDowell, "Perhaps most telling are numerous inconsistencies between the accuser's description of the rape and the presence or absence of physical evidence."[333] In the Wilkerson case, there is zero physical evidence to support Hanks' story but actually some evidence to cast significant doubt on it. Her version of where she slept, the light in the room, the stairs, the way she exited the house, etc., all fail to pass the truth test when compared with the physical layout of the Wilkerson home. Unfortunately, Judge Brown ruled the jurors could not see the house for themselves. Therefore, the jurors must have been unable to understand the contradictory physical evidence disproving Hanks' story.

There is no evidence that places Lt. Col. Wilkerson in the same room with Hanks after he left the living area to go to bed for the evening. There is no evidence Hanks had any injuries (bruising, etc.). There is no evidence Hanks even slept in the bed (or any bed) at the Wilkerson home. Only her story says she got into a bed. And then, Col. Christensen said it was a different bed. There is no evidence to support any piece of Hanks' version of events after 12:43 a.m. Additionally, the inconsistencies in Hanks' story, such as the light, lamp, hallway access, stairs, exits from the house, counter, etc., are both numerous and telling. They don't add up.

Dr. McDowell found the nature of physical injuries may be "the most significant of all indicators of a false allegation. Physical injuries sustained by false victims tend to be inconsistent or 'odd.'" Hanks describes a slight pain as the finger curled and uncurled.[334] She describes the injury to the "left side of her inner labia." She is a physician's assistant, so perhaps this is not an "odd" or "inconsistent" injury to a physician's assistant, but it appears to be "odd" under Dr. McDowell's description.

Dr. McDowell's factors, by themselves, individually or independently, are not conclusive that a rape did or did not occur. "Rather, the presence of one or more of the criteria suggests the possibility of a false allegation that should be carefully and sensitively investigated and explored."[335] We have discussed six of McDowell's factors present in Hanks' story. They should have caused OSI investigators and the Lt. Col. McCarron to investigate the possibility of a false allegation. Why didn't they?

The organization Respecting Accuracy in Domestic Abuse Reporting assessed Dr. McDowell's article to be "credible."[336] "McDowell adopted a conservative approach more likely to yield an undercount of false allegations rather than an overcount. Such caution is a hallmark of objective research." The bottom line is that, according to credible research, the probability of Hanks' allegation being false is high, tripping at least six indicators.

Dr. McDowell's study is not the only research that supports the theory that Hanks filed a false allegation. *The Rape Investigation Handbook* by John O. Savino and Brent E. Turvey lists nine "red flags" that help identify potential false reports of sexual assault:

> Initiation of the report, or pressure to report, by someone other than the complainant herself.[337]

Hanks stated repeatedly she did not want to report the incident. She was urged by everyone she confided in to report the allegation. Even then, she wanted to file only a "restricted" report.[338]

> The complainant is unable to say where the sexual assault occurred, or locate it when pressed, when nothing would appear to prevent her from being able to do so (e.g. no blindfold, no drugs or alcohol to impair memory).[339]

At the trial, Hanks claimed she was not drunk but could not identify the bed or the room where the alleged assault occurred. When shown pictures of all the bedrooms in the Wilkerson home, Hanks stated, "I know I did not sleep in any of these beds." When specifically shown the room in which the alleged assault occurred and asked by the judge, "Does that look like the bed you slept in that night?" she answered, "Oh, no, definitely not."[340]

If Hanks were more inebriated than she admitted, as we showed through the testimony of others, it is possible she may not have remembered the details of the room, etc., due to alcohol. More likely, Hanks trips this red flag — unable to say where the alleged assault occurred or locate it when pressed — because it did not happen.

> A vague description of the attacker is provided, when descriptions of other parts of the crime are more detailed.[341]

Hanks could not identify whether Lt. Col. Wilkerson had a mustache or not, even though she had spent the better part of three hours around him and conversing with him earlier in the evening. On the contrary, she offered vivid details of exactly what was alleged to have occurred in her pants, an event that would have occurred in less than three seconds. "I woke up and felt a hand that was down my pants being removed. I opened my eyes and saw a man about six inches from my face squinting with his eyes closed."[342] She had only a "vague description" of her alleged attacker but very minute detail of the one to two seconds.

> While able to discuss details before and after the alleged sexual assault, the complainant avoids answering specific questions about the attack by crying hysterically, becoming angry without provocation, or engaging in other deflective behavior.[343]

Every witness who either filed a statement or testified about Hanks' demeanor, said Hanks "teared up" — did not want to discuss the details of the event — and swore them to secrecy only after being pressed for information. MSgt. Dunnivant said: "When I first saw Kim as I got there (to pick her up at 3:20 a.m.), she seemed okay ... As Kim was talking to me, she was upset, crying, and confused."[344] Remember, MSgt. Dunnivant also said Hanks was "tipsy, somewhat intoxicated" when she picked her up.[345] Lt. Col. McCarron, the Article 32 IO, said Hanks "became teary on a few occasions." Again these episodes only occurred during questioning for further detail.[346] At no time did any witness write or testify that Hanks was upset prior to the person asking for more information. Whenever pressed, Hanks "teared up." As Turvey and Savino write, she avoids answering specific questions by crying or engaging in other deflective behavior.

Hanks also deflected questioning about her story from Captain Manning. Captain Manning testified she "spoke to Kim Hanks the Monday or Tuesday after the concert. She did not mention a sexual assault. I gave her a hug." Captain Manning asked, "What happened?" Hanks told her "she didn't remember or didn't remember much. I don't recall her exact words. There were no red flags at that time. We talked about going to Spain together in July. Kim said she didn't think she was going to go. At that point, there was a distinct change in her mood. She said she was too old for the party scene. I noticed something wasn't right. I asked her about it. She said: 'I don't know. I don't want to talk about it.' I asked her if something happened. She repeated, 'I don't remember.' "[347]

The complainant appears to be interested in something
other than reporting the sexual assault.[348]

Hanks oddly "doodled" during her portion of the Article 32
hearing.[349] Additionally, as mentioned above, Hanks showed interest in
anything but the allegation when Captain Manning questioned her about
specifics.[350]

The report of a sexual assault serves to provide an alibi of
some kind.[351]

To Hanks, the assault provides a reason for leaving the house
without shoes and a convenient denial of a possible report of an alcohol-
related incident in case "the wife" tried to get her in trouble.

Reconstruction of the physical evidence is at odds with
the story of the victim.[352]

Embodied in the processes of sexual assault protocols is a forensic
reconstruction and comprehensive assessment of the crime scene;
interviews with complainants, the accused, and witnesses; and the results
of victim and suspect sexual assault examination protocols. Standard
sexual assault protocols require a physical examination known as a
Sexual Assault Forensic Examination. The technician who saw Hanks the
next day should have accomplished this physical examination. It may
have revealed bruising or tearing from the alleged assault that would
corroborate her story. But Hanks refused the examination. She was a
physician's assistant, fully aware of what these examinations would and
would not yield. Hanks' refusal prevented the gathering of physical
evidence to possibly support (or refute) her allegation. The bottom line is
there was no physical evidence in this case.

In the Wilkerson investigation, the only actions taken by the OSI
were witness interviews. The "five English-speaking men" were never
interviewed, despite Hanks saying they were Air Force Airmen in the last
sentence of her OSI statement.[353] The house was never examined or

photographed, the bed was never analyzed, measured, or examined, and no evidence was seized to search for DNA or other trace evidence.

The story of exiting the house cannot have occurred as Hanks testified: "The room with the French doors is a straight shot from the room I slept in. The doors lead to the yard, not the driveway."[354] This description in her testimony is not consistent with the physical evidence — the layout of the Wilkerson home. To exit the room Hanks said was "a few steps down" requires walking down a hallway, making a left 180-degree turn and climbing seventeen stairs to get to the main floor. Only then can one walk to the French doors and only then by making a turn and going through the kitchen.[355]

> Injuries sustained by the complainant are consistent with known patterns of self-inflicted injuries.[356]

This does not apply, as there were no injuries reported and no examination conducted.

> The complainant's details are similar to information seen commonly in movies and television.[357]

The complainant puts the wife catching her husband at the exact moment that: 1) the hand is down the pants and 2) she wakes up. In the matter of one second, all three of these events occur in perfect harmony. She did not wake up as he allegedly got under the covers. Nor did she wake up as he alleged put a hand down her buttoned and buckled pants. She only woke at the precise moment the light came on. Arguably, only in the movies does this amount of drama occur all at once.

Hanks trips eight of Savino and Turvey's nine red flags defined as being "helpful in identifying potential false reports of sexual assault." OSI investigators at Aviano failed to notice or take action on any of them.

CONCLUSION

My belief, based on the evidence I have gathered and researched, is that Hanks was afraid her drunk and disorderly conduct — being asked to leave a colonel's house in the middle of the night — would be reported, and that an alcohol-related incident might cause her job, currently up for renewal, not to be renewed. I believe Hanks fabricated the assault story, as Dr. McDowell says, as a cover story to avoid getting into trouble — one of the most obvious reasons for a false allegation. According to Dr. McDowell, "for the vast majority of false reports, the allegation of rape solved a perceived problem the accuser was, *or anticipated*, facing. The same cannot be said for proven rape victims as, for most, rape marks the onset of numerous, long-term, and not easily resolved problems."[358]

Kim Hanks repeatedly referred to her concerns about an alcohol-related incident affecting her job, and it is abundantly clear that Hanks did not want to go back on base for fear of getting in trouble. The offers of a ride back to the base meant she would be dropped off at the gate and would have to walk through the security checkpoint after she had been drinking. She was concerned about doing so. She testified: "I didn't understand why, but you know I talked to people later. It's ah — you know they — if you go through and you have alcohol on your breath and you're going through the gate, it's a big deal. I didn't know — I didn't really want to be dropped off. I didn't know how far I'd have to walk in to the TLF. And I, you know, I had been drinking, so I was concerned about getting in trouble."[359]

"It's a big deal." "I was concerned about getting in trouble." MSgt. Dunnivant said "Hanks appeared concerned that she (Hanks) could be fired because she was a civilian contractor or that Wilkerson's wife would try to get her in trouble."[360] Hanks said "Wilkerson's wife would try to get her (Hanks) in trouble." The wife, not the husband; the wife. How could Beth get Hanks in trouble? For what? For only one thing — being drunk and disorderly in the middle of the night. Beth had told her either go to bed or leave, so Hanks left. Now she had to explain why.

In the end, Hanks' story actually puts her where Beth Wilkerson said she found her — on the main floor of the Wilkerson home — not in the guest room that Hanks testified was downstairs. Hanks said she didn't remember how/why she got there. I believe she was looking for her shoes and was planning to leave anyway. Beth, fed up with Hanks not settling down for the night, asked her to leave, and so Hanks did, without her shoes. Beth said she found Hanks' shoes in the bedroom where the boys slept the next day.

Hanks had far more to drink than she admitted. She was still intoxicated at 3:20 a.m. and still smelled of alcohol at 8:30 a.m. Given the testimony, it is probable Hanks continued drinking throughout the night. The effects of Red Bull and vodka include a "greater chance of experiencing several side-effects related to over-stimulation, including increased speech speed, sleeping difficulties, agitation, irritability, and tension."[361] Energy drinks only mask the effects of alcohol; they do not counter them.[362] Hanks was up walking around, restless and unable to sleep. She still needed a ride home, so she called MSgt. Dunnivant to come get her. When questioned why she was out at 3 a.m., at first, Hanks said, "They threw me out." Only after additional questioning did she relate a story. She needed a story to cover her own actions.

Kim Hanks did not act rationally. Perhaps the Red Bull and vodka or the sheer amount of alcohol affected her, but in any event, her behavior that night was not rational. Hanks said, "I was freaking out that I had been left at the house," but she refused to leave.[363] She refused multiple offers of a ride, and she repeatedly misplaced her shoes, to where even others who were looking for them could not find them. Her trip to the Medical Group the next morning was not an "all in" plan. She got a lot of attention, but she said she would only file charges if the drug test came back positive. She's a physician's assistant and refused a Sexual Assault Forensic Examination. She knew what an examination might or might not reveal. She kept getting attention but was noncommittal about going forward. She attempted to file a restricted report — again, not an "all in" plan.

It is my opinion that Hanks craved attention. Why turn down so many offers to drive her back to the base, including one from her best friend? She turned them down because each person who asked was showing her attention. She turned down Berrong's offer to come get her, too, stating it was too far, but she really had no idea how far it was. It could have been the same village for all she knew. But she clearly got Berrong's attention during the phone call. She got more attention from Beth by staying up. She got more attention from each person to whom she told her story. They were all concerned for her. She was smothered with attention, especially from the Air Force. The accusation against a colonel fighter pilot was too juicy to investigate as a false allegation. The Air Force would certainly look good if it prosecuted this one. In fact, that is close to what Brig. Gen. Zobrist actually said: "The USAF should certainly not be criticized for failing to put the right emphasis on this case…"[364]

Berrong said she thought Hanks had something to hide. Berrong wrote to Lt. Gen. Franklin: "I repeated to them (the prosecuting attorneys) that I did not believe her (Hanks) and there was more to what was going on. They asked if I thought that something consensual occurred, I replied that I wasn't implying that anything sexual occurred, but *something did that I felt was not in her favor and she was afraid it would come out, whatever it was.* Needless to say, I was not called for the prosecution." [365]

According to Dr. McDowell, "as with all of human behavior, there are numerous reasons why a person would lie about being assaulted." In McDowell's study, more than half of false accusers fabricated the rape to serve as a "cover story" or alibi. "The perceived problem was typically something that caused feelings of shame and guilt in the accuser which was bound to be discovered and received negatively by family or friends."[366] Berrong was convinced Hanks was afraid something happened "that was not in her favor and she was afraid it would come out." I believe Hanks was afraid her drunk and disorderly conduct in a colonel's house would get out, and she was afraid she would lose her job. She said it repeatedly.

Why didn't the OSI investigate this possibility? By reading her statements, they should have seen that it was possible Hanks was embarrassed at her situation. She had been associated with the military for less than a year. Her job, at more than $180,000 per year, was under review for a continuation of her contract. An alcohol-related incident would not look good. She said she was concerned about being fired. She might lose her job; she needed a cover story. They should have seen it. But I found nothing in their report or investigator notes to indicate they ever doubted Hanks' version.

Dr. McDowell wrote: "Their goal was not to harm or cause problems for the acquaintance, but *to protect themselves in what they perceived to be a desperate situation.* As with most lies, the false rape accusation allowed the accuser to *deny responsibility by creating an alternate reality* into which to escape."[367]

My firm belief is Hanks made up this false accusation to protect her high-paying job. Hanks told one version of a story to MSgt. Dunnivant, a slightly different version to Berrong, wrote something different in her first statement, then changed it considerably, to add digital penetration. When confronted, she feigned confusion but finally admitted she had offered conflicting testimony. She said she "passed out drunk" but then Berrong said, "No, we were on the phone," so the story changed to, "I must have been drugged." Hanks tried to file only a restricted report, which involves no law enforcement, but oops, civilians can't do that. It was too late. Her story was in official channels. It grew. It changed.

Hanks' friends pushed her to report an assault — Red Flag No. 1. She cannot identify the room or the bed —Red Flag No. 2. She cannot remember if her attacker had a moustache and gave only a vague description — Red Flag No. 3. She avoided answering specific questions by crying and engaging in deflective behavior such as doodling — Red Flags Nos. 4 and 5. Her story provided an alibi to cover up her fear of losing her job because of an alcohol-related incident — Red Flag No. 6. The physical evidence did not support her story. She could not remember the twenty-minute phone call with her best friend, and she refused a Sexual Assault Forensic Examination — Red Flag No. 7. And her story is strikingly like a scene from a movie — Red Flag No. 9.

Hanks tripped eight out of nine red flags and six warning indicators of a false allegation. It doesn't get much clearer for investigators. She had more than $180,000 reasons to make up a false allegation. Perhaps most telling is that her best friend and one of the women with her that night did not believe her story. I don't believe it, either.

19

CLEMENCY, PART 1

"It's easy to convict an innocent man.
But it's almost impossible to get him out once you have."
— *John Grisham*

Post-trial clemency is a discretionary option of a convening authority — the officer on whose authority the court-martial was convened.[368] It may involve reducing the sentence, sending the case back for another trial, or setting aside the conviction altogether. Clemency is exceptionally difficult to receive from a Convening Authority and, if any is granted, it usually comes in the form of a reduced sentence for the convicted person. However, there are times when something new and mitigating comes up during the clemency period. In the Wilkerson case, there were plenty of mitigating issues brought to the attention of the Convening Authority during this phase.

During the clemency phase, the defense may submit additional information on the defendant's behalf. Friends and family of the Wilkersons were told that they could write letters to the Convening Authority (Lt. Gen. Craig Franklin) and that these letters should focus only on asking for a lighter sentence.

Here is the email and portions of the letter friends received from the Air Force Defense Attorney (Area Defense Counsel or ADC):

Request for Clemency Letter for Lt. Col. Wilkerson
Mon 11/19/2012 7:51 AM
Sir/Ma'am:

On behalf of Lt. Col. Wilkerson, I am asking for your support in writing a letter of clemency to Lt. Gen. Franklin so that he may be persuaded to grant some form of clemency to Lt. Col. Wilkerson. I know all of you in some manner provided Roscoe and Beth with support for the court-martial, but I ask again for this portion of the military justice process. I have attached a letter/template which explains further how the letter should be addressed and the information it should contain. We would like your letter to ask that Lt. Col. Wilkerson receive some amount of confinement be taken off his sentence (currently at 1 year). We will also be asking that his forfeitures be provided to Beth but I will handle that request.[369]

Request for Letter in Support of Clemency Request — Lt. Col. James Wilkerson
19 November 2012

We are now about to enter what is commonly known as the "clemency" phase of the court-martial process. Clemency is a procedure under military law that allows the commander who convened the court-martial (Lt. Gen. Craig Franklin, 3AF/CC) to either reduce Lt. Col. Wilkerson's sentence, or potentially disapprove the entire findings and sentence. We propose to request that Lt. Col. Wilkerson's sentence be altered, specifically that his confinement be reduced. Given the political climate, we do not believe Lt. Gen. Franklin would disapprove the findings of the court or remove the dismissal. We are focusing instead on what we believe he might be willing to do.

You can help Lt. Col. Wilkerson with his clemency petition, if you choose to do so, by writing a letter of support. Your statement can assist this request for clemency by highlighting positive aspects of Lt. Col. Wilkerson's character and by showing support for granting relief. Military members have the absolute right to provide a clemency statement for an individual.

Say whatever you want the Convening Authority to know about my client. Give your opinion of Lt. Col.

Wilkerson. Discuss his work performance, military bearing, civic activities, attitude, goals, and anything else you wish to discuss. **I know emotions are still high and we are all upset/surprised/angry at the decision of the panel members, however there is a respectful way to convey that feeling and we just ask, if you want to do so, to please be mindful of how you are saying that to a 3-star General. However, you should bear in mind this is not an opportunity to degrade military justice system.** [Emphasis in original.] Please use specific examples to support your opinion. If you know of instances where Lt. Col. Wilkerson particularly stood out, please note them here. Don't be afraid to use multiple examples.

The adjudged sentence: This is where you would talk about the sentence Lt. Col. Wilkerson received at his court-martial. Explain what you feel would be a more appropriate punishment considering the circumstances. Lt. Col. Wilkerson is asking that his forfeitures be waived to Beth for her benefit and the benefit of (their son). Additionally he is asking for a reduction in confinement so he can get home to his family sooner. Remember, the Convening Authority can only approve the sentence as adjudged or reduce it; the Convening Authority can *never* make the punishment more severe.[370]

The email support group I helped establish after the verdict grew rapidly to seventy-seven people. Those were the ones I was aware of. Many others stepped in to help, as well, by contributing their own clemency letters. I passed the attorney letters on to friends and family via the email listing.

Contrary to media and congressional writings, these clemency letters focused far more on the lack of a proper investigation and errors in the trial than on the idea that Lt. Col. Wilkerson was a "model family man." As has been clearly documented, there were plenty of opportunities to point out mistakes and misconduct in the investigation and trial. Once the Record of Trial transcript was released, errors and misconduct jumped off the pages, screaming for justice. Those were the focus of the majority of letters to Lt. Gen. Franklin.

As soon as the trial was complete, the Air Force began transcribing the audio recording to a written format called the Record of Trial, which I've referenced throughout this book. That took about six weeks. When the Record of Trial was complete, the Air Force provided a copy to the defense, and from that point, the defense had two weeks to submit the clemency package.

Lt. Col. and Beth Wilkerson provided me with a copy of the Record of Trial, and I began to conduct in-depth research of the entire record. The official record includes all documentation from the initial opening of the investigation through the sentencing phase. This includes all the witness statements, Lt. Col. Wilkerson's taped interrogation, and the OSI report written by the agents as the investigation progressed. It also includes a copy of OSI agent notes, which provided insights otherwise not in statements, the OSI report or testimony. Finally, the official record also includes the Article 32 Investigating Officer's report and the entire transcript of the trial.

I wanted to see for myself if Lt. Col. Wilkerson could be guilty or how the jurors could have reached this verdict. When I read the Record, I was shocked and disappointed. It was still my Air Force, and I was dismayed at how otherwise good people would succumb to political pressure to the point where they overlooked obvious discrepancies, failed to follow clues to their logical conclusion, and outright failed to perform professionally. During my review, I found many inconsistencies (a majority of which you have now read). In my opinion, the verdict was a clear-cut injustice — a wrongful conviction. I began extensive research in preparation for both clemency and the appeal process. I consulted with Lt. Col. Wilkerson and Beth Wilkerson individually via phone. I researched the jury selection process, prosecutorial misconduct, witness intimidation, and Unlawful Command Influence. I wrote point papers on these last three issues for distribution to Lt. Gen. Franklin and Congressional staffers who were polite enough to listen.

I reached out to the South Carolina legislative delegation, because Lt. Col. Wilkerson's family is from South Carolina, and he is a constituent. Members of Congress hear many complaints from constituents. Their staff members are trained to have patience and to recognize issues worth their effort and their representatives' time. I was pretty well stonewalled by most of the staffers I interacted with. In particular, an attorney staffer for Senator Lindsay Graham was actually rude and hung up on me. On the other hand, three separate staffers from three separate Congressmen from South Carolina did meet with Beth and me in January 2013 to listen. We presented the issue of a wrongful conviction based on intimidation, Unlawful Command Influence and an inadequate investigation. These staffers were in the process of communicating with the Air Force Liaison officers when other actions intervened.

I discussed the case with attorneys from Washington and from Houston, Texas, both military and civilian. Most attorneys thought the case had a strong chance at being overturned on appeal. In fact, most thought the case should never have gone to trial and would not have if it had been in civilian court. I decided I would point out these many inconsistencies and errors in the investigation in my clemency letter. I wanted to prove to Lt. Gen. Franklin what I found — that this was a wrongful conviction.

I wrote my letter of clemency listing many inconsistencies in Hanks' various versions of the story. I highlighted the statements and testimony where Hanks alluded to her fear of an alcohol-related incident and how she said she "had to get her story out before they did theirs." I pointed out what I believed to be the two errors by Judge Brown, the conflicting statements between Hanks and Berrong, and the differences between the stories Hanks relayed to each of her friends according to Berrong's and MSgt. Dunnivant's statements. Finally, I asked for a complete dismissal of charges or, at a minimum, a new trial.

I discussed the clemency letter restrictions with the attorneys and shared my letter with them. We agreed to open all the letters up to writing anything that could be substantiated with documentation from the Record of Trial. In effect, we changed the way clemency letters had always been. I forwarded these ideas to the email group and asked others to write what they wanted with no limitations as well. I passed my letter of clemency to the group as an example. Below is my email to the group.

> 19 November Clemency update
>
> All,
>
> The attached letter is a request from Jay Wilkerson's attorney asking for letters from people willing to write to Lt. Gen. Franklin, the Convening Authority in Jay's case. I specifically asked him if it was okay to share with you. He said yes; he would like letters for General Franklin from anyone willing to write. Please send them directly to him per the guidance below.
>
> Despite what Jeff says in his letter, my letter will ask Lt. Gen. Franklin to read the ever changing accounts provided by the witness, how she cannot say which room she was in, she cannot tell if he had a moustache, how she wanted a restricted report, how she told the girl who picked her up her pants were undone but the technician at the med group that they were not, etc., — basically that her story is not true. I will then ask for a new trial as I know he will not set the entire thing aside. I'd like to see a new trial without command influence (SECDEF guidance of 17 April). I don't think he could get a fair trial in Europe given all the AFN commercials and the SECDEFs guidance.
>
> Bottom line is that your letter should say what you want it to say and cover those required items listed in Jeff's letter of guidance (attached).
>
> On another front, I have not had any luck with Senator Graham's office — cannot get past the staff. If any of you know him, perhaps you could call. We are asking that he 1) request a transcript, 2) review it, and 3) offer his thoughts to us on what we can do. In particular, I would like to ask his thoughts on the climate to convict and whether or not that may have influenced the prosecution

and jury to the degree that Jay could not receive a fair trial.

Finally, Beth saw Jay this past weekend and another visit is scheduled on this Wed-Sun (extended visitation due to the Thanksgiving holiday). He is holding up as well as can be expected.

This is Roscoe's mailing address for the time being:
JAMES H. WILKERSON
UNIT 29723 BOX LL
APO AE 09055

Please keep praying and helping. We do not know where the big break will come from. Please keep helping in any way you can. Please share this with all friends of the Wilkersons. If you do not want these updates, please tell me. If you know anyone else who does want them, please provide a name and e-mail address.

Thanks
Bob Harvey[371]

With Lt. Col. Wilkerson's permission, I shared the Record of Trial with a small group of others who offered to read it as well. This provided a fresh set of eyes and thinking from other, less impacted and less involved people. They became instrumental in writing letters that contain detailed accounts of facts in the record and discussions of the errors in the investigation and trial. The information provided to Lt. Gen. Franklin was in the Record of Trial, but it required extensive reading and research to find the important and relevant issues. No Convening Authority is expected to accomplish the amount of detailed research several of us who wrote letters did. I am confident, due to the references to specifics in the Record of Trial, our letters had an important impact on the subsequent decision.

When General Franklin received the first clemency package, it included eighty-five letters of support for Lt. Col. Wilkerson. Seeing so many letters, he may have sensed something was wrong. As I understand it, rarely, if ever, are there that many letters. And, evidently, it was unusual for letters to point out errors and omissions in the trial. The general's duty is to read the entire clemency package, including all the letters, before making any decision. I have only included a few letters here because of who wrote them and the significant importance of what they say.

During the clemency phase, I also reached out to several witnesses who, I had heard, had misgivings about the verdict. In particular, I reached out to three key people: Captain Tanya Manning, Suzanne Berrong, and another co-worker of Hanks.

Captain Manning, who accompanied Hanks to the Wilkerson home that evening, also wrote a letter to Lt. Gen. Franklin. In it, Captain Manning, a physician's assistant herself, expressed doubts about the validity of Hanks' version of events:

> One thing I will say that may have been overlooked was the events that occurred after. *In my opinion, Ms. Hanks' initial reaction did not seem consistent with someone that had been sexually assaulted.* When I called her the next day, she said she missed my call because she was at a movie. When I saw her 3-4 days later, she greeted me with a smile and a hug asking "what happened" the other night? At the time, I did not know of anything that had happened. Looking back, I am just curious why she would greet me with open arms when she claimed I left her. Why would she be happy to see me if I left her at some strangers' house? The same house she claimed she was assaulted in. *It does not make sense to me.* Every interaction we have had since, she has apologized for getting me involved. I told her I was sorry, and that I had no idea she had not left. She constantly told me it was not my fault and that 'I have a great heart'. Never once did she ask me why I left her there. *That seems very odd to me.*
>
> Lt. Col. Wilkerson received confinement for 12 months and a Dismissal from the service at his court-martial. I have served as a juror on a court-martial so I

was quite shocked at the guilty verdict and punishment given the lack of evidence. I understand that this is a hot topic right now, but I think we would be doing an injustice by making an example out of someone due to poor timing. Only three people really know what happened that night. *Something about this story does not seem right.* I am not taking sides, but I thought people are innocent until proven guilty. Lt. Col. Wilkerson's request that his forfeitures be waived to benefit his wife and son seem very reasonable. Why should his family be punished for this too? I ask that you also consider a reduction in confinement. This will be a hard transition for the family. They will need each other's support to make it through these tough times. I thank you for the opportunity to share some of my thoughts on this case.[372]

I added the emphasis (italics) in Captain Manning's letter to stress that Captain Manning had doubts regarding Hanks' story. She said it was not consistent, did not make sense to her, seemed odd, and did not seem right. As a reminder, Captain Manning is Hanks' co-worker, is also a medical professional, was with her the night of the concert, and has discussed the night with Hanks several times since.

I also reached out to Suzanne Berrong. I had heard through the email support group that Berrong did not believe Hanks, so I contacted her and asked if she would write a clemency letter. I have come to learn Berrong is a strong person. She told me she wanted the truth to be told. She did not know the Wilkersons, but in her heart, she believed Kim Hanks was not truthful. In my opinion, her letter was the most powerful:

> As time progressed, I would continually play everything over and over in my head, comparing what she said happened with her behavior. Several times she had come into my office to speak of concerns of her contract which was up for renewal and the impact this could have. So, yes, there were $150K+ reasons for her to make this

up, if an inappropriate alcohol related incident were to come forward, she also talked of speaking vengeance, to "get him for this," in such a way that sounded of a woman scorned. I don't know of any other way to articulate her tone and manner. This ongoing behavior continued to strengthen my opinion that she is not telling everything, that there is more to this.

My telling all of this is to show that not everything came out at the trial. The prosecution knew that I did not believe her. I told them early on in their questioning that I didn't believe her, that there was more to the story. They did not seem interested in discovering the truth, but in the hunting of the man, the rank and the pilot. How is it that everyone else is lying and only Kim is telling the truth?

General Franklin, I have no stake in any of this. I had no prior relationship with Lt. Col. Wilkerson or his wife that was social or would be in any way influence of my recollection of the events described by Kim. *I tell you honestly and sincerely that I absolutely, to my heart do not believe that the evening events are as Kim claims.*[373]

That last sentence carries a lot of importance. Again, I added the emphasis. This is Hanks' best friend at Aviano, the woman who picked her up in the morning and took her to the clinic. In hindsight, one might say she was the woman who convinced Hanks to go to the clinic in the first place. In her Article 32 testimony, Berrong said: "Kim said she didn't want anyone to know, didn't want me to tell anyone and we discussed making a restricted/unrestricted report. Since Kim was a PA she had access to the back of the clinic. We went back and found Major Michael O'Keefe ..."[374]

Hanks appeared to be a "reluctant" witness all throughout the reporting process. She only progressed through the reporting process as a result of the encouragement (attention) of others, specifically Berrong, who drove her to the clinic. Even then, Hanks entered through the back door and allowed only a drug screening while refusing the Sexual Assault Forensic Examination. Berrong's letter was significant.

The third person I reached out to in the early clemency phase was another of Hanks' co-workers. Two days after sentencing, Hanks approached this person, who was also a Wilkerson family friend. Hanks apologized for Lt. Col. Wilkerson's punishment. She told her co-worker that she had not wanted his benefits to be taken away. She said she "did not know they would be taken away from Beth and (their son), that she tried to make a statement at the sentencing that his retirement not be taken away but that she was not allowed to do so."[375] That seemed unusual for two reasons. First, it has been my experience with other sexual assault cases in the military, that when a woman has been assaulted, she is not remorseful when the person who assaulted her has been punished. Instead, the typical victim desires severe punishment and often thinks whatever sentencing handed down was not strong enough. The second reason Hanks' actions seemed unusual was because if she truly tried to make a statement not to take Lt. Col. Wilkerson's retirement, why was she not allowed to do so? Was this the prosecution putting their values in her words and not allowing her to voice her own? Or, was she saying this to her co-worker for other reasons?

Finally, one more clemency letter to Lt. Gen. Franklin that may have had significant impact was from the visiting boys' mother. As we have seen, her letter corroborated the Wilkersons' story of Beth's phone records:

> ... the prosecution made mention that Beth's phone was being utilized at 7:00 am on the morning of March 24th, an attempt to correlate this in contradiction to Beth's direct testimony that she slept till 9:00 am on March 24th. The lead prosecutor presented this with dramatic flair in his closing argument which prevented any defense counter. It is true Beth's phone was utilized. I personally called her cell phone and Jay answered it because he said Beth was asleep, just as she testified in court. The prosecutor used this in closing as proof she had lied,

when in fact, she was completely truthful. I spoke with Jay and my children and even went as far as to stop by and say hello prior to 8:00 AM on Saturday March 24th. I saw Jay, my boys and JW that morning and I did not see Beth because the boys told me she was sleeping. How this was bent into a lie by the lead prosecutor is unforgivable.[376]

During the clemency process, Lt. Gen. Franklin's JAG also had the opportunity to comment. Colonel Joseph Bialke was the 3rd Air Force Judge Advocate General — Lt. Gen. Franklin's command attorney. One of his primary duties was to advise Lt. Gen. Franklin concerning legal matters. This is Col. Bialke's recommendation to the general:

> I reviewed the attached clemency matters submitted by the defense. I recommend you approve the findings. I recommend you approve the adjudged sentence of confinement of one year, and I further recommend you commute the adjudged sentence of a dismissal to confinement of one year, approving a sentence of confinement for two years.[377]

Col. Bialke's letter recommended changing the punishment given Lt. Col. Wilkerson during the sentencing phase of the trial. Col. Bialke recommended giving Lt. Col. Wilkerson back his retirement in lieu of "dismissal" from the service in exchange for one additional year of imprisonment. Dismissal is a complete forfeiture of all credit for military service and stripping of any retirement benefits, a lifetime pension. Col. recommended increasing the prison sentence by another year in trade for removing the dismissal. He offered no explanation for this recommendation.[378]

Col. Bialke's letter was surprising and yet revealing. The defense team viewed this compromise proposal as a "blink." They thought Col. Bialke saw the weakness of the case and/or knew Lt. Gen. Franklin was uncomfortable with the outcome of the trial, so Col. Bialke was attempting to salvage the conviction. Regardless, Lt. Col. Wilkerson refused the "compromise."[379]

20

CLEMENCY, PART 2:
ANOTHER CHANCE

"Truth will ultimately prevail
where there is pains to bring it to light."
— *George Washington*

During the review of the clemency package, including all the letters, Lt. Gen. Franklin read the allegations of prosecutorial misconduct — bullying — on the part of Col. Christensen and his team. Lt. Gen. Franklin, through his JAG Col. Bialke, asked Col. Christensen and two other prosecution team members to write statements responding to the allegations in some of the clemency letters.[380]

When Col. Christensen responded to Lt. Gen. Franklin, he addressed issues raised in the clemency letters beyond the issue of bullying. In summary, he discussed at length the interaction with the major who accused him of bullying. Although he did admit to raising his voice, Col. Christensen wrote counter accusations of unprofessional behavior and denied accusations about his behavior in the courtroom, including an aggressive approach to Beth while she was on the stand. Additionally, he strongly denied targeting pilots: "Contrary to the many clemency letters, we did not put the 'pilot community' on trial." Further, he rebuffed the testimony of Brig. Gen. Milligan, current spouse to Hanks' former husband, saying she only wanted to "smear Ms. Hanks with her general dislike for her." He said he doubted "the opinion of the wife of an ex-husband that has had no contact with the victim in over ten years would have had any weight with the members," and he said the judge properly denied her testimony.[381]

Because the prosecution was afforded an opportunity to respond to the clemency letters, the window opened for the defense to submit additional information. The Wilkerson team, including me, embraced the opportunity. By that time, I had done extensive additional research and was thoroughly familiar with the transcript, and I felt confident I could prove Col. Christensen's response and characterization of his (Col. Christensen's) behavior and actions as the lead prosecutor were wrong. I knew I could provide proof that Col. Christensen had indeed put the fighter pilot community on trial. There were also an additional seventeen letters submitted on Lt. Col. Wilkerson's behalf during this second round of clemency.

As I read Col. Christensen's letter, it appeared to me to contradict what I heard him say firsthand during the trial, reinforced by what I had read when I researched the Record of Trial. Therefore, I chose to focus my addendum to the clemency package on Col. Christensen's response. In my view, Col. Christensen's affidavit did not agree with his actual comments in the trial transcript. Specifically, in his affidavit, Col. Christensen denied bullying of any witnesses. While he specifically denied bullying the major, by the time the second clemency window closed, I had located three other people who were willing to write letters detailing how the prosecution team, including Col. Christensen, had also bullied them. These are listed later in the chapter on prosecutorial misconduct.

As has been well established, Col. Christensen's claim that "we did not put the pilot community on trial" simply did not ring true under examination of the transcript.[382] Col. Christensen disparaged the pilot community in general and insinuated it was a good-old-boy culture that would cover for each other. Again, he was attempting to paint traditional fighter pilot heritage as conduct unbecoming in an effort to bolster a weak case. Combat aviation morale-building traditions are part of Air Force heritage and have nothing to do with sexual assault. Here are some examples. This list is not all-inclusive:

> Page 187, opening remarks: Friends of the accused introduced as fighter pilots — "fellow pilot," "also a pilot."
> Page 358, speaking about Major Goldsberry: "Okay, and he is a major, and he's a pilot, correct?"

> Page 477, direct examination of Colonel Ostovich: "And you're a pilot, obviously?"
>
> Page 484: "And I would imagine, in the pilot world, that this happens quite frequently — people get together?"
>
> Page 739: "It's not really unusual in the fighter pilot world to kind of have an impromptu get-together is it?"
>
> Page 740, questioning Beth about her father, step-father, and first husband:
>
> > "And almost all of these people are fighter pilots as well, right?"
> >
> > "So, you're ingrained in the fighter pilot culture as well?"
>
> Col. Christensen in the closing argument: "He's a fighter pilot — a fighter pilot — he — we can rely on our common sense and knowledge of the ways of the world…"

These references to pilots and the insinuation that pilots are "different," that in the "pilot world" things like this happen frequently, were clearly intended to stir anti-pilot biases in the non-pilot jurors. It was a tactic used on purpose, and it worked, although it was completely irrelevant to the charges in the case. Most damning was Col. Christensen's comment, "we can rely on our common sense and knowledge of the ways of the world." There can be no denying the implication intended by Col. Christensen with that statement. His affidavit denying that he put the fighter pilot culture on trial in the Wilkerson case was laughable and false and probably not lost on Lt. Gen. Franklin, who now had additional testimony and statements indicating Col. Christensen was willing to bend rules and say half-truths to further his agenda.

In the chapter on Prosecutorial Misconduct, I discuss how Col. Christensen approached Beth Wilkerson on the stand in such a fury that spittle flew on her and she withdrew in fear; how others said he placed his head down on the table and in other ways repeatedly showed disdain for pilots and senior officers on Aviano. All of this information, if not already clear, came to the general's attention as a result of Col. Christensen's affidavit.

Another interesting aspect of Col. Christensen's letter is how he maligned Brig. Gen. Milligan's character when he accused her of only wanting to "smear Ms. Hanks with her general dislike for her." He doubted "the opinion of the wife of an ex-husband that has had no contact with the victim in over ten years would have had any weight with the members."[383] Wouldn't that be something the members of the jury should have the wherewithal to understand and make their own judgment? Col. Christensen said the judge "properly denied her testimony."[384] But he didn't. As subsequent references to case law prove, Judge Brown erred.

The final defense letter of the second round of clemency is from Lt. Col. Wilkerson's Air Force attorney. In this letter, he cites the two cases of law in which the defense believes Judge Brown erred: denying Brig. Gen. Milligan's testimony and denying any testimony as to Lt. Col. Wilkerson's character for truthfulness. You will recall Judge Brown turned the tables on the defense, shifting the burden of finding case law to support Brig. Gen. Milligan's testimony to the defense away from the prosecution. Judge Brown afforded the defense a forty-seven-minute recess to research and find applicable case law before ruling against it. The Air Force Defense Attorney was able to find and cite case law supporting two major points for the defense only after the trial was completed (more than forty-seven minutes were required).

> MEMORANDUM FOR 3AF/CC
> 22 February 2013
> FROM: Area Defense Counsel
> SUBJECT: Response to SJAR Addendum — United States v. Lt. Col. James H. Wilkerson, III
> 1. Sir, I write this letter to you after recently separating, my date of separation was 31 January 2013. I know many letters have been submitted to you for review and my

intention here is just to summarize the main points I see which demonstrate the need for clemency in this case.

a. *Brigadier General Milligan* not being able to provide her opinion testimony on the complaining witness' character for untruthfulness was a grave error by the military judge. In *US v. Toro, 37 MJ 317*, the court states opinion evidence should be admissible provided "the character witness personally knows the witness and is acquainted with the witness well enough to have had an opportunity to form an opinion of the witness' character for truthfulness." Brigadier General Milligan had personally seen the lengths the complaining witness was willing to lie in past court proceedings, and these dealings were more than sufficient for her to form an opinion on her character for truthfulness. Not being able to provide this opinion to the members seriously undermined Lt. Col. Wilkerson's ability to put on a defense, especially when this came down to credibility.

b. *Truthfulness evidence for Lt. Col. Wilkerson* was prevented from being admitted by the military judge, again causing substantial harm to the defense's case in what came down to a credibility determination. In *US v. Goldwire, 55 MJ 139*, the Court indicated that evidence of the accused's character for untruthfulness could be presented even though the accused did not testify at trial. Here, a number of OSI agents on video called Lt. Col. Wilkerson a liar and the Trial Counsel continually called him a liar. Yet despite these numerous character assassinations against Lt. Col. Wilkerson, we were barred from introducing evidence as to his strong character for truthfulness.

c. The Prosecution was more interesting [*sic*; interested] in putting the *Air Force fighter pilot culture* on trial vice putting Lt. Col. Wilkerson on trial. Trial Counsel routinely brought up burning couches and singing songs as trying to portray Lt. Col. Wilkerson as some sort of monster without morals, ethics or integrity. To insinuate this at trial, when fighter pilots around the Air Force have done the same things, shows you the lengths the prosecution was willing to go to get a conviction.

d. The *Prosecution tactics* in this case were unlike anything I have ever seen in any other case. In previous submissions, we submitted the opinions of Major Lowe, Major Goldsberry, and others who questioned the tactics they observed in being involved with the court-martial. In this new package, we now have the letter of (name withheld), a spouse of a F-16 pilot at Aviano who felt she had her job and livelihood threatened if she did not cooperate with the prosecution. Due to the tactics used in this case, an entire base population has a level of distaste for the military justice system that they once had high regard for. These people are also the future leaders of the Air Force and will pass on these feelings in mentoring sessions and future discussions with those that come after them. It is a shame to think that one case, one team could cause such distaste to so many.

e. The *physical impossibility* of the act occurring as alleged is the last main point I want to bring to your attention. The complaining witness testified that when the act allegedly occurred, she was still fully clothed with her pants still buttoned and her belt still fastened. Next she would have you believe that a grown man's hand was able to go down her pants, without waking her up. Given the purpose of the belt alone (to keep pants tight around the waist to prevent them from falling off), this account is impossible to comprehend; impossible because it never happened. This is just one of the logical inconsistencies and physical impossibilities the complaining witness would need you to believe to find Lt. Col. Wilkerson guilty.

2. I started my first clemency letter asking you to remember that our justice system is not foolproof, that mistakes are made and innocent people are found guilty. Again, it is in my opinion still the greatest justice system in the world but from time-to-time mistakes are made. We have even now submitted the clemency letter from Commander (redacted), USN, who went through a very similar process of being falsely accused and found guilty (albeit through a different forum). This is just meant to show you that false allegations do happen and innocent people are found in the same place where Lt. Col. Wilkerson finds himself now.

3. Again sir, on behalf of Lt. Col. Wilkerson I request you order a new trial or in the alternative lessen his confinement to time served. I thank Col. Bialke for recognizing the strength of our first clemency package and changing his recommendation to get rid of the dismissal but I assure you, it should not come at the expense of two additional years. I also believe that to be an arbitrary number given the lack of explanation by Col. Bialke on why adding time in place of the dismissal is appropriate and if appropriate, why two years is proper. Sir, Lt. Col. Wilkerson is living the worst punishment every day because he is an innocent man sitting in jail apart from his family. Please end this now.

4. Thank you for your favorable consideration of this request. As I am no longer on active duty, please email my personal email account at (redacted) if you need any additional information or have concerns with this request.[385]

Another highly unusual event occurred as a result of Lt. Gen. Franklin's request for additional information. The prosecution asked Hanks if she would "write" her own letter to Lt. Gen. Franklin. Normally, an accuser is not afforded the opportunity to write a letter directly to the

Convening Authority because she has already been heard from several times. She had previously written a statement, testified at the Article 32 hearing and trial, and was asked for her feelings during the sentencing phase.

Submitting a letter from Hanks was unusual, if not unprecedented, as was allowing her access to the clemency letters. According to Hanks' letter, the prosecution showed her the clemency letters submitted by the defense.[386] This shocking and highly questionable release of information may have been illegal and was certainly unethical. I can find no documentation supporting an accuser being permitted to see clemency letters outside of normal Freedom of Information Act laws. Hanks, as the accuser, has no particular right or benefit that would allow her to read the letters. According to privacy laws, if she wanted access, she should have filed a Freedom of Information act request as others have. If access had been granted, the clemency letters should have been redacted in the same manner as when the Air Force posted them on the Freedom of Information website. In my opinion, this action was not only unethical, but a clear violation of privacy laws, and it further demonstrates willingness of this prosecution team to bend or break rules. It clearly indicates the prosecution feared Lt. Gen. Franklin might not concur with the conviction or sentencing. They got lucky with their dream jury of non-pilots and tried desperately to preserve their conviction without evidence.

The Air Force is not publically saying why Hanks was shown these letters in violation of the privacy act. As with the other irregularities, complaints have been filed with the Inspector General for these actions. As with the other complaints, it is unlikely the Air Force will share the results of the Inspector General investigations, if they conduct any.

The letter purported to be from Hanks is questionable in itself. In testimony she refers to Col. Ostovich as a "big wig." In her statements, she confused Lt. Col. Wilkerson's rank with that of a Master Sergeant. Yet her letter correctly addressed the Lt. Col. Investigating Officer as only "Colonel." I use Lt. Col. here in the book to avoid confusion for non-military readers. The proper way to address a Lt. Col. in writing or speaking is simply "Colonel." It is highly unlikely Hanks knows that given her testimony and written communications to this point. Hanks' letter also correctly refers to "panel members" instead of "jurors" and calls them "field-grade officers." After repeatedly admitting to not clearly understanding differences in rank, all of a sudden, in this letter, Hanks gets all of these subtleties correct? More likely, she didn't write the letter herself. Finally, Hanks' letter is written as if she were present during the entire trial when in fact she did not attend the overwhelming majority of testimony. As a witness, she was not permitted in the courtroom.[387] How then, was she able to characterize what was argued, etc.?

Hanks' letter said: "There is no possible motive for me to lie," again going back to the prosecution's central theme from the Article 32 hearing right through clemency. The text and style of this letter suggests, strongly, that it was written by someone other than Hanks, most likely someone in the prosecution's office. Here again, the prosecution is attempting to influence the case with more unethical and unprofessional behavior.

This chapter is about the second round of clemency. The additional opportunity to submit information is an unusual event, this one generated by an allegation of bullying against the prosecution. It afforded the defense an opportunity to add information in rebuttal to Col. Christensen's affidavit, the most critical of which were statements by three additional witnesses indicating they were intimidated, one in tears and threatened with the loss of her job (these letters are further explained in the chapter on Prosecutorial Misconduct). These statements all agree that the prosecution bent rules and used strong-arm tactics to get their way.

Col. Christensen said in an *Air Force Times* interview: "I'm not willing to risk my integrity ... to convict somebody just for political purposes."[388] That may be true. But then, wouldn't it also be true of those who wrote letters explaining how Col. Christensen and his team threatened them? It is unlikely the four people who wrote letters describing misconduct by Col. Christensen and his team were willing to risk their integrity either. So what did happen? Four people independently say they were bullied or threatened by the prosecution. And one woman even produced an email from the prosecution threatening her with the loss of her job if she did not cooperate. Those four people came from all walks of life on Aviano: a visiting Lt. Col.; a young pilot; one captain's spouse, also a working civilian on the base; and more important, Suzanne Berrong. So, whom should we believe?

This information is included to show that there are two sides to the story. Col. Christensen denied inappropriate behavior, yet several witnesses were willing to write statements saying otherwise. It is important to discuss this alleged pattern of behavior involving many Air Force personnel associated with this case, particularly those connected with the prosecution. The record suggests a trend of rationalizing poor behavior to get a conviction, to "do what the boss wants" no matter what. The second opportunity to submit clemency letters definitely shone a light on misconduct.

21

EXONERATION

"The truth will make you free."
— *John 8:32*

Lt. Gen. Franklin, the Convening Authority in U.S. vs. Wilkerson, declined to accept the verdict and threw out the charges in their entirety. Lt. Col. Wilkerson was fully acquitted by this action. He was released after four months in prison and reinstated to the Air Force. To date, the Air Force has not returned his security clearance, has not allowed him to fly, and has not promoted him to the rank of Colonel, which he had previously earned. In fact, late in 2013, the acting Secretary of the Air Force took personal action to have Lt. Col. Wilkerson retired at an even lower rank. That will be discussed later.

While it was not required of Lt. Gen. Franklin to provide any explanation for his dismissal of the charges, due to an uproar in the media and U.S. Senate, he wrote a letter to the Secretary of the Air Force explaining his decision:[389]

DEPARTMENT OF THE AIR FORCE
HEADQUARTERS THIRD AIR FORCE (USAFE)

12 March 2013
Secretary Donley

I am keenly aware of the significant Congressional interest and media coverage of my 26 Feb 2013 decision as a General Court-Martial Convening Authority (GCMCA) to disapprove the findings and dismiss the charges in the court-martial U.S. vs. Lt. Col. James H. Wilkerson III. I am troubled by the recent wave of continuing negative and biased dispersions being cast upon the Uniform Code of Military Justice (UCMJ), the constitutional court-martial process, and the weighty and impartial responsibility of a convening authority to fairly administer justice.

Accusations by some that my decision was the result of either an apparent lack of understanding of sexual assault on my part, or that because I do not take the crime of sexual assault seriously are complete and utter nonsense. I unequivocally view sexual assault as a highly egregious crime. I take every allegation of sexual assault very seriously. As a commander, I cannot think of a more destructive act to good order and discipline and to the maintenance of a cohesive and effective fighting force. Likewise allegations that I made this decision to protect a Lieutenant Colonel pilot or because I was a former Aviano/31 Fighter Wing Commander are equally preposterous. I have many responsibilities as the Commander of Third Air Force, one of those being a GCMCA. In this role, I review and decide all matters of military justice fairly and impartially. I review each court-martial thoroughly and independently.

The UCMJ directs that a convening authority may, in his or her sole discretion, set aside any finding of guilty in a court-martial. This broad and independent discretion is a direct function of military command. There are legitimate reasons, past and present, why the UCMJ does not require a convening authority to explain his/her actions, and in some ways, it even appears rightly to discourage convening authorities from explaining their decisions so as not to cause even a perception of Unlawful Command Influence.

I have no desire to set an unfortunate and potentially damaging precedent for present and future convening authorities. By law and in the interests of justice, they should not believe they are obliged to provide such explanations. No one has asked or directed me to provide this information to you or to anyone else. Yet due to the ongoing controversy that I have recently observed in the "court of public opinion," it is appropriate, in this case only, to provide you a sense of what I considered in arriving at my decision.

To begin, this was the most difficult court case that I have ever faced as a convening authority.

The case was comprised of mostly consistent testimonies of a husband and wife in contrast to the testimony of an alleged victim. There was no confession or admission of guilt by the accused and no physical evidence. I even struggled with referring this case to a court-martial after reviewing the results of the Article 32 Investigation. As you know, the evidentiary standard of probable cause to refer charges to a court-martial is much less than the very high standard of proof beyond a reasonable doubt to convict in a court-martial. Consequently, after my review of the evidence within the Article 32 investigation report, and after my many discussions with my Staff Judge Advocate (SJA), I concluded that sufficient probable cause existed to refer the case to trial.

After the court-martial, I was somewhat surprised by the findings of guilty based upon the evidence that I had previously reviewed and the high constitutional standard of proof beyond a reasonable doubt in a court-martial. However, I gave deference to the court-martial jury because they had personally observed the actual trial. I subsequently received the request for clemency by Lt. Col. Wilkerson and his defense counsel along with its many compelling clemency letters.

To be honest, this was the most extensive clemency request package that either my SJA or I had ever seen. I read all of the clemency letters (91 of them) in detail and some I read several times.

Most pleaded with me to review the entire court transcript and all the evidence in detail because of grave concerns that they had with the fairness of the trial.

Letters from Lt. Col. and Mrs. Wilkersons' family, friends, and fellow military members painted a consistent picture of a person who adored his wife and 9-year-old son, as well as a picture of a long-serving professional Air Force officer. Some of these letters provided additional clarity to me on matters used effectively by the prosecution in the trial to question the character and truthfulness of both Lt. Col. Wilkerson and Mrs. Wilkerson. Some letters were from people who did not personally know the Wilkersons, but wanted to convey their concerns to me about the evidence and the outcome of the case.

Due to my previous concerns with Lt. Col. Wilkerson's case prior to referral and the concerns identified in defense clemency matters, my deliberation became extensive. Accordingly, I began to personally review and consider the entire record of the trial and its accompanying papers. I reviewed the Article 32 investigation report again. I reviewed the entire court transcript and all the other evidence the jury reviewed (captured on compact discs or in hard copy photos). I looked at some evidence a second and third time and I re-read particular portions of the court transcripts. I reviewed affidavits provided after trial by the prosecuting attorneys and I also read a personal letter to me from the alleged victim. I carefully looked at everything, evidence supporting the findings of the court-martial and evidence against. The more evidence that I considered, the more concerned I became about the court-martial findings in this case.

After my extensive and full review of the entire body of evidence and my comprehensive deliberation spanning a three-week period, I only then finally concluded there was insufficient evidence to support a finding of guilt beyond a reasonable doubt. Based upon my detailed review, I could not conclude anything else. Accordingly, I could not in good conscience let stand the finding of guilty.

Please note, at the beginning of my thorough review, my SJA recommended approving the court-martial findings and approving the sentence of one year confinement. In consideration of Lt. Col. Wilkerson's family and his lengthy military service, my SJA also recommended commuting the sentence of dismissal to an additional two years of confinement. However, after we engaged in numerous subsequent conversations during my extensive deliberation of the evidence, he told me that he had come to fully respect my concerns with the evidence in the case and my conclusion that the evidence did not prove Lt. Col. Wilkerson guilty beyond a reasonable doubt. At the end, he advised me that I could only approve court-martial findings and a sentence that I found correct in law and in fact. Based upon his personal knowledge of how extensively and thoroughly I had reviewed and deliberated on this case, my SJA said he fully respected my decision to disapprove findings in this court case.

Below is a portion of the considerable evidence which caused me, in part, to form my reasonable doubt as to Lt. Col. Wilkerson's guilt. I reviewed all the evidence below, and other evidence, holistically and comprehensively in reaching my conclusion:

a) The evidence indicated that the alleged victim turned down at least three distinct offers of a ride from the Wilkerson home back to her room on base. Whenever she was offered a ride, she seemingly had a different reason to stay at the Wilkerson home;

b) When shown clear photos of all bedrooms of the house, the alleged victim could not identify the bed in which she slept and/or where she claimed the alleged assault occurred;

c) At different times, the alleged victim's description of the hours leading up to the alleged assault varied, as did her description of the state of her clothing during and immediately after the assault;

d) In her initial statement, the alleged victim said that she "passed out" (went to sleep) between 0045 hours and 0100 hours in the morning, and in her court testimony she said that her next memory was that she was in a dream state and was subsequently awoken at about 0300 hours by Mrs. Wilkerson turning on the light. Yet the alleged victim's phone records and her testimony in court showed that she was texting on her phone to a friend at 0143 hours;

e) The alleged victim did not remember whether or not the man who she says assaulted her had facial hair. In addition, she said his face was only 6 inches away from hers. Lt. Col. Wilkerson had a full mustache and the alleged victim had already seen him throughout the recent evening;

f) The alleged victim's version of events describes a path out of the house from the downstairs bedroom (the only room that she could have logically stayed in). This path was not feasible based upon the actual layout of the house;

g) The alleged victim claimed that she woke to a bright light being turned on in the room in which she was sleeping, and Mrs. Wilkerson yelling at her to "get out of my house." The room that she stayed in had an energy-saving ceiling light that is dim for the first few minutes of operation. Although the military judge did not allow the members of the jury to visit the house, the defense counsel made a video to document what would have been the alleged victim's actions based upon her testimony. I watched the entire video twice. It shows the very dim light and the only path to get out of the house from the only room that she could have logically stayed in. It was not consistent with her description of the path that she said she took out of the house;

h) Mrs. Wilkerson's version of the events at her house the night of the alleged incident was substantially consistent from her initial OSI interview statement, to her Article 32 investigation statement, and through her court testimony. And my detailed review of all phone records (of all the key witnesses) validated Lt. Col. and Mrs. Wilkerson's combined version of what occurred on the night in question and the next morning. Please note, I spent close to 4 hours looking at phone record evidence alone. In particular, I determined that the alleged victim's cell phone records (times and durations of incoming/outgoing calls and text messages) when aligned with the testimony and phone records of the friend of the alleged victim, all merged to a common picture that was more consistent with Lt. Col. and Mrs. Wilkerson's combined version of events;

i) Regarding the next morning after the alleged incident, Mrs. Wilkerson claimed she slept in until 0900 hours. In closing arguments, the prosecution argued she was "lying" because she had outgoing calls, incoming calls, and texts before 0900 hours. The defense counsel countered that it was possible that Lt. Col. Wilkerson was using her phone (I am aware that occasionally wives will use husbands' phones, husbands will use wives' phones, kids will use adults' phones, etc.). The prosecution argued that the defense explanation was impossible since phone records showed Lt. Col. Wilkerson was on his own phone/texting at apparently the same time. When I closely checked the phone records to verify this prosecution argument, I determined the times of Lt. Col.

Wilkerson's phone-use were different from his wife's cell phone-use — thereby making it entirely possible that Lt. Col. Wilkerson was using Mrs. Wilkerson's phone before 0900 hours. Likewise, the letter of clemency from the mother of the two guest-children (who were staying overnight at the Wilkerson house), specifically indicated that she called Mrs. Wilkerson's phone that morning at approximately 0700 hours and that Lt. Col. Wilkerson answered it, saying his wife was still asleep. She also said that she spoke with her children during this same phone call. In addition, when she subsequently stopped by the house prior to 0800 hours to check on her children, she said Lt. Col. Wilkerson was awake/up and that her children said that Mrs. Wilkerson was still sleeping;

j) The Office of Special Investigations (OSI) interviewed these two guest-children, ages 13 and 9 who were guests in the Wilkerson house the night of the alleged incident. Neither awoke or heard any yelling during the time of the alleged incident. Yet, the alleged victim at one point said that Mrs. Wilkerson yelled at her to "get out of my house";

k) In addition, the mother of these two children observed her kids and the Wilkersons the very next day following the alleged incident. She did not notice any change in the Wilkersons' behavior or her children's behavior, or that her children sensed any tension between the Wilkersons. Further, these two children apparently stayed at the Wilkerson house the following night. If an incident occurred as claimed by the alleged victim, it would be highly peculiar for the Wilkersons to volunteer to take care of these two children again the following evening;

l) Additionally, witness testimony about the Wilkerson marriage before the night in question and in the immediate days and weeks after that night, showed no perceptible tension or change in their relationship. Had the alleged sexual assault taken place as the alleged victim claimed, it would be reasonable to believe that their relationship would change and that close friends would perceive this change;

m) Witness testimony from a female friend of the alleged victim (who also works at the 31st Medical Group, and who took the alleged victim to the hospital the next day) and her subsequent letter of clemency (in support of Lt. Col. Wilkerson), caused me notable additional doubt about the alleged victim's stated version of events. The friend's comments in this clemency letter also indicated a potential reasonable motivation for the alleged victim to have been less than candid in her stated version of the events;

n) One particular witness was not allowed to testify in court. The primary rationale was that the applicable events of which she had knowledge in regard to the character and truthfulness of the alleged victim occurred 10 years earlier (when the alleged victim was approximately 39 years of age). I reviewed this excluded testimony, as well as the clemency letter of this witness which detailed court proceedings that involved the alleged victim 10 years earlier. The excluded witness had a strong opinion that the alleged victim (now 49 years old) might lie in a court proceeding when it would be in her personal interest to do so;

o) Significantly, I closely watched the video of the entire OSI interview of Lt. Col. Wilkerson (3 hours and 25 minutes). I watched it not once; but twice (and several portions I watched additional times). The prosecution effectively used small segments of the video in closing arguments in attempts to portray Lt. Col. Wilkerson as a liar, or as someone who was trying to cover up misconduct. However, when I twice viewed the video in whole, and I considered his answers in the context of the questions and paths that the OSI attempted to take him down, I believed the entire OSI interview portrayed him as truthful;

p) In addition, Lt. Col. Wilkerson waived his rights to remain silent, did not request a lawyer, and appeared cooperative throughout. The Special Agents who conducted the interview utilized a full gamut of investigative interviewing techniques in attempts to garner incriminating statements from Lt. Col. Wilkerson. He maintained his innocence throughout the interview, provided a written statement, never stopped the interview, nor did he ever ask for a lawyer at any time. As I viewed the entire interview in whole (twice), it was my consistent impression that Lt. Col. Wilkerson answered all the questions in a manner like an innocent person would respond if faced with untrue allegations against him;

q) Lt. Col. Wilkerson voluntarily agreed to take an OSI polygraph examination. I am fully aware of and considered the polygraph results. As you are aware in a criminal investigation, a polygraph is only an investigative tool to assist in the potential focus of the investigation and/or to attempt to elicit admissions of guilt. It is not a "lie-detector test," nor is it "pass" or "fail." Because of the inherent unreliability of polygraphs, they are entirely inadmissible in a court-martial. Ultimately, Lt. Col. Wilkerson has consistently maintained his complete innocence — throughout two lengthy OSI interviews, through the entire court-martial, and throughout his nearly four months in prison (following the court-martial and during the post-trial process);

r) Finally, I do not assert in any way that the event as argued by the prosecution was out of the realm of the possible. However when I considered all the evidence together in total, the evidence was not sufficient to prove this alleged version by the prosecution beyond a reasonable doubt. In addition, and as simply one more point of reference, I was perplexed in relation to this conundrum — Lt. Col. Wilkerson was a selectee for promotion to full colonel, a wing inspector general, a career officer, and described as a doting father and husband. However, according to the version of events presented by the prosecution, Lt. Col. Wilkerson, in the middle of the night, decided to leave his wife sleeping in bed, walk downstairs past the room of his only son, and also near another room with two other sleeping guest-children, and then he decided to commit the egregious crime of sexually assaulting a sleeping woman who he and his wife had only met earlier that night. Based on all the letters submitted in clemency, in strong support of him, by people who know him, such behavior appeared highly incongruent. Accordingly, this also contributed, in some small degree, to my reasonable doubt.

There were some matters of evidence that I could not reconcile. For example, I did have questions about differences in some witnesses' respective versions of events that conflicted with the combined testimony of Lt. Col. and Mrs. Wilkerson. Accordingly, I scrutinized the allegations and arguments that the Wilkersons were untruthful in these instances. The majority of these inconsistencies had plausible alternate explanations. Those that did not were not independently conclusive, nor did all of them put together satisfy me beyond a reasonable doubt of Lt. Col. Wilkerson's guilt.

Moreover, minor inconsistencies between Lt. Col. Wilkerson and Mrs. Wilkerson's versions of events indicated to me that they had not colluded to manufacture a "unified story." In fact, if their two separate versions were too consistent, I would have reasonably been skeptical of them.

After I reviewed all the evidence, it appeared to me that, at the time of their OSI interviews, the two

Wilkersons were simply trying, in good faith, to recall an evening that had occurred almost 3 and 1/2 weeks prior. After consideration of all the matters I have mentioned, as well as other matters within the record of trial, I impartially and in good faith concluded that there was insufficient evidence to prove beyond a reasonable doubt that Lt. Col. Wilkerson was guilty.

Obviously it would have been exceedingly less volatile for the Air Force and for me professionally, to have simply approved the finding of guilty. This would have been an act of cowardice on my part and a breach of my integrity. As I have previously stated, after considering all matters in the entire record of trial, I hold a genuine and reasonable doubt that Lt. Col. Wilkerson committed the crime of sexual assault. As a result, I would have been entirely remiss in my sworn military duty and responsibility as a GCMCA if I did not release someone from prison whose guilt I did not find proven beyond a reasonable doubt Accordingly, I knew that my court-martial action to disapprove findings and to dismiss the charges was the right, the just, and the only thing to do.

In summary, I exercised the obligation of a GCMCA exactly as required by the UCMJ, when after my lengthy review and deliberation of the evidence, I had reasonable doubt as to Lt. Col. Wilkerson's guilt. Sir, I provide this letter for you to use or to share with others as you deem appropriate in relation to this case or in relation to the lawful and necessary discretion of a court-martial convening authority.

Very Respectfully,
CRAIG A. FRANKLIN, Lieutenant General, USAF
Commander, Third Air Force

How could Lt. Gen. Franklin have arrived at this conclusion when the jury did not? Clemency offers the defense an opportunity to submit information to the Convening Authority in the hope of reducing the sentence or overturning the conviction. The Wilkerson defense team submitted case law showing that Brig. Gen. Milligan's testimony and testimony for Lt. Col. Wilkerson's truthfulness should have been permitted during the trial. Brig. Gen. Milligan's testimony went straight to the heart of the untruthfulness of Hanks, attesting to her willingness to falsify court papers to get her way. Many clemency letters attested to the truthfulness of Lt. Col. Wilkerson and pointed out multiple inconsistencies in Hanks' various versions of the story, and detailed a possible motive for a false allegation.

Lt. Gen. Franklin also had the letters from Captain Manning and Suzanne Berrong, both of which clearly indicated their doubts about the validity of Hanks' story. And, he had the letter from the visiting boys' mother explaining the phone calls to Beth's phone, corroborating Beth's testimony, and refuting a key point made by the prosecution.

During his deliberations, Lt. Gen. Franklin zeroed in on prosecutorial misconduct and asked for affidavits from the prosecution team. Col. Christensen's affidavit denying he bullied a witness (or witnesses) or put the fighter pilot culture on trial, opened the door for others to write letters describing prosecution threats, intimidation tactics and unprofessional behavior. Those additional letters and statements may have influenced the general's decision. They surely pointed out the win-at-all-costs tactics employed by the prosecution.

According to Nancy Montgomery's June 3, 2013, article in the *Stars and Stripes*, "Lt. Gen. Franklin has no regrets about his decision to overturn a fighter pilot's sexual assault conviction... 'I made the right decision even amidst all the attacks... I can sleep well at night because I know I made the right call.' "[390] (Notice how Montgomery always connects "fighter pilot" to her articles, echoing again Col. Christensen's theme.)

No matter how this case turns out in the long run, Lt. Gen. Franklin proved himself to be a man of courage. Surely he understood the pressure inside the military to "do something" about sexual assault. Just as surely, he also understood the political backlash he might face. He did the right thing.

22

WHY THE DEFENSE LOST

"The evil that is in the world almost always comes of ignorance,
and good intentions may do as much harm as malevolence if they
lack understanding."
— *Albert Camus, "The Plague"*

In my opinion, the defense team in the Wilkerson trial was caught off guard by the political pressure on the Air Force to "do something" about sexual assault and by the attack on fighter pilots throughout the trial. Since this was a pretty clear-cut case of "she-said, she-said," and there was zero evidence of any kind, the defense did not object to what it thought were small issues raised by the prosecution, such as fighter pilot behavior, the Korea incident and the burning of a couch. When Kim Hanks could not identify the room where the alleged incident took place, the defense thought the case was won.

Additionally, the defense attempted to prove Hanks was not drunk. This was part of a strategy to refute all the possibilities of substantial incapacitation. I believe this was an error. Hanks had more to drink than she admitted. I believe she was drunk and disorderly and, along with the effects of Red Bull and vodka combined, that she was doing exactly what Beth said she was — making noise walking around the house. Lt. Col. McCarron, the Article 32 Investigating Officer, said, "Most who observed or talked to Ms. Hanks during the evening of 23-24 March, described her as drunk, slurring her words and stumbling. She describes herself as 'out of it,' and admittedly does not remember many details of the evening."[391] I believe Hanks was drunk, despite the toxicologist's assessment. He was in error because he based his calculations on what Hanks said she had to drink, not what she actually drank, and there was no discussion of the effects of Red

Bull and vodka during the trial. MSgt. Dunnivant said Hanks was tipsy and somewhat intoxicated at 3:20, and Berrong said Hanks still smelled of alcohol at 8:30. MSgt. Dunnivant's assessment of Hanks' level of intoxication was only found in the OSI investigator's notes. She did not put that in her OSI statement, and when she testified, she said Hanks "seemed okay" when she picked her up. I do not believe the defense found this discrepancy prior to my research. In hindsight, the defense should have shown that Hanks was indeed drunk, and she was disorderly, just as Beth said. That is why she left the house before 3 a.m., and that is why she needed a cover story to keep Beth from getting her in trouble by reporting an alcohol-related incident.

At this point in history, there seems to be a common theme throughout the Department of Defense (DoD). Later I discuss guidance from Secretary of Defense Panetta and Chairman of the Joint Chiefs of Staff General Dempsey to "ensure that cases of sexual assault receive a high level of command attention," and "increase prosecutions," and we have also seen comments from other senior leaders as well.[392] The most famous (infamous) comment is from the Commandant of the Marine Corps, General James F. Amos, who publically stated his view that most men accused of sexual assault were guilty (without offering any evidence to support his assertion). The Commandant said: "I know fact from fiction. The fact of the matter is 80 percent of those are legitimate sexual assaults." The Commandant is telling his subordinates that 80 percent of those charged with sexual assault are guilty and suggesting anyone charged with sexual assault should be dismissed from the service.[393] Guess what, general: If 80 percent are guilty, that leaves 20 percent who aren't. Where is your support for those wrongfully accused? Shouldn't the services fully and aggressively investigate those cases as well? And shouldn't accusers who falsify reports be prosecuted? Where is the balance?

Political pressure like this has some senior military officers going along. As in the case of Tracy West from Simi Valley, California, cited in the chapter on false allegations, prosecutors sometimes bend to pressure or fail to do the right thing. In the Wilkerson case, Col. Christensen fell in line with the Marine Corps Commandant's comments. He "detailed himself" to the Wilkerson case and published his commentary, "My job is prosecuting sexual assault," on the Ramstein website. Col. Christensen also relayed the philosophy of guilty without the presumption of innocence to the court-martial panel when he questioned Col. Walker, Lt. Col. Wilkerson's boss. Col. Christensen said: "If the boss has made it clear he wants something to happen, we expect a good officer to salute and make sure those things happen, correct?"[394] By this statement, was Col. Christensen suggesting that good soldiers will seek convictions regardless of innocence? His actions might be perceived as supporting that attitude. During the trial, as is required, the Aviano JAG office notified the Mannheim Military Detention Center that they were trying Lt. Col. Wilkerson but not to expect a conviction. Telling the prison not to expect a conviction clearly indicated the prosecution team didn't think there was a strong enough case to convict Lt. Col. Wilkerson. Why, then, did the prosecution proceed? Remember, the Investigating Officer based her recommendation to proceed based solely on "the apparent lack of motive" for Hanks to fabricate a story (without investigating that motive). Is there an unwritten policy now in the military to go to court-martial regardless of the level of evidence?

Pressing to a full court-martial without evidence does seem to have become a trend inside the military. The United States Navy tried a Marine Corps major in May 2013 on charges of sexually assaulting a female Navy midshipman two years after an alleged incident, despite having three witness statements saying it didn't happen. The three witnesses wrote that they were either with the defendant or the accuser during the time of the alleged assault and that the defendant and accuser were not together at that time.[395] Evidence in the case also included texts between the accuser and a friend indicating collusion as to the "story" they would fabricate to charge the major. Despite the three alibi witnesses and collusion evidence, the Navy tried the major anyway. He was found innocent of sexual assault, but the Navy did find him guilty of committing an indecent act, having an unduly familiar relationship and conduct unbecoming an officer.[396] I found no evidence the Navy punished the female lieutenant for perjury or false police reporting.

Similarities between the Navy case and the Wilkerson case include the alleged Navy female victim "describing a day of heavy drinking that preceded the incident that had created lapses in her memory." It was "like some out-of-body experience," the alleged Navy victim said. You recall Hanks saying it "felt like she as dreaming."[397] During the Navy case testimony, the alleged victim described her level of intoxication as "8 out of 10" but insisted she could "walk in heels without help and get to the bathroom herself to vomit."[398] In the Wilkerson case, Hanks said she wasn't drunk, but we have discussed evidence to the contrary.

Did the Wilkerson defense lose because of political pressure? Philip Cave, a defense attorney based in Washington, D.C., who specializes in defending sexual assault cases, stated: "These cases are political. There is significant and robust media attention, congressional attention, and attention from special interest groups, so commanders are scared of appearing soft on sexual assault. That means that *in almost every case you are going to be prosecuted at court-martial.*"[399] Cave said this can happen even in cases where a UCMJ Article 32 investigation hearing officer does not recommend court-martial because the case is weak or non-existent.

According to Cave: "Law enforcement will tell you that they are only there to get the truth. That's not accurate. They are there to get you to confess or say something that can be twisted into a confession or admission of guilt."[400] As we saw in the Wilkerson case, Cave said investigators generally practice what is called confirmation bias, meaning they search out evidence they think will convict you. They don't spend time looking for evidence to clear a defendant or hurt their case. He said investigators will ignore information that might be helpful to the defense, even to the extent of leaving helpful information out of their reports. The investigators in the Wilkerson case did not ask MSgt. Dunnivant to include that Hanks was intoxicated into her written statement. That might be an example of the type of actions, helpful to a defendant, that Cave is concerned about. He went on to say prosecutors who may fail to independently verify the case proceed based on an incomplete investigation. The Wilkerson OSI taped interview is a textbook example of this statement. OSI investigators lied repeatedly to Lt. Col. Wilkerson in their attempt to get him to admit guilt. They also repeatedly ignored evidence of innocence. Prosecutors equally never questioned the OSI report.

Attorney Cave again: "The events of most military sexual assault cases are typically a he-said/she-said situation. The most important theory you (as the defense) must identify is 'why?' Why would she lie, why would she put herself through this, why would she come to court and talk about this?"[401]

Cave was right. As in the Wilkerson case, the burden of proof has shifted to the defense. Defense attorneys must now offer reasons why the accuser would lie. It is no longer sufficient to provide reasonable doubt, but one must now actively offer substantial evidence as to why the accuser would lie in each case. A failure to do so may result in a (another) wrongful conviction. In the Wilkerson case, defense attorneys did not address motives for Hanks to lie. They were trying the case by old rules. They thought all they had to do was provide reasonable doubt. But the rules had changed.

Without knowing about the Wilkerson case, Cave seems to have defined it completely. There was no evidence; it was a weak or nonexistent case. The Investigating Officer told Beth it would not go forward but then changed her recommendation. Finally, there was a lot of special-interest group and political pressure. There was a one-sided investigation ignoring evidence that would prove innocence. While the defense did rigorously cross-examine the OSI agent for his lack of investigation, the defense did not ask if the OSI investigated the possibility of a false allegation. This was a classic (modern) case of sexual assault in the military — going to court-martial no matter what.

Investigators have also been known to bend to pressure. As in is the case of Ron Williamson of Pontotoc County, Oklahoma, detailed in John Grisham's book *The Innocent Man*, investigators sometimes fail to act in a professional manner or otherwise rationalize poor behavior in the name of what they believe is right.[402] Later, we discuss the investigators who questioned Beth Wilkerson and how Beth said it was a reservist she discussed Hanks' shoes with, not the active duty agent. The active duty agent said Beth refused to give them the shoes, but Beth said she offered the shoes to the other agent. Perhaps, in trying to do what they thought was right, they got their story confused. Lt. Col. Wilkerson's attorneys merely questioned the active duty special agent and let his story that Beth misled him go unchallenged. They did not question the professionalism of these investigators. In hindsight, now that we know investigators sometimes get it wrong, perhaps the defense should have called the reservist to testify.

Finally, jurors also bend to pressure. In the Air Force today, men and women stationed overseas cannot go a week without seeing an article on sexual assault in the *Stars and Stripes* or a day without seeing a public service announcement on Armed Forces Network television aimed at the perpetrators of sexual assault.[403] It is not an understatement to say Air Force personnel in Europe are inundated with awareness of sexual assault. They are bombarded with the need to "do something." It is not difficult to believe many Air Force members believe anyone accused of sexual assault is guilty even before a trial. The Wilkerson defense team believed jurors could remain impartial, despite pressure from the Secretary of Defense and the Chairman of the Joint Chiefs and comments like those of General Amos and Brig. Gen. Zobrist. I am not sure they can. In fact, I believe political pressure contributed to the Wilkerson jury rationalizing sending Lt. Col. Wilkerson to prison with no evidence to support Hanks' story. The pressure simply helped them convict a fighter pilot because, as Col. Christensen said, "we can rely on our knowledge of the ways of the world," meaning he's guilty of something. Pressure to convict anyone accused of sexual assault likely played a significant role in this verdict.

The military is a cross-section of American society. Just as in civilian society, investigators, prosecutors, judges, jurors and others involved in the justice process sometimes rationalize unprofessional actions, poor investigations and unethical behavior and sometimes convict innocent men.

The defense strategy was not to sweat the small stuff. An example is the couch-burning incident the prosecution used to paint Lt. Col. Wilkerson with "conduct unbecoming of an officer."[404] The defense chose not to object to references or questions concerning the tradition. It would have been pretty easy to object. The visiting fighter squadron commander wrote an affidavit saying his squadron was responsible. Lt. Col. Wilkerson did not light the couch and was not present when the couch was lit on fire. Lt. Col. Wilkerson discovered the fire and, as senior officer present when the Security Forces Airmen arrived, chose to take charge and speak with the Security Forces. The only relevant testimony in the entire incident was that of the Security Forces Airmen who testified Lt. Col. Wilkerson wasn't nice to him. In the Airman's mind, the first impression Lt. Col. Wilkerson gave him was "less than professional."[405] A two-minute interaction was used as a reference to support and substantiate a charge of conduct unbecoming. There were no corroborating witnesses called, and, as mentioned, the defense did not dispute or challenge the testimony. It should have. The entire incident was irrelevant.

In hindsight, I believe the defense attorneys should have challenged testimony about the couch, the Korea bathroom incident, the singing of songs with explicit words, and for the prosecution laying blame on Lt. Col. Wilkerson for other officers not wearing seatbelts in a car where he was not the driver or owner. These issues were all irrelevant to the sexual assault charge, and none were specified in the charges. The defense should have objected to these sideshow issues. The Korea incident was pure hearsay. The young Security Forces Airman did not see Lt. Col. Wilkerson burn the couch (he arrived after the fire started). Most specifically, the defense should have strenuously objected to the allegation of conduct unbecoming by Lt. Col. Wilkerson vis-à-vis the seatbelts. Testimony related to any and all of these issues should have generated defense objections; Lt. Col. Wilkerson broke no rules.

The defense should have suspected something was different when Col. Christensen detailed himself to the case and showed up at the Article 32 hearing. As mentioned, Col. Christensen's presence at the Article 32 hearing itself was an unusual occurrence and may have given some insight into how the prosecution intended to proceed, i.e., "Ms. Hanks has no obvious reason to lie," as Lt. Col. McCarron wrote.[406] Col. Christensen convinced the jurors that someone was lying. He said Hanks had no reason to lie, but the Wilkersons had a lot to lose, therefore they must have been the ones lying. Understanding the prosecution strategy earlier may have allowed the defense to realize the burden of proof had shifted to them. As attorney Phillip Cave suggested, the defense should have submitted a motive for Hanks to lie, or the accused was guilty by default.

With pressure from Congress and the President, is it any wonder the rate of convictions is increasing? Defense attorney Philip Cave said, "Allegations of sexual assault in the military are no longer criminal allegations; they have become politically charged." In the Wilkerson case, the lead defense attorney had been practicing law for more than thirty-five years, including experience as an active duty Air Force JAG. He knew the case was a "she-said, she-said" with no evidence and confidently thought it would result in a not-guilty verdict. Unfortunately, in my opinion, he misjudged the "political" nature of the allegation and the atmosphere of convict-no-matter-what pervasive in the military today. It appears Cave was right, at least about why the Wilkerson case went to trial. It certainly appears to have been politically motivated.

According to the *Stars and Stripes*: "The Air Force prosecuted 96 sexual assault cases last year, *including 15 cases in which civilian jurisdictions where the off-base assaults occurred declined the cases as unwinnable.*" Of those fifteen cases civilians declined to prosecute, Col. Christensen said "so far, we have eight convictions. We don't shy away from a tough case."[407] (Emphasis added.) Meaning, the Air Force takes cases to court even when the civilian jurisdictions don't believe there is a case. Now that we have discovered the new military way of doing business, it makes one wonder how many of those eight convictions might be innocent men.

Why take on cases others won't? According to McClatchy Newspapers, the DoD budget for "Sexual Assault Prevention and Response leapt from $5 million in fiscal 2005 to more than $23 million in fiscal 2010. Total Defense Department spending on sexual assault prevention and related efforts now exceeds $113 million annually."[408] The services have a win-win if they go to trial. They either get a conviction or, at a minimum, they can say, "See, we take this seriously." Unfortunately, innocent men are going to prison to make them look good.

Ironically, that is exactly what Captain Beliles said during the sentencing phase of Lt. Col. Wilkerson's trial: "It must not be said. It must not be said that we as an Air Force did not take this crime seriously."[409] One female civilian employed on the base at Aviano who was also a retired lieutenant colonel (non-pilot) wrote to Lt. Gen. Franklin. She said this about the jury of non-pilots and the comments of Captain Beliles, the assistant prosecutor: "I am saddened by the obvious pressure the jury succumbed to when the prosecution told them it was their 'duty' to find him guilty and remove the Air Force's current black eye."[410] So it was about making the Air Force look good. The Air Force went to trial because it had unlimited resources. It got lucky with a jury comprised entirely of non-pilots, so it put the pilot culture on trial and got a guilty verdict when even it did not expect one. Justice?

Evidence shows, in the Wilkerson case, there was concern about how the Air Force looked in the eyes of the public/media before the Article 32 hearing. As early as June 3 — before the Investigating Officer recommended court-martial — Brig. Gen. Zobrist wrote to Lt. Gen. Franklin about Col. Christensen in Washington. To be absolutely clear, there was no impartiality in Brig. Gen. Zobrist's emails. Here is what he wrote in June: "Col. Christensen is THE senior prosecutor for the USAF. ALL other Air Force prosecutors work for him, and he has decided to take this case on himself. The USAF should certainly not be criticized for failing to put the right emphasis on this case regarding our legal team."[411] The emphasis is in the original email. So, at least in Brig. Gen. Zobrist's mind, it was about the Air Force not being criticized. There is no mention of the possibility of innocence or of ensuring a fair trial in any of the emails released by the Air Force on August 26, 2013. Lt. Col. Wilkerson, once accused, was guilty, at least in its emails.

Sexual assault is the focus of effort in the military right now. One could argue even the war in Afghanistan has taken a back seat. The political pressure is stifling, and so it goes. Defense attorneys across all the services are fighting a new type of courtroom/system. No longer is truth the goal. Defense attorneys must offer motivation, and probably some proof, of a false allegation or the defendant is going to prison, guilty or not. The Wilkerson case has become a bellwether warning for defense attorneys. They have to learn to play by new rules. It is much more difficult to prove innocence these days. It is a new game.

After the Wilkerson verdict, word passed through the grapevine that at least one juror said that Hanks' story never changed while Beth's was "all over the place." Had defense attorneys objected to hearsay and irrelevant fighter pilot traditions, and disputed each of Hanks' inconsistencies in a more aggressive manner, i.e., gone to greater lengths to show the changes in Hanks' multiple versions and to prove motivation for a false allegation, it might have become clearer to the jurors whose story was actually all over the map.

To be fair, the defense did try to do so, but in a gentlemanly way. The lead defense attorney summarized in his closing argument:

> She gives you one story and she gives an inconsistent story to the SARC, where she says she's passed out. Now here's how that works. That goes to her credibility about these allegations. She's told different stories about what happened. In this court she said — she said, that she was awake during part of this time, but to the SARC she said she was passed out. And, of course, then she modified the words "passed out" to mean "I was just sleeping." So at this point she's telling inconsistent stories even about what happened. Now who knows what happened? All we know is she's told inconsistent stories. And, ultimately, how can you believe her beyond a reasonable doubt when she's telling inconsistent stories about the very things that happened that night?[412]

Obviously this was not strong enough or memorable enough for those particular jurors. Perhaps the defense should have gone to greater lengths to detail more of these inconsistencies. Perhaps they should have driven the point home for each of the multiple changes in Hanks' story. Perhaps the attorney should have raised his voice as Col. Christensen did when cross-examining Beth Wilkerson? Then perhaps the jurors would have understood whose story was "all over the map." One can lead a horse to water, but...

The clemency letters and additional written statements and testimony painted a clearer picture. They helped Lt. Gen. Franklin reach his decision to dismiss all charges and reinstate Lt. Col. Wilkerson to active duty. However, that decision led to media and political uproar.

2 3

PRESUMPTION
OF GUILT

"People only see what they are prepared to see."
— *Ralph Waldo Emerson*

The Air Force Office of Special Investigations (OSI) is the investigative arm of the Air Force. Like a civilian police detective division, the OSI's duty is to investigate alleged crimes. It is the primary resource of the Air Force for investigating crime.

According to an OSI fact sheet, "The Air Force Office of Special Investigations has been the Air Force's major investigative service since Aug. 1, 1948. The agency reports to the Inspector General, Office of the Secretary of the Air Force. AFOSI provides professional investigative service to commanders of all Air Force activities. Its primary responsibilities are criminal investigations and counterintelligence services." It is "a federal law enforcement and investigative agency operating throughout the full spectrum of conflict, seamlessly within any domain; conducting criminal investigations and providing counterintelligence services," whose mission is "to identify, exploit and neutralize criminal, terrorist and intelligence threats to the Air Force, Department of Defense and U.S. Government." It advertises its pillar cornerstone is to "Vigorously solve crime; protect secrets; warn of threats; exploit intelligence opportunities; operate in cyber."[413]

One would reasonably assume the OSI would "vigorously solve crime" in an impartial and professional manner. A conversation with high-ranking officers in the Pentagon confirmed the OSI is supposed to remain neutral, and OSI investigators do not work for the prosecution but should investigate with no favoritism for either side of a case.[414]

In the Wilkerson case, the Aviano Office of Special Investigations began an investigation on April 17, 2012, based on the Sexual Assault

Response Coordinator's unrestricted report.[415] The OSI interviewed Hanks on April 17. Lt. Col. Wilkerson's voluntary OSI interrogation occurred on April 19, simultaneous with OSI agents visiting his home and interviewing Beth Wilkerson.

One might reasonably assume that to vigorously solve crime, the investigators would want to gather all evidence available. Then, only after gathering all evidence available, one might expect the investigators to make decisions about the validity or usefulness of that evidence. However, during the OSI visit to the Wilkerson home on April 19, investigators did not take photographs of, or gather evidence of any kind from, the alleged crime scene. Nor did they, at any time, attempt to gather evidence from Hanks.

OSI Special Agent Derrick Neives, of the Aviano office, testified during the trial as to why the OSI did not make any effort to gather evidence:

> Neives: Based on the fact that at the time the allegation was brought forward to OSI, three weeks — approximately more than three weeks later, it was ruled out that any trace evidence from his skin cells or hand that would have transferred to the underwear probably would not have been there. [416] ... Based on the nature of the allegation and the time from when the incident occurred, we were not given search authority.
> Q . Did you seek search authorization?
> A. No, sir, we did not, based on the consultation and the recommendation of our forensic science consultant.

Special Agent Neives further explained why the OSI did not attempt to gather evidence:

> Well, sir, based on the nature of the allegation, which was a victim alluding to subject using or potentially placing his hand within her waistline. Once we relayed that information to the forensic science consultant, he opined that the chances of any evidence being at the

scene with that amount of time in between was unlikely. And, therefore, we didn't seek the search authority.

That may be a reasonable assumption, but what about looking at the layout of the house — at the lighting in the room, at the exits and counters, and where the bedrooms were located? Each of those issues could have provided considerable information to a jury about to destroy a man's career and family by putting him in prison and taking away twenty years of service to his country.

The bottom line is the OSI just didn't bother to look. It seems reasonable to expect a professional investigator to go look for evidence and to check on the reliability or plausibility of the story being told, regardless of timing, because you don't know what you will find. If you don't find anything, then and only then, you testify there wasn't any evidence. You don't not look and then testify you didn't do a professional job because you assumed there wouldn't be anything to be learned. You don't avoid looking because of time. The OSI evidently did not think anything in Hanks' statement was worth questioning or verifying.

The Aviano OSI began its investigation by first interviewing Hanks and Captains Brock and Manning on April 17-18, 2012. They asked Lt. Col. Wilkerson if he would come to their office on April 19 and visited the Wilkerson home to interview Beth on April 19. The two Wilkerson interviews were simultaneous, and both were voluntarily given. While at the Wilkerson home, Beth showed the investigators the basement room she offered Hanks. The investigators took no photographs and collected no evidence.

Investigators asked Lt. Col. Wilkerson to return to their office on April 26, where he voluntarily agreed to take a polygraph exam. Throughout the polygraph, Lt. Col. Wilkerson remained consistent in his denial of any wrongdoing. The OSI investigators used a legal, and often used, tactic of telling Lt. Col. Wilkerson he failed the polygraph. They told him he failed and then yelled in his face that he was a liar. However, this did not get Lt. Col. Wilkerson to "break" and confess to any wrongdoing. Investigators changed tactics slightly, telling him he failed only one question, and they asked him to confess to which one. Still, Lt.

Col. Wilkerson denied wrongdoing — even with a very intense interrogator inches from his face screaming at him that he was a liar. [417]

With regard to the polygraph, the OSI report states: "After analysis of the physiological data collected during the Series I examination, it was the opinion of the examiner that the subject's physiological responses to the relevant questions were indicative of deception. During post-test interview, SUBJECT continuously denied he was in bed with VICTIM and did not put his hands down her pants or penetrate her vagina in any way. SUBJECT related he did not leave his bed on the third floor until the following morning and there is no way he would have gotten up in the middle of the night to go downstairs for anything. SUBJECT stated his spouse would not and did not lie to cover up this incident as she is very independent and would have kicked him out of the house and gone back to her parents if she had caught him in bed with another woman."[418]

Also according to the OSI report, part of this analyst's interpretation was based on the accused not being able to "explain why the accuser would make up an allegation like this."[419] Again, because Hanks had no obvious reason to lie (that anyone investigated), Wilkerson must be guilty.

According to the American Psychological Association, The validity of polygraph testing is questionable and unreliable. "There is no evidence that any pattern of physiological reactions is unique to deception," and "most psychologists and other scientists agree that there is little basis for the validity of polygraph tests." [420]

Polygraphs have been refuted many times; courts, including the United States Supreme Court, have repeatedly rejected them because of their "inherent unreliability."[421]

In this case, after being accused of failing all and then only part of the polygraph, Lt. Col. Wilkerson consistently maintained his innocence.[422] No evidence was offered to support that he failed a polygraph during the trial, and it was not pursued by the prosecution. One would think if the polygraph was of any value, the prosecution would have found a way to include the information.

Polygraphs are so unreliable, their "results," which are only an individual's interpretation of the subject's nervousness, are inadmissible. In reality, they are used only as an investigator's tool to get a subject to confess. As psychologist Leonard Saxe, Ph.D., has argued, "the idea that we can detect a person's veracity by monitoring psychophysiological changes is more myth than reality."[423]

The OSI had all the witness statements and access to the Wilkerson home. Reasonably, they should have compared Hanks' statement with those of Lt. Col. and Beth Wilkerson and others. The OSI then should have visited the Wilkerson home and assessed the credibility of the allegation in Hanks' statement. Given the layout of the Wilkerson house, they should have been able to see some of the inconsistencies. They also should have noticed the inconsistencies in what Hanks told others and the statements that suggested Hanks may have a motivation for a false allegation.

However, rather than a balanced investigation, it appears the OSI made zero inquiry into the possibility that Lt. Col. Wilkerson might be innocent. In fact, after a lengthy review of the OSI report and the Record of Trial, it appears the OSI acted solely as the prosecutor's investigators without concern for where the evidence led them. They appear to have accepted Hanks' story as truth without any questions. They were attempting to vigorously solve a crime without verifying one occurred. They presumed guilt and avoided any investigation into the possibility of innocence. They were not neutral in this case. They saw only what they were prepared to see — guilt.

OSI investigators did not collect *any* evidence from the Wilkerson home or from Hanks' person or clothing, not even photographs. In fact, the record shows their only effort on the case was an attempt to coerce Lt. Col. Wilkerson into a confession.[424]

The OSI relied heavily on Hanks' statement, but that statement seemed odd. I have never seen a statement like this before in my experience in the Air Force (twenty-seven years total with four years in command positions that included experience in four sexual assault court-martial cases).

Hanks' first two pages are not on the formatted paper the OSI uses. They are on blank paper. The third page of her statement is on a different, formatted piece of paper — the type normally used by the OSI. The second page is marked as if it is the end of a statement. It is "Z'd" out at the bottom, signifying "I have nothing more to write." But then, the third and subsequent fourth and fifth pages add additional information, as if as afterthoughts or answers to specific questions.

Following are the pages of Hanks' statement. Notice the format of the paper of the original written statement — blank. Then notice the additions on lined and formatted paper, used by the OSI. No other witness statements in the entire Record of Trial appear in this manner. All others are on the standard, formatted paper provided by the OSI. Only Hanks' statement is different.

It is not uncommon for the OSI to ask questions based on the witnesses' statement, or for a witness to add detail.[425] As an example, the fourth page of Hanks' statement lists the people whom Hanks interacted with that night, while the fifth page lists what she had to eat and drink. So, it is possible these additional pages are in response to questions. But then, when and where did Hanks write the first two pages? And why did digital penetration — a critically important aspect of the alleged assault — only show up as a response to a question or as an afterthought?

What OSI question would have solicited the paragraph alleging "digital penetration"? Wouldn't something as critical as that have been important enough to include in the first draft of any statement when accusing someone of sexual assault? Why was such a critical and serious piece of information only added later?

Hanks' first two pages may have been written prior to her meeting with the OSI, while the remaining information would seem to indicate the presence of OSI investigators asking questions.

The critical question is why, only on page three, on a different format of paper, appearing to be after consultation or in response to a question, does Hanks first mention digital penetration. Added as an afterthought to Hanks' original statement, this elevated the seriousness of the case.

Here are the first three pages from her OSI statement:

3 Mar 17:30 - Met friends at TLF where we'd reserved rooms ('5 other people) - <1 I know well, 3 fairly new acquaintances.

1900 - Walked over to USO concert

time? 2030-2100 - Walked to La Bella Vista after concert

3 people went home of our group (including my two friends).

We were talking with some people the other 2 women knew. I know one of them peripherally. They wanted to go somewhere, I thought I heard them mention the pub, and thought we were going there where some friends of mine were. One of the women asked me to come and I said yes.

time? Instead we drove to someone's house, the man who sat in the front passenger seat. I asked how we were going to get home and where were we to one of the people in the car and he said he wasn't sure.

The man who lived there ✱ I asked someone today prior to this appointment with OSI the name of person who lived there ✱ Wilkerson - poured us a glass of wine and we toasted. We all met his wife Beth. The others went outside, I was not comfortable there, I didn't know anyone very well and did not want to drink more so I hung out with Beth, her friend who was visiting and their kids.

time? At some point I told both women I'd come with that I was ready to go home whenever they were, and went back to talk with Beth and the kids.

4 March ? 0030-0100 - Beth told me the people I came with left without me. She explained they could drive me back to the TLF but would have to drop me off outside the gate, and that they had done that for one of the other women. The second woman had gotten a ride home with the person who drove us over. She asked me to stay over but I didn't want to.

≈ 0030 Beth went off to do something - make up a bed I think her husband asked me if I wanted a drink. Initially I said no but I may have had a glass of prosecco or asked for a non-alcoholic drink, I can't remember.

≈ 0045 called my girlfriend. I didn't remember calling her until she told me - she said "you were slurring your words. you were making sense and sort of not making sense, it didn't sound like you." I remember telling her I didn't know where I was but that it is too late and too far to drive and I will stay there. Beth made a twin bed up in a downstairs room and said they would get me up in time to check out of the TLF. I was so tired, I remember crawling into the bed fully clothed and turning out the light and went to sleep.

I.O. Exhibit 3
page 3 of 7

4 Mar ≈ 0300-0320 I was having a dream, it felt like I was floating, and I was being touched over my body. I felt a little initial pain when being touched between my legs.

A very bright light came on, I rolled over to cover my eyes and I heard a man say loudly "what the hell is going on?" I woke up and felt a hand that was down the front of my pants being removed. I opened my eyes and saw a man about 6 inches from my face squinting with his eyes closed.

I didn't know at first who he was or where I was. I heard "Get the Hell out of my house", looked up and saw Beth at the light. I realized where I was. I don't know if her husband was dressed or not or what he did, I didn't look at him. I sat on the side of the bed and felt very woozy. I looked down and saw I was still fully clothed, with my belt buckled.

She asked me to get up and leave, I didn't know where my shoes or sweater were. I started to walk out of the door she had open and saw my wallet and glasses on the counter. I went back in. She said "I really liked you" I said I really liked her too and of course I was leaving. I checked my phone it was I think 0320.

0320-0415 I had to climb over their low wall in front and walked into some town in my socks. I do not remember but was told I called twice the same friend I called before. I do remember calling one of my friends I had gone to the concert with, who had gone home early. I was really foggy, crying and didn't know where I was! There was a group of english speaking young men walking down the street luckily, they told my friend where I was and stayed with me until she got there to pick me up.

0430-0730 back at TLF I slept, got a phone call from the friend I'd called but did not remember. She was concerned I hadn't seemed myself, as was I, and I still felt out of it, and we decided to go to the clinic to get tested.

0900 - my friend drove me to clinic where I requested a full drug panel including GHB (? spelling) and Rohypnol.

I have had a follow up appt. with PCM Maj. O'keefe (who was working the sat. clinic)
I have had 2 meetings with MH Tom Horan for issues regarding the assault.
I have met 3 times with SARC

I.O. Exhibit 3 pg 4 of 7
page 4 of 7

Name of Individual Making Statement: Kimberly Hawks   Date: 17 Apr 12

In Continuation of what I have provided the OSI officers

I fell asleep fully clothed. I was dreaming that I was on my back floating and was being touched. I don't remember any talking. I was touched over my breasts but can't recall if under clothes just dream-like.

I felt pain initially being touched on the left inner labia, then it stopped hurting and I felt being touch just inside my vagina with the

When the light got really bright I rolled over to my left and heard a man say, "What the Hell's Going On?" and his hand was inside the front of my pants and his finger was in my vagina and he pulled his hand out. It didn't feel like his entire finger, it was curled/flexed and felt like perhaps to middle interphalangeal joint. KEE

Signature of Individual Making Statement: Page 5 of 7

There is another troubling conflict in trial testimony concerning the OSI investigation — it has to do with the OSI investigator who interviewed Beth Wilkerson. Two OSI agents visited the Wilkerson home on April 19 to interview Beth; Special Agent Derrick Neives and another agent (the Air Force has decided to withhold his name, so I will call him Agent No. 2). According to Special Agent Neives' testimony, "we" asked her (Beth) for Hanks' shoes.[426] It is another subtlety, but he never says he was present when asking. He only testifies multiple times that "we asked her." Beth testified that she offered Hanks' shoes to the OSI when they visited her home on April 19.[427] She said the other agent — Agent No. 2 — was the person with whom she discussed the shoes, not Special Agent Neives. Beth said she offered the shoes to Agent No. 2 while Special Agent Neives was *outside on the phone* talking with the OSI office where her husband, Lt. Col. Wilkerson, was being simultaneously interrogated.

There is no dispute about the phone call back to the OSI on base, only about with whom Beth had this conversation. Unfortunately, Special Agent No. 2 was not present for the trial. He is a reservist not stationed in Italy. A couple of months later, as I researched the Record of Trial, I contacted Special Agent No. 2 and asked if he would answer some questions concerning the trial and his interview with Beth Wilkerson. He refused to answer any of my questions, including my specific question of whether Special Agent Neives was present when Beth offered the shoes. To quote Col. Christensen, "What is he hiding?" If there were nothing to this issue, why should he refuse to answer the question? There remains a dispute over the actual conversation at the Wilkerson home.

The Air Force, including its investigative force, the OSI, has a duty to protect the military member equally, whether he or she is the accused or the accuser. The OSI charter is to investigate each case impartially and follow every lead, no matter where it leads them. The investigators did not. Instead, there appears to be a presumption of guilt throughout this investigation. These investigators seemed never to have considered the possibility that Lt. Col. Wilkerson was innocent. There was no investigation into the inconsistencies in Hanks' versions of the story, nor was there any physical evidence gathered. They behaved as if Lt. Col. Wilkerson was guilty and failed to notice or investigate evidence that didn't fit the guilty scenario.

There was no visible action taken by law enforcement from March 24 until April 17. The SARC report was filed on March 29. But, while nothing was happening related to Hanks' allegation between March 24 and April 17 at Aviano Air Base, Italy, quite a bit was happening in the Department of Defense's proclaimed war on sexual assault.

On April 17, The Secretary of Defense and The Chairman of the Joint Chiefs of Staff (CJCS — the senior military officer in the United States Military) announced a new Pentagon initiative to combat sexual assault that reads in part: "Most significantly" this is "a move expected to lead to more prosecutions."[428] (See Appendix 1.) This directive/guidance was briefed to every officer in Europe, including JAG (attorneys) and OSI officers at Aviano, and all potential jurors throughout U.S. Air Forces in Europe. On April 17, on the same day as the public announcement of the SECDEF's new guidance, the Aviano OSI began an investigation. On April 19, just two days after the new guidance, OSI agents interviewed the Wilkersons. OSI agents visited the Wilkerson house but did not take photos or gather physical evidence, such as the bedding. They never investigated the possibility of any outcome other than guilt. Perhaps the pressure from on high to "do something" influenced their actions.

2 4

PROSECUTORIAL MISCONDUCT

"Wrong does not cease to be wrong
because the majority share in it."
— *Leo Tolstoy*

Defense witnesses and others in the court observed a pattern of prosecutorial misconduct, zealousness and aggressive behavior in pursuit of a conviction without proper decorum in the courtroom or common courtesy to witnesses.

The Judge Advocate General of the base acts as the prosecutor and the staff as the prosecution team for criminal cases. Because this case was so "high-profile" — a Colonel-select fighter pilot accused of sexual assault — Col. Don Christensen from Air Force Headquarters in Washington detailed himself to the case as chief prosecutor. Col. Christensen said he "was asked by the Aviano staff judge advocate to assist in the Wilkerson case because of the fighter pilot's rank and position, and because the vice wing commander was expected to testify."[429] (Note the continued and constant reference to "fighter pilot.") With Col. Christensen overseeing the effort, there were a number of troubling actions on the part of the prosecution team.

Early on, the Aviano JAG office failed to portray complete truthfulness. They misled the Convening Authority, Lt. Gen. Franklin, as to the charges against Lt. Col. Wilkerson in two letters sent to the general. The two letters requested testimonial immunity for Col. Ostovich and Captain Manning and are misleading because they include the word "rape."

This is the text of the letter sent by the Aviano JAG office to Lt. Gen. Franklin requesting testimonial immunity for Colonel Ostovich. The letter for Captain Manning is identical, so only one is printed here. Highlighted are the inflated references to rape.

DEPARTMENT OF THE AIR FORCE
31ST FIGHTER WING (USAFE)
29 May 2012

MEMORANDUM FOR 3 AF/JA
FROM: 31 FW/JA
SUBJECT: Request for Grant of Testimonial Immunity and Order to Testify — Col. Dean R. Ostovich

1. This is a request for a grant of testimonial immunity and an order to testify for Col. Dean R. Ostovich, 31 FW/CV, Aviano AB, Italy. I request that this immunity cover any information he provides during any administrative hearing, deposition, or interview conducted by legal counsel and their legal assistants in preparation for a potential trial involving Lt. Col. James H. Wilkerson, 31st Operations Group, Aviano AB, Italy. I have spoken with Brigadier General Scott J. Zobrist, 31 FW/CC, at length regarding this request, and he fully concurs with granting testimonial immunity to Col. Ostovich.

2. 31 FW/JA personnel are investigating allegations against Lt. Col. Wilkerson. *The alleged misconduct includes, but is not necessarily limited to Rape,* in violation of Article 120, Uniform Code of Military Justice (UCMJ).

3. Evidence currently indicates that Col. Ostovich witnessed Lt. Col. Wilkerson's actions immediately prior to the alleged offenses and can corroborate statements made by other witnesses that may incriminate Lt. Col. Wilkerson. Specifically, Col. Ostovich was present at Lt. Col. Wilkerson's house immediately prior to *the alleged rape.* According to his statement, he was the last person to leave the house with Captain Tanya L. Manning, 31 AMDS. Presently, his statements are relevant to

information provided by three other witnesses who were also present at Lt. Col. Wilkerson's home who left at various times throughout the evening. Investigation has further revealed a number of telephone calls and text messages between Col. Ostovich, Lt. Col. Wilkerson, and a number of other relevant witnesses very close in time to the alleged offenses. Col. Ostovich's immunized testimony is necessary in order to ensure an accurate account of events which took place that evening.

4. If Col. Ostovich were asked to testify without testimonial immunity, he could risk criminal liability and would be placed in a position where he could have to make self-incriminating statements under oath. Furthermore, because he left Lt. Col. Wilkerson's house with a junior officer, he will likely be reluctant to testify truthfully, or at all, without the protections afforded under this process. I note that Col. Ostovich has already refused to answer AFOI investigator's questions involving this matter on at least one occasion.

5. Given these circumstances, it is in the Air Force's best interest to grant Col. Ostovich testimonial immunity and order him to cooperate with investigators and testify. Testimonial immunity prohibits the use of testimony, statements, and any information directly or indirectly derived from such testimony or statements by a person granted immunity in a later court-martial of that person, unless evidence is derived from a source wholly independent of his immunized testimony. Ordinarily, immunity is granted when testimony or other information from the person is necessary to the public interest, including the needs of good order and discipline, and when the person has refused or is likely to refuse to testify or provide other information on the basis of the privilege against self incrimination. A grant of testimonial immunity does not bar a later court-martial for perjury,

false swearing, making a false official statement, or failure to comply with an order to testify. Additionally, a grant of testimonial immunity does not bar a later prosecution for the underlying offense(s) that is the subject matter of the statement of the immunized individual, provided such evidence is derived from a legitimate source wholly independent of the compelled testimony and where the decision to prosecute is determined before immunity is granted or the evidence otherwise establishes that the prosecutorial decision was not tainted by the immunized testimony.

6. In accordance with Rule for Courts-Martial (R.C.M.) 704(c), only a general court-martial Convening Authority may grant immunity. The decision to grant immunity is within the sole discretion of said authority. (R.C.M.) 704(e).

7. If you have any questions, please contact me at DSN 632-7843

BRYAN D. WATSON, Lt. Col., USAF

Staff Judge Advocate

Article 120 of the UCMJ defines rape this way: "Any person subject to this chapter who commits an act of sexual intercourse by force and without consent is guilty of rape." The charges, listed in chapter five, do not include, nor did they ever include, rape. Hanks never alleged rape.

The use of the word rape inflames and escalates the seriousness of the charges. Lt. Col. Bryan Watson was the Aviano Judge Advocate General and signed the letters. As the JAG, Lt. Col. Watson was aware of the exact allegations, charges and specifications and knew these did not include the allegation of rape. As the senior officer of the Aviano JAG office, it was his duty to fully and completely understand the details. It cannot be anything but intentional that he used the word rape in these letters to the Convening Authority — the very general who would later decide whether to convene a court-martial. This appears to be a deliberate attempt to influence the general's upcoming decision in favor of proceeding to a court-martial.

The members of a court-martial panel must outrank the accused.[430] In the Wilkerson case, the Air Force could not select the jury from Aviano Air Base, because there were not enough officers senior to Lt. Col. Wilkerson on Aviano, and those that were at Aviano and senior to him were in his chain of command. The jury was selected solely from officers at Ramstein Air Base.

Before the trial began, Col. Christensen posted on the Ramstein AB, Germany, website ads concerning the new "get tough" policy announced by the Secretary of Defense. Additionally, the Ramstein Air Base website carried an article by Col. Christensen (see "My job is prosecuting sexual assault," in Appendix 2) for a two-month period. Basically, the article says that Col. Christensen and his team are specialists in prosecuting the really bad guys and that usually the defendants he prosecutes have used alcohol to take advantage of their victims. He claims his "special victim's unit" is "very effective" because "prosecuting this kind of case is one of our core specialties."

The jury nomination and selection process began with the Aviano wing commander, Brig. Gen. Zobrist, nominating potential jurors. Brig. Gen. Zobrist nominated twenty officers from Ramstein Air Base.[431] For various reasons, these were whittled down to twelve officers who traveled to Aviano just prior to the trial. These twelve were interviewed by the attorneys, and a final five, all men, were selected. The only female officer nominated had a previously known conflict with the defense counsel and was dismissed. There were no female officers on the jury and several women commented in clemency letters that the lack of women on the jury might have negatively affected the outcome for Lt. Col. Wilkerson.[432]

Lt. Col. Wilkerson is a pilot. None of the officers in the jury pool were pilots. Nine of twelve potential jurors were from the medical career field, the same career field as Hanks. Five men were selected: three colonels and two lieutenant colonels. The only two non-medical officers available in the jury pool were selected for the jury. The three senior officers were all from the medical career field. The odds against selecting twelve non-flying officers from an Air Force base with a fully operational flying wing and an operational headquarters must be staggering. The odds against nine of the twelve being from the medical career field are astronomical.

The article on sexual assault by Col. Christensen was posted on the Ramstein Air Base website, and only on the Ramstein website, and allowed to remain for more than two months prior to jury selection, knowing all of the jurors would be selected from the Ramstein populace.

The composition of the jury brings into the spotlight the prosecution theme of putting the fighter pilot culture on trial, as has already been discussed. With no pilots of any kind on the jury, it was easier for Col. Christensen to play on institutional biases. It is what Col. Christensen was overheard calling his "dream jury."[433]

The pilot culture is unique in the Air Force, and medical officers are perhaps some of the least likely people in the Air Force to understand it. Many officers outside the pilot career field hold prejudices against pilots in general and fighter pilots in particular. A review of the Record of Trial shows a clear bias toward fighter pilots in the statements of both trial counsel and assistant trial counsel. There is no doubt that this was the tactic Col. Christensen used for the jury of non-pilots. With routine comments and testimony that pilots are wild and break rules, it appears Col. Christensen was able to capitalize on this predisposition and institutional bias.

It is clear the prosecution theme was to reference fighter pilots and the fighter pilot culture repeatedly. The Air Force defense attorney also made note of it as mentioned in his letter to Lt. Gen. Franklin. In addition, a civilian non-pilot who works on the base and observed the entire trial said: "The prosecutor wove a fabric of misbehavior involving acceptable fighter pilot practices of couch burning, song singing and nights at Bruni's. I neither condone nor condemn these actions, as I know they permeate the history of combat aviators. To use these fighter pilot traditions as examples of bad behavior is twisted in the extreme and leads anyone with knowledge of aviation history to say, 'He who is without sin, cast the first stone.' "[434]

The bottom line is that, in fact, Colonel Christensen did attack and indict the fighter pilot culture to get a conviction. It worked. But that was not the only tactic Col. Christensen used. There was also a pattern of witness intimidation and bullying.

The *Air Force Times* reported, "Some said Christensen bullied witnesses" but "Christensen denies those accusations."[435] However, there are statements from at least four witnesses attesting to direct threats and bullying. All four letters went to Lt. Gen. Franklin as part of the clemency package. As of this writing, there are several Inspector General complaints against Col. Christensen for these allegations. As of December 2013, the Air Force has not responded to any of these complaints.

The following letters from the clemency package allege misconduct, bullying and intimidation. If the Air Force investigates this alleged inappropriate behavior, it is doubtful it will publically release the results of the investigation. Nonetheless, these letters are all part of the official, and now public, record.

> Sir/Ma'am,
>
> The following describes the verbal abuse I endured as a witness by the Lead Prosecutor, Col. Don Christensen during Col. Wilkerson's trial.
>
> When I arrived back in Aviano Air Base for the trial, the Prosecution asked me to come in on Sunday, 28 October for a pre-trial interview, as they were planning on calling me as a witness. I agreed and I met them at the JAG office to discuss some questions that they had. During the line of questioning, I got the impression that Col. Christensen was trying to make me give definitive answers as to me not recalling something specifically happening in order to prove his case. I said that the prosecution did that during the Article 32 hearing and that during the trial I wasn't going to be forced into answers that I did not know either way. At this point Col. Christensen completely shocked me when he yelled at me claiming he'd "never been disrespected like that by an officer." This was completely unprofessional conduct from both a Colonel and as a Prosecutor, and at this statement I asked him if I was free to leave. He said I

could not leave, and I asked why. His reason for me having to stay and answer his questions was that he was a Colonel and that he "out-ranked" me. I am not sure he actually does "out-rank" me because he is a staff officer and I am a line officer, but I did not bring it up there as he was obviously trying to elicit a reaction from me. Additionally, by his logic, I would not have to answer his questions if I was a Colonel or higher or if I was a civilian, which does not seem to advocate a fair trial. He could not cite a legal reason for me to stay and answer questions other than his rank.

The incident did not end there. He continued to ask me questions and I asked if I could contact my Commander. He asked who my Commander was, and then when I told him that my Commander was Lt. Col. (name withheld), he agreed to allow me to phone him. This led me to believe that he only allowed me to talk to my Commander because he had a rank advantage over him as well. I had (my Commander) talk to him on the phone, and Col. Christensen once again cited his rank advantage as the sole reason for me having to answer his questions. He then told my Squadron Commander, in front of me, that I was a "punk" and was "a punk the last time I was in there." (My Commander) advised me not to self-incriminate and to hold off on answering any other questions until he got answers from the Aviano JAG about whether or not I legally had to talk to Col. Christensen. I held off on answering questions for another couple of minutes, as I was awaiting a call back from (my Commander) about the legal precedent for me to answer questions. This angered Col. Christensen to no end, and he leaned forward towards my face and began blatant name calling. He said I was a "punk" and "the worst officer he'd ever seen." He continued to ask questions and repeatedly denied my requests to leave. I answered his questions referencing my legally signed statement from months previous to the incident and said I had nothing more to add. Finally, he let me leave. Captain Beliles and the Forensic Psychologist for the Prosecution were witness to all of the above events.

In my opinion, he abused his rank and displayed poor conduct as a JAG when he started calling me names and forcing me to answer questions against my free will. I was an innocent witness in this event, and he treated me as an OSI agent would treat a suspect. I was actually afforded fewer rights than a suspect during an OSI interrogation. Nobody could produce an actual regulation that said a witness had to answer the prosecution's questions during pre-trial interviews. Finally, on the last day of the trial, I was informed that I had to answer the questions because he was granted Special Convening Authority from Lt. Gen. Franklin and that I must answer any questions that the SCA asks.

This revelation of Col. Christensen being delegated as the SCA sparked a whole new round of questions for me. He was the one who was responsible for the overall conduct of the trial, yet he was also the Lead Prosecutor. Could Col. Wilkerson have been given a fair trial if the Prosecutor was also the one who was instructing the jury members and the judge? I still don't know the answer to this. Based on the questions he was asking and the logic chains he was trying to go down, I got the distinct impression that he was not out for the truth, but only out for a conviction. Combine this with the fact that he excluded testimony about the accuser's previous perjury under oath, I am now sure that once this went to trial, he was out for only a conviction. Personally, this has left a complete lack of faith in the Military Court-martial system, and from talking to others in the Air Force, I am not alone.

The bottom line is that the Air Force deserves better behavior from JAGs than they received from Col. Christensen, and it is my hopes that Captain Beliles and Captain (another JAG officer) do not attempt to emulate his improper methods and behavior as they mature as officers in the JAG Corps. Furthermore, I question whether this was truly a fair trial since the Prosecutor was essentially running the entire trial.[436]

A co-worker of Hanks wrote this about Col. Christensen:

I was interviewed by the prosecution team about one week before the trial. There were three lawyers present for the interview, two captains and Col. Christiansen. The two captains were very friendly and professional. Col. Christiansen asked most of the questions. I was very disturbed by the interview and left shaking in tears. I had been questioned before by the defense team and was accustomed to being asked questions and giving my answers honestly without being judged. I felt Col. Christiansen was condescending and he had a response or rebuttal for every answer I gave to their questions.[437]

"I left shaking in tears!" But Col. Christensen and Captain Beliles denied bullying anyone.

A wife of another pilot in the 31st Fighter Wing is so afraid of Col. Christensen and reprisals from Brig. Gen. Zobrist that she wishes to remain anonymous. She stated she was threatened with the loss of her job if she did not tell prosecution attorneys about the incident in the bathroom of the squadron bar in Korea. She included a copy of an email from an Aviano attorney with the not-so-veiled threat of losing her job to Lt. Gen. Franklin with her clemency letter.

I never spoke to Col. Christensen personally. I was approached by another lawyer here at Aviano, Captain Nguyen. Not wanting to be involved in the case, I told a close friend at the legal office that I did not want to talk to (him) about the case and would decline an interview if asked. I was then informed that the terms of my employment were on the line and per AFI36-703, my employment (as a federal employee) could be terminated if I did not cooperate and answer Captain Nguyen's questions. I wrote an email to Captain Nguyen stating that I would like time to look into the terms of my employment and what I had to comply with as a federal employee. I ultimately gave him his interview (I did not know how much power he actually could have over my job and couldn't chance getting fired) and then told the Area Defense Council everything I had spoken to Captain Nguyen about.[438]

Note: Captain Vy Nguyen was an attorney in the Aviano JAG office and an assistant trial counsel for the prosecution.

This Air Force Instruction (AFI) requiring compliance, in fact, does say removal from the job is an option if a civilian employee fails to cooperate with an investigation.[439] It is important to note, this woman's testimony was not firsthand knowledge, but rather hearsay about the incident in Korea; an incident where she was not present and had no personal knowledge. She simply had heard a story. She also had no knowledge of the alleged event for which Lt. Col. Wilkerson was charged. Nonetheless, she felt so strongly intimidated and threatened that she wrote to Lt. Gen. Franklin.

Remember in the closing argument where Col. Christensen insinuated perhaps Suzanne Berrong might be lying about Hanks slurring her words? Col. Christensen said this about Hanks' best friend at Aviano: "There's absolutely no evidence that Kim was slurring her speech other than Suzanne Berrong. Again, maybe that was intentional on Suzanne's part."[440] Perhaps he felt the need to attack Berrong because she did not believe Hanks' story and was willing to testify to that effect. Notice in this letter to Lt. Gen. Franklin where Berrong said she wanted to tell the truth but felt threatened:

My only concern was the last day during the trial, while waiting to testify, (the defense attorneys) called me in to review my testimony regarding Kim's cursing and other discussion. I was told that the prosecution wanted to see me after. I was taken to a room with Captain Beliles and Captain Nguyen. Captain Beliles asked me what was discussed. I told him it was regarding the text messages and phone call. He then told me between his teeth that I was not to speak about why I don't believe her/my opinions and that if I did he would object. It did make me uncomfortable and for lack of a better word, I did feel threatened by his manner in how and what I was to say. I knew that I was already on the "bad side" as I had already told them in prior interview that I did not believe Kim but would be truthful in anything they asked. It was during this interview the prosecution asked about the cursing statement, I did say that yes, she was cursing a bit about her situation. A facial expression with Captain Nguyen, Captain Beliles and Col. C, who asked the question, was exchanged. I repeated to them that I did not believe her and there was more to what was going on. They asked if I thought that something consensual occurred, I replied that I wasn't implying that anything sexual occurred, but something did that I felt was not in her favor and she was afraid it would come out, whatever it was. Needless to say, I was not called for the prosecution.

In court, when the Defense Attorney asked me about what Kim had said, referring to her "they fucking left me," I hesitated because I was unsure if this was something that I could say, not only because it was cursing but because Captain Beliles had said what he had said and I was unsure if this is something I wasn't suppose to say or he would object. I said to them prior to departing that I know that I can sometimes ramble or go on and if I do that if they will let me know. Regardless, it impacted my thought process as to what I could or could not say.

This sticks in my head because at that moment I wish I would have had (Defense staff — name withheld) or asked for someone to go in the room with me. Had there been a witness in the room outside of Captain Nguyen, I do not think Captain Beliles would have said this. I was too trusting of them to do the right thing. I called back after my testimony thinking that I needed to clarify that I did say yes to telling Col. Ostovich about the trip to the Medical Group, but it was also a No answer. I spoke with Captain Nguyen who told me that he couldn't really talk to me about it and they had already gone to deliberation. (?) I think is what it is called when both sides have "rested."

This has been so impactful, I no longer blindly trust in the legal system. This very act is something, one of many; I play over and over again that should not have occurred. As a result, I would not engage again without some legal advice or a witness in the room. I had no idea this was how this would work. As soon as the prosecution realized you are on the side of Jay, the manner in which you are treated is different. I can't explain it. But I felt it. Very different from the first interview, and then later interviews.

Rather eye opening and disappointing experience. I think it was the prosecution or OSI ... don't remember, did ask if the experience was good or bad, at some point and I indicated not good. While this experience may be every day for legal folks, it is not for me. As an outsider, I was expecting more on the side of honor, integrity to be in play. I have said before, this was not about the truth, but going after the rank and person. I'm sure someone got a good bullet out of it.

As far as Kim reading my statement, she already knows how I feel. I sent it to her in a previous email. My life is now in some ways "crap" because I'm not on the side of the "victim" ... but I'm on the side of "right." So I guess it is a tradeoff I knew would happen. I would prefer she not have seen what I wrote, but I don't care if she does. I stand behind what I believe. For what that is worth.[441]

"He then told me between his teeth that I was not to speak about why I don't believe her... I did feel threatened." It is important to emphasize, Suzanne Berrong had never met the Wilkersons prior to March 23. She simply didn't believe Kim Hanks' story, and she only wanted to testify to that. But the prosecution team only wanted to hear testimony against Lt. Col. Wilkerson. *"As soon as the prosecution realized you are on the side of Jay, the manner in which you are treated is different. I can't explain it. But I felt it. Very different from the first interview, and then later interviews."* Berrong felt different treatment when she wanted to tell the truth about what she thought. The prosecution clearly was not interested in the truth, to the point where they threatened Berrong through clenched teeth. It appears the prosecution team rationalized overzealous and unethical behavior in an effort to get a guilty verdict.

Their poor behavior didn't stop there.

Col. Christensen's team crossed another line: "Prohibition against Unlawful Command Influence includes attempts to interfere with access to witnesses" or attempts to discourage "witnesses from providing character statements for accused."[442] The prosecution team called Brig. Gen. Milligan, who was prepared to testify to a history of untruthfulness and questionable character by Hanks. During the telephone conversation, the prosecution attempted to dissuade Brig. Gen. Milligan from testifying for Lt. Col. Wilkerson. They insinuated that Lt. Col. Wilkerson was guilty and she might not want to testify for him. They asked her: "You do know he failed a polygraph, don't you?" She said they wanted her to believe Lt. Col. Wilkerson was a liar and not to testify.[443] This was both a violation of the privacy act and an unethical attempt to influence a witness to alter or change her testimony.

Other clemency letters to Lt. Gen. Franklin indicated unprofessional conduct inside the courtroom:

> Sir, I would like to discuss my perception of how the chief prosecutor acted in the courtroom. While I was questioned by the defense I saw Col. Christensen put his head down on the table with his arms folded. He continued to keep his head down and shake it back and forth to the answers I provided the defense. I was in disbelief that a Colonel in the Air Force will behave that way in the courtroom.[444]

Another lieutenant colonel, a pilot who attended the trial in his flight suit, wrote:

> I sat behind the prosecution team after asking an enlisted member of the JA where I could sit. She pointed to the seats behind the prosecution. Col. Christensen told me to move. I told him the Aviano JA told me I could sit here. He said, "you are going to have to move. These seats are reserved." I said, "I know the reporter for *Stars and Stripes* is sitting in the reserved seat, but the others are open." He then told me, "you need to address me by, Sir, when speaking." I said, "Sir, the Aviano JA said it was ok for me to sit here. Are these seats reserved for someone that isn't listed?" He then rolled his eyes and turned around.
>
> Later during that day I noticed him putting his head on the desk during defense witnesses' testimony. I observed many loud and disruptive sighs during times of defense witness testimony as well as a couple of times in which the judge overruled his objections. There was continuous leaning back in the chair as well as body language of disrespect for the court.

The worst behavior was his obvious hate for all pilots in the room during his closing arguments. Since Aviano is a fighter wing and flying daily training sorties there were interruptions in the proceedings by jets taking off. Each time a jet took off, Col. Christensen stopped his closing arguments, sighed, leaned on the podium, and glared at the section of the court room where we, the pilots, were sitting until the noise subsided. This was an obvious intimidation tactic for the court room observers there to support the defense as well as an attempted connection with the non-operational members of the jury. Defense Attorney experienced the same interruptions, but handled it much differently. He would simply stop speaking, stand by the podium and wait for the jet to take off.[445]

Finally, Col. Christensen's bullying behavior continued in his treatment of Beth Wilkerson, the wife of the accused, on the witness stand. The *Air Force Times* reported: "Wilkerson's defense attorney wrote that Christensen was 'overbearing in the courtroom when he cross-examined' the wife of the accused, 'was disrespectful and mischaracterized facts in evidence.' "[446]

Most, if not all, courts have rules of behavior. Among them, prior to approaching a witness, the attorney will ask the judge for permission: "May I approach the witness?" This helps maintain order and civility. Whether only a rule or simply customary etiquette, Col. Christensen violated both.[447]

According to the transcript and testimony from several witnesses, at one point, Col. Christensen abruptly approached Beth Wilkerson in the witness chair without asking permission from the judge, raised his voice such that spittle was coming from his mouth and hitting Beth, and shouted the word "vagina" in her face. As one observer noted, "The entire court watched the prosecutor stand so close to Beth as to spit on her and yell 'VAGINA!' in her face multiple times."[448]

Col. Christensen said in an *Air Force Times* newspaper article: "If we were so overbearing ... they had a duty to get their butt out of the chair and object."[449] In fact, the defense counsel did object but was overruled by Judge Brown.

An Air Force civilian working on Aviano wrote the following in her clemency letter to Lt. Gen. Franklin:

> The most shocking behavior was that of the Air Force's number one prosecutor ... the entire court watched the prosecutor stand so close to Mrs. Wilkerson as to spit on her and yell "VAGINA!" in her face multiple times to shake her, which he did not accomplish...[450]

The defense attorney said of Christensen's examination of Beth Wilkerson: "I have never in thirty years as an attorney seen a prosecutor treat a witness with such disrespect. Col. Christensen was leaning over into Beth's face, and spittle was flying. I objected strenuously but was repeatedly overruled."

The toxicologist expert witness for the defense stated that in more than seventy court cases in which he had testified, "he had never seen a prosecutor express such disrespect for a witness." Yet, Judge Brown ruled that behavior could continue. One has to wonder why Judge Brown felt Col. Christensen should be permitted this unsavory behavior.

As the defense counsel stated in the *Air Force Times* article, Col. Christensen also mischaracterized facts in evidence. During his summation, Col. Christensen simply changed the story. He said "nobody, nobody said Ms. Hanks was drunk that evening." This is directly contradicted by Lt. Col. McCarron's Article 32 report, when she wrote: "Most who observed or talked to Ms. Hanks during the evening of 23-24 March, described her as drunk, slurring her words and stumbling. She describes herself as 'out of it,' and admittedly does not remember many details of the evening."[451] Beth Wilkerson's statement and Lt. Col. Wilkerson's taped interview also indicate they both thought Hanks was drunk.[452] MSgt. Dunnivant told the OSI Hanks was still "tipsy" and "somewhat intoxicated" at 3:20 a.m.[453] Col. Christensen also said, "Only Beth, and nobody else, only Beth says Kim Hanks slept in that daybed."[454] Of course, that is directly contradictory to

Kim Hanks' own testimony. She refers to "going down" to the bedroom several times during cross examination, and she described the bedroom as "this room that had like an Italian style twin bed in this little room a few steps down."[455]

There were ample "facts in evidence" that Col. Christensen mischaracterized during his summation. It was the old trick of getting the jurors to believe the last thing they hear. Only the jurors know how they resolved the conflict between what Col. Christensen said last and witness testimony provided as evidence.

25

KNOWLEDGE
IS POWER

*"The world is a dangerous place to live,
not because of the people who are evil,
but because of the people who don't do anything about it."*
— *Albert Einstein*

Military judges are usually more senior attorneys from the Judge Advocate General Officer Corps. They are, like their civilian counterparts, assigned as impartial overseers of the process and should remain neutral.[456] Judge (Colonel) Jefferson Brown was the presiding judge in the Wilkerson court-martial. Judge Brown is a circuit judge in Europe. Judge Brown, as all Air Force JAG officers, works for The Judge Advocate General (TJAG) in Washington. Col. Christensen also works for the TJAG and his (Col. Christensen's) office is in the Washington area. In short, Col. Christensen works with Judge Brown's boss, is much nearer to the boss, and sees the boss far more often, than Judge Brown.

Judge Brown made several significant and controversial rulings during the trial. First, he ruled a key defense witness' testimony was too old (stale) to be entered into evidence before the jurors.

No testimony impeaching the character or truthfulness of Hanks was permitted during the trial. The defense scheduled a witness, Brigadier General Pamela Milligan (U.S. Air Force Reserves), to testify to the untruthfulness of Hanks. Brig. Gen. Milligan is married to Kim Hanks' former husband and has personal firsthand knowledge of Hanks' actions in a prior court case. Brig. Gen. Milligan intended to offer evidence that Hanks had previously falsified court documents and to testify that Hanks lied in that previous court case. Brig. Gen. Milligan intended to testify that, in her opinion, Hanks would lie again in court to get her way.

Judge Brown interjected himself into the case when he suggested Brig. Gen. Milligan's testimony was too old — stale — to be relevant. This is unusual in that normally it is either the prosecution or defense attorney who is required to object. In this case, Judge Brown himself intervened to say the testimony was stale. This move clearly shocked the defense counsel, who stated, "First of all, I didn't hear the government raise a 403 objection, so it strikes me that the court is interjecting itself here by bringing up 403, and the fact of the matter is confusion of the issues, waste of time."

Judge Brown, in a closed-door session, ruled that Brig. Gen. Milligan's testimony would not be heard by the jury. However, since this testimony was critical to the defense and would be important in an appeal should one be required, the defense asked that Brig. Gen. Milligan be permitted to testify without the jury present, so that her testimony was a part of the Record of Trial (for use on appeal). Judge Brown permitted Brig. Gen. Milligan to testify without the jurors present (via a video teleconference). The court case in which Brig. Gen. Milligan says Hanks was untruthful was ten years earlier, when Hanks was 39 years old. At the time of the previous case, Hanks was an adult and fully capable of understanding the difference between false statements and the truth, and Brig. Gen. Milligan intended to show Hanks was, at that time, willfully untruthful. After Brig. Gen. Milligan testified in the absence of the jurors, Judge Brown asked for a prosecution objection: "In light of that testimony, government, do you have an objection as to her testifying…"[457] The prosecution then stated that the testimony was too old and should be excluded, parroting Judge Brown's initial interjection.

The defense attorney pointed out that the prosecution cited no case law on the issue for his objection. Judge Brown then turned the tables on the defense attorney, asking him for case law to allow the testimony. This is a highly unusual event. Normally, the party voicing the objection is the party required to find case law to support the objection. In this case, the judge reversed normal practice and shifted the burden to the defense. The defense was given a forty-seven-minute recess to find case law precedent that would allow Brig. Gen. Milligan's testimony. They were unable to do so during the short recess, and Judge Brown ruled the jury could not see Brig. Gen. Milligan's testimony.[458] The end result was the jurors were unaware of the evidence of Hanks' previous untruthfulness in prior court proceedings.

Subsequent to the completion of the trial and the conviction, defense counsel was able to locate case law precedent that proved Judge Brown erred in his ruling. This is one significant piece of information Lt. Gen. Franklin had access to that the jurors did not.

As Lt. Col. McCarron said in her Article 32 report, "this case comes down to the credibility of two witnesses, Hanks and Beth Wilkerson."[459] The jury was not permitted to hear testimony about Hanks' untruthfulness, while Col. Christensen repeatedly and vigorously asserted his character assassination of both Lt. Col. and Beth Wilkerson.

Judge Brown also ruled no evidence or testimony as to the truthfulness of Lt. Col. Wilkerson could be admitted.[460]

Post-trial, the defense found supporting case law to prove Judge Brown erred again and submitted that to Lt. Gen. Franklin:

> Truthfulness evidence for Lt. Col. Wilkerson was prevented from being admitted by the military judge, again causing substantial harm to the defense's case in what came down to a credibility determination. In *US v. Goldwire, 55 MJ 139*, the Court indicated that evidence of the accused's character for untruthfulness could be presented even though the accused did not testify at trial. Here, a number of OSI agents on video called Lt. Col. Wilkerson a liar and the Trial Counsel continually called him a liar. Yet despite these numerous character assassinations against Lt. Col. Wilkerson, we were barred from introducing evidence as to his strong character for truthfulness. [461]

Attorneys will understand this, but for us laymen (and fighter pilots), this meant no one was allowed to testify that they knew Lt. Col. Wilkerson to be truthful. The prosecution was able to enter into evidence

OSI investigators calling Lt. Col. Wilkerson a liar, and the prosecuting attorneys were permitted to say Lt. Col. Wilkerson was a liar, but no one who testified on his behalf could say they knew him to be truthful, i.e., not a liar.

The judge also prevented jurors from seeing the Wilkerson house.

The layout of the Wilkerson house is confusing. It is a three-story home with two bedrooms on the top floor, one on the main floor with the kitchen, living and dining areas, and one bedroom in the basement. Because the defense contended it was not physically possible for Hanks to have exited the house as she claimed, at the beginning of the trial, the defense requested the court visit the home. Judge Brown denied the motion: "At this time, the court does not believe that it would be helpful in resolving this issue for the court to do a viewing of the accused's residence."[462]

Judge Brown refused a second request to visit the Wilkerson home, this time when during deliberations, one of the jurors asked to do so. "Members, a (juror) asked a question regarding whether the (jury) would be able to see the inside of the house." Judge Brown said, "You will *not* have an opportunity to personally view the inside of the house."[463]

Why not visit the house? If the goal is the truth, why not permit the jurors to visit the house, where they could understand which account of the evening was more probable (truthful) based on the physical layout of the house? Imagine having to understand the layout of this home only from the verbal description. (You have the benefit of the schematic drawings in chapter one. The jurors did not.) The jurors had some photos of the home, provided by the defense, but were not permitted to visit the home. How much they looked at the photos or how well they understood the layout of the house is unknown. They deliberated only three and a half hours.

Col. Christensen seems to have capitalized on the confusion over the layout of the house during his summation when he claimed Hanks slept in the room occupied by the two visiting boys — directly contradicting Hanks' own testimony. The jury must have been confused. What else could explain their disregard for Hanks' testimony in favor of Col. Christensen's version? Much of this confusion about the house and Hanks' inconsistencies would have been cleared up with a visit to the

Wilkerson home. But Judge Brown would not allow a visit. It was only 1.6 miles away.

The judge also prevented the defense from seeing emails that might have proved undue influence.

The defense asked for copies of emails sent to and from the wing commander, Brig. Gen. Scott Zobrist, from the time of the alleged incident to the date of trial. At the time of the Wilkerson investigation and Article 32 hearing process, General Mark A. Welsh III was testifying at his Senate confirmation hearing to become the new Chief of Staff for the Air Force.[464] One of the topics of his questioning was sexual assault. Additionally, the Secretary of Defense, Leon Panetta, had just released new guidance on handling sexual assault in the military.[465] It is reasonable to think this high-profile case may have generated some email traffic between the wing commander and his superiors and perhaps guidance from the wing commander to his wing personnel. The actions of command leadership may influence an investigation, the decision to go to trial, and the opinions of the jurors. Unlawful Command Influence is discussed in its own chapter. The defense wanted to review these emails for Unlawful Command Influence.

The Investigating Officer, Lt. Col. McCarron, in her Article 32 report, said: "Email communications between leadership (e.g., Brig. Gen. Zobrist, Numbered Air Force leadership and email in Inspector General channels) were not protected by a privilege. I asked the government representative to gather responsive documents. To date, they have not been provided."[466] They were not provided prior to the trial, either. The defense counsel moved for discovery of the emails again during the trial. This is when Judge Brown ruled against the defense, stating, "The defense has failed to demonstrate any probability that the requested emails would affect the outcome of the trial ... wherefore the defense motion is denied."[467] How can the defense demonstrate the probability an email might change the outcome of the trial without seeing them? If they discussed improper actions that constitute Unlawful Command Influence, then they could have affected the outcome. But Judge Brown didn't think so and ruled against compelling the government to produce them. As we will see in another chapter, Unlawful Command Influence was a major issue ignored by the court.

Subsequent to the trial, a friend of Lt. Col. Wilkerson submitted a Freedom of Information Act Request (FOIA) for the emails: FOIA 2013-01345-F, Tue, 18 Dec 2012 07:18:03: *"Any and all non privileged emails or correspondence detailing this case between the 31ˢᵗ Fighter Wing, Prosecution and Air Force or DOD Leadership (for the purposes of this request 31ˢᵗ Fighter Wing and Higher)."* In late August 2013, the Air Force published more than 570 pages of email amid other information on its Freedom of Information website, stating this release of information complied with the FOIA request. And yes, there is some interesting information published there, such as Brig. Gen. Zobrist hand-picking the "known commodity" as the Investigating Officer.

There were other issues.

Judge Brown stopped the defense attorney in the middle of his opening statement.[468] Judge Brown decided to take a break. The judge interrupted defense counsel again during closing arguments.[469] It seems odd that Judge Brown interrupted defense counsel during both his opening statement and his summation and did not interrupt the prosecution during these critical phases of the trial.

Judge Brown also made a significant ruling concerning Col. Christensen's behavior during his cross-examination of Beth Wilkerson. We have previously mentioned how, without permission, Col. Christensen aggressively approached Beth Wilkerson on the stand and yelled in her face. In this case, Col. Christensen did not follow courtroom etiquette when approaching a witness, which is to ask the judge for permission, but rather he rapidly approached Beth, raising his voice to a point where spittle was coming out of his mouth.[470] Beth actually drew back in shock, as she feared that Col. Christensen was going to touch her physically.[471]

Spinner objected to Col. Christensen's behavior but Judge Brown overruled the objection and permitted Col. Christensen's abusive and unprofessional behavior to continue. Judge Brown decided this unusual and intimidating behavior from the Air Force's senior litigator was acceptable in a military courtroom. At least, in Judge Brown's courtroom, it was.

These decisions by Judge Brown were favorable to the prosecution: allowing intimidating tactics, ruling against Brig. Gen. Milligan's testimony on the untruthfulness of Hanks, refusing a juror request to visit the Wilkerson home, withholding e-mails otherwise required by law (FOIA) to be released, and refusing to permit character for truthfulness testimony in support of Lt. Col. Wilkerson. It is certainly possible the lack of information for the jury, restricted by Judge Brown, may have affected the outcome of this case. In at least two of his decisions, Judge Brown was later proven in error by case law, and he may have also been in error when he refused repeated requests to visit the Wilkerson home. If truth were the goal, there were many errors.

Judge Brown is junior in rank to Col. Christensen, and Col. Christensen is in a position of authority coming from Washington. Could that relationship have influenced some decisions? Only Judge Brown knows.

2 6

Unlawful Command Influence

> "All concerns of men go wrong
> when they wish to cure evil with evil."
> — *Sophocles*

Unlawful Command Influence (UCI) occurs when a senior person, or any commander or leader, wittingly or unwittingly influences court members, witnesses, or any other Service member participating in the military justice system. Unlawful influence undermines the morale of military members and their respect for the chain of command, causes a loss of public confidence in the military, and jeopardizes the validity of the military judicial process. Unlawful influence is discussed in article 37 of the Uniform Code of Military Justice.[472]

The employment of Unlawful Command Influence by members of the uniform services during military court-martial proceedings is a prohibited practice as it has the ability to influence the actions of subordinates and jurors regarding the guilt or innocence of the accused. This chapter outlines a chronology of Unlawful Command Influence actions executed by Brig. Gen. Scott Zobrist, Commander, 31st Fighter Wing (31 FW), preceding the court-martial of Lt. Col. James Wilkerson. Brig. Gen. Zobrist's actions and emails display a perceived immediate and unwavering attitude of guilt toward Lt. Col. Wilkerson, one that was communicated both to the members of the 31 FW conducting the investigation and to potential jury members throughout the United States Air Forces in Europe (USAFE). Brig. Gen. Zobrist's actions are an example of how a military commander can influence not only his own wing personnel, who will fail to conduct a thorough investigation, but also the jurors he nominates.

The definition above does not mean that senior personnel are, by definition, guilty of malicious intent if or when they commit Unlawful Command Influence. They may be innocently influencing the case. Their intent is not relevant. It is the outcome — the influence — that is important to the case. Commander actions can be perceived by subordinates as approval to act similarly, i.e., to presume guilt. In this case, Brig. Gen. Zobrist's actions readily and repeatedly presented the perception that he thought Lt. Col. Wilkerson was guilty, which possibly contributed to the poor OSI investigation and prosecutorial misconduct. On August 26, 2013, the Air Force posted relevant emails to and from Brig. Gen. Zobrist on the Freedom of Information website. These emails present a picture of Brig. Gen. Zobrist's belief that Lt. Col. Wilkerson was guilty. As early as May 25, 2012, Brig. Gen. Zobrist relayed that belief in written format. In an e-mail to Lt. Gen. Franklin, his superior and the Convening Authority in this case, Brig. Gen. Zobrist wrote: "it is now clear that Col. Ostovich knew of the sexual assault allegations but failed to take any action on them. ... I believe he did this to protect his friend, the alleged assailant. There is also the possibility of criminal activity by Col. Ostovich in that he potentially obstructed justice by communicating this info to Lt. Col. Wilkerson."[473]

As early as June 3, 2012, long before the Investigating Officer concluded her Article 32 investigation and recommended court-martial, Brig. Gen. Zobrist revealed his attitude that Lt. Col. Wilkerson was guilty. He wrote to Lt. Gen. Franklin about Col. Christensen coming from Washington. "Col. Christensen is THE senior prosecutor for the USAF. ALL other Air Force prosecutors work for him, and he has decided to take this case on himself. The USAF should certainly not be criticized for failing to put the right emphasis on this case regarding our legal team. We've got the top prosecutor in the entire AF working for us."[474] Note the "us." Brig. Gen. Zobrist is clearly communicating that he is on the side of the prosecution. There is no impartiality. In his email, as in his actions, Brig. Gen. Zobrist implies that he believes Lt. Col. Wilkerson is guilty.

This is not an accusation that Brig. Gen. Zobrist intentionally or maliciously sought to injure Lt. Col. Wilkerson or negatively affect the outcome of the investigation or the trial. This chapter shows that Brig.

Gen. Zobrist's actions, wittingly or unwittingly, constituted Unlawful Command Influence based solely on facts and evidence.

A brief chronology of actions taken by Brig. Gen. Zobrist follows. A review of these facts provides ample evidence that Brig. Gen. Zobrist's actions probably materially affected both subordinates conducting the investigation and jurors.

March 24, 2012: Alleged incident occurred; Hanks visited Aviano Medical Clinic.

Sometime between March 24 and April 17: Hanks said she "met with SARC three times."[475] Hanks filed what she stated was intended to be a restricted report. However, civilians do not have the option of a restricted report. Therefore, Hanks testified that after consulting again with the SARC, she agreed to make the report unrestricted.[476] We know now, because Hanks filed any type of report that day, that it went unrestricted and she had no choice — it was out in the chain-of-command and law enforcement channels. Hanks' only option was either to cooperate with law enforcement or not. She went on a trip to Croatia to think about it (and was again influenced by a friend to continue).

April 13, 2012: The SARC board officially informed the vice wing commander, Col. Ostovich, of the unrestricted report during a regular monthly meeting of that board.[477] Remember, Col. Ostovich was aware of Hanks' story on Sunday after the alleged incident, because Suzanne Berrong told him on the phone. He took no action before the official notification.

It is reasonable to assume, though I have no evidence, that Col. Ostovich notified Brig. Gen. Zobrist shortly after he was notified by the SARC board. Regardless, by April 13, both command and legal channels on Aviano AFB were officially aware of this allegation.

No statements, interviews, or investigation occurred for another four days.

April 17, 2012: Secretary of Defense and The Chairman of The Joint Chiefs of Staff issued guidance to "prosecute more" alleged sexual assaults.

This guidance was publically announced on April 17 and briefed to every officer in United States Air Forces Europe (USAFE), including the jury pool.[478]

April 17, 2012: Date of Hanks' statement to the OSI.[479]

April 19, 2012: Lt. Col. Wilkerson and Beth Wilkerson were interviewed separately by the OSI. Agents visited the Wilkerson home to interview Beth but took no photos and gathered no evidence (bedding, etc.).[480]

April 18, 2012: OSI briefed Brig. Gen. Zobrist, erroneously, that Lt. Col. Wilkerson had been "missing" for four workdays immediately following the alleged event.

A review of Lt. Col. Wilkerson's flight records prove he was flying each of those four days. OSI investigators did *not* investigate the flight records, nor did Brig. Gen. Zobrist, or anyone else, ask Lt. Col. Wilkerson his whereabouts during that time. [481]

April 26, 2012: Brig. Gen. Zobrist grounded (removed from flying) Lt. Col. Wilkerson.[482]

In operational flying units, grounding is universally seen as adverse action — punishment. At this point, it became public knowledge that something was wrong with Lt. Col. Wilkerson; he was being investigated.

May 11, 2012: Brig. Gen. Zobrist "removed" Lt. Col. Wilkerson from his duties as Inspector General (IG).[483] Another clear adverse action.

Brig. Gen. Zobrist never spoke to Lt. Col. Wilkerson again.[484]

May 14, 2012: Brig. Gen. Zobrist directed the new Inspector General to distribute an email to base leadership indicating Lt. Col. Wilkerson has been removed from his duties and was under investigation.

Air Force Instruction 36-6001 on Sexual Assault directs commanders to "Strictly limit information pertinent to an investigation to those who have an official need to know" and "Emphasize that the alleged assailant is presumed innocent until proven guilty."[485] This email, sanctioned by Brig. Gen. Zobrist, violated both of those rules.

This is the IG's email to base leadership, sent by order of Brig. Gen. Zobrist:

Subject: IG change

Commanders,

FYI — Brig. Gen. Zobrist re-assigned Lt. Col. Wilkerson as an assistant to the Operations Group. Lt. Col. Wilkerson is the subject of an on-going investigation and could not remain in place as the IG until that issue is resolved. Brig. Gen. Zobrist assigned me as the IG over both inspections and complaints resolution. GP/CCs were updated by the boss. If you have questions, please engage with them until the WG/CC can provide more information. Both IGQ and IGI will operate as before. I apologize for the quick email, but it is important to keep you updated. Your professionalism will help keep the rumint (rumor intelligence) to a minimum.[486]

June 29, 2012: Brig. Gen. Zobrist nominated potential jury members to 3rd AF/CC.[487]

August 3, 2012: Brig. Gen. Zobrist suspended Lt. Col. Wilkerson's top-secret security clearance.[488]

This is another adverse action and also implies the perception of guilt.

August 16, 2012: Brig. Gen. Zobrist was quoted in the *Stars and Stripes* newspaper discussing the removal of Lt. Col. Wilkerson amid sexual assault charges:

"Brig. Gen. Scott Zobrist, 31st Fighter Wing commander, issued a statement when the charges were announced, emphasizing that 'sexual assault is simply unacceptable and will not be tolerated.' "[489]

The article clearly and unequivocally ties Lt. Col. Wilkerson's removal from office to Brig. Gen. Zobrist's comments about sexual assault. It is inferred that Brig. Gen. Zobrist believes Lt. Col. Wilkerson is guilty. Ramstein AFB, Germany receives and distributes the *Stars and Stripes*. Every member of the jury pool nominated by Brig. Gen. Zobrist resided at Ramstein Air Base and had access to this article.

August 17, 2012: Brig. Gen. Zobrist suspended Lt. Col. Wilkerson's additional security clearances and banned him from all classified secure areas in the fighter wing.[490]

Both of these last two actions by Brig. Gen. Zobrist were clearly adverse actions, detrimental to Lt. Col. Wilkerson. At this point, Lt. Col. Wilkerson was removed from all official duties as a direct result of Brig. Gen. Zobrist's actions. Brig. Gen. Zobrist himself ties his actions to the allegations in the case and nothing else.

November 1 2012: Brig. Gen. Zobrist was called to testify at the Wilkerson court-martial.

Brig. Gen. Zobrist was called to testify because Captain Beliles (the assistant prosecutor) stated, in front of the jury, that Brig. Gen. Zobrist "fired" Lt. Col. Wilkerson: "And these are also after he had fired both Lt. Col. Wilkerson and Colonel Ostovich, correct"?[491] This statement by Captain Beliles that Brig. Gen. Zobrist "fired" Lt. Col. Wilkerson, if true, is clear, unequivocal, and hard evidence of Unlawful Command Influence. Remember, Captain Beliles was stationed at Ramstein Air Base, where the jurors were from, and had access to the *Stars and Stripes* article where Brig. Gen. Zobrist said he had removed Lt. Col. Wilkerson and would not tolerate sexual assault. For UCI, it is the perception that matters, not the action.

Following the defense counsel's immediate objection to Captain Beliles' reference to "fired," and a defense request for a mistrial based on Unlawful Command Influence, Judge Brown ruled the trial could continue. This was perhaps another questionable ruling given the evidence of Unlawful Command Influence in its totality.

Brig. Gen. Zobrist testified: "I did not 'fire' Lt. Col. Wilkerson. I removed him from the position, and I use the terminology "removed" very explicitly to ensure that it did not affect the investigation that was ongoing. I used also the descriptive words of 'It is neither temporary nor permanent.' "[492]

It is interesting what the prosecutor himself said about the semantics of the words "removed" and "fired": Col. Christensen stated there is no difference between "relieved" and "fired." In fact, he contends there is no word in the military for "fired."

Col. Christensen said: "The government, obviously, opposes, Your Honor. I believe, although the question — the term 'fired,' and there is no 'fired' or 'not fired' within the military construct — relieved, fired — I don't know if there's really a lot of difference, but he's relieved from his position."[493]

Webster's II, New Riverside University Dictionary (a U.S. Government publication) 1988, defines "remove" as: "dismiss from office." Webster's further defines "dismiss" as "to discharge, as from employment."

Dictionary.com defines "removed" as "to dismiss or *force* from a position or office; discharge: *They removed him for embezzling.*"[494]

No matter the word, the point conveyed to all who heard about Lt. Col. Wilkerson's "removal" was that Brig. Gen. Zobrist fired, discharged or removed Lt. Col. Wilkerson because of the sexual assault charge, thereby implying, *wittingly or unwittingly*, that Brig. Gen. Zobrist thought Lt. Col. Wilkerson was guilty. Captain Beliles may have inferred that Brig. Gen. Zobrist "fired" Lt. Col. Wilkerson from the *Stars and Stripes* article, just as Brig. Gen. Zobrist's subordinates on Aviano may have, including the OSI investigators and JAG office personnel.

Further proof that Brig. Gen. Zobrist believed Lt. Col. Wilkerson was guilty and that his actions were a message to the wing was provided during the testimony of the former Aviano Wing Director of Staff, Col. (USA, retired) Scott Cusimano. His position as director of staff had been discontinued just prior to the court-martial, and he was flown back to Aviano to testify for the prosecution. Basically, Col. Cusimano didn't like Lt. Col. Wilkerson. He testified as a negative character witness, saying he told Brig. Gen. Zobrist he didn't like Lt. Col. Wilkerson. He had also filed a complaint against Col. Ostovich at some time in the past.[495] Col. Cusimano went on to testify that he had voiced his concerns to Brig. Gen. Zobrist but that Brig. Gen. Zobrist had not listened to him.

Q. Now, Sir, prior to your leaving here (Aviano) on 2 October, 2012, did General Zobrist ever apologize to you for not taking your advice about Colonel Wilkerson and Colonel Ostovich?

A. Ah, he apologized to me several times throughout the last six months. Specifically, on the Thursday before I left, whatever date that was — 27-28 September — he again apologized to me and said, "I know, Scott, you take issue with the fact that I didn't respond quickly enough, but you need to understand, too, that you know I do things behind the scenes and don't think that I haven't held people accountable.[496]

Brig. Gen. Zobrist said to his outgoing Director of Staff: "I do things behind the scenes" and "don't think that I haven't held people accountable." Brig. Gen. Zobrist had been "doing things behind the scenes" and "holding people accountable" for months. He started by grounding Lt. Col. Wilkerson. Then he removed Lt. Col. Wilkerson from his position and contrary to Air Force policy, announced it to wing leadership via email. He took away Lt. Col. Wilkerson's security clearances, and finally, he went public announcing Lt. Col. Wilkerson's removal in the *Stars and Stripes* simultaneous with publicly stating he would "not tolerate" sexual assault.

According to Air Force instruction 36-6001, 29 September 2008, "Sexual Assault Prevention and Response (SAPR) Program," Brig. Gen. Zobrist violated written Air Force guidance to:

"Strictly limit information pertinent to an investigation to those who have an official need to know," and

"Emphasize that the alleged assailant is presumed innocent until proven guilty."

As of this writing, several Inspector General complaints have been filed against Brig. Gen. Zobrist for his Unlawful Command Influence throughout the investigation into this alleged assault. The complaints were submitted with the hope that the Air Force, corporately, will learn from these actions and provide additional training to commanders in the future. Whether the Air Force will actually investigate now Major General Zobrist is unknown. It is unlikely in any event that it will share results of an investigation if one takes place.

All of these actions occurred with an audience that not only included the members of his wing who would conduct the investigation, but also in full view of all potential jurors in the case. Wittingly or unwittingly, Brig. Gen. Zobrist's actions "behind the scenes" influenced both the personnel in his own wing and the jurors from Ramstein. OSI investigators ignored a lack of physical evidence and multiple discrepancies in Hanks' story. They knew the boss thought Lt. Col. Wilkerson was guilty, so there was no need to investigate the possibility of innocence. Wittingly or unwittingly, Brig. Gen. Zobrist influenced the witnesses, investigators, jurors and others as to the presumed guilt of Lt. Col. Wilkerson. He outwardly portrayed an attitude of guilt toward Lt. Col. Wilkerson. That was demonstrated when he removed Lt. Col. Wilkerson from flying status and his duties as Inspector General and announced to wing leadership that Lt. Col. Wilkerson was under investigation. Brig. Gen. Zobrist also suspended Lt. Col. Wilkerson's security clearances and violated Air Force instruction 36-6001 when he publicly released throughout United States Air Forces Europe that Lt. Col. Wilkerson was accused of sexual assault and had been removed from his position. Through these actions, the presumption of guilt was effectively relayed to the members of the Aviano wing and the juror pool at Ramstein Air Base. It was Unlawful Command Influence.

27

The Uproar

"Political correctness is tyranny with manners."
— *Charlton Heston*

When Lt. Gen. Franklin dismissed the charges against Lt. Col. Wilkerson, freeing him after nearly four months in prison, no one could have foreseen the uproar that was about to happen.

That decision by Lt. Gen. Franklin triggered a storm of protest from groups representing victims of military sexual assaults as well as several United States senators, who "demanded answers from senior military leaders on why an Air Force commander dismissed charges against a lieutenant colonel after he was convicted of sexual assault."

Under the Uniform Code of Military Justice, the convening authority has the right to grant clemency to a convicted military member. Clemency can be a reduction in punishment all the way to complete dismissal. Lt. Gen. Franklin was personally attacked for his decision. He was accused of being a "good ol' boy" who pardoned a fellow F-16 pilot for personal reasons.[497] Noticeably, the senators vehemently condemned Lt. Gen. Franklin's decision, apparently without receiving any information except what someone else said about the case.

It is unknown how much effort, if any, senate and congressional staffers put into researching the actual case. It appears from the immediacy of the senators' comments that there was no time to conduct research and that the statements were based either on their own opinions or what they were told from someone else, who likewise did not have time (or attempt to) research the case. In all of the statements and posturing by these senators, congresswomen, and Protect Our Defenders, they clearly assumed Lt. Gen. Franklin was wrong and Lt. Col. Wilkerson was guilty.

Attorneys I have spoken with do not believe the Wilkerson case would have gone to trial in a civilian world. But the military is under significant pressure to reduce sexual assault. There were several high-profile sexual assault cases pending, in particular the case against several basic training instructors at Randolph Air Force Base in Texas, where more than thirty instructors were accused of sexually assaulting recruits.[498] This was a highly controversial and very public case. As a result of the Lackland case, the Air Force was under significant pressure to combat sexual assault. As Col. Christensen and Brig. Gen. Zobrist indicated in their email communication, the Wilkerson case gave the Air Force an opportunity to have all the right "optics."

Brig. Gen. Zobrist wrote: "The USAF should certainly not be criticized for failing to put the right emphasis on this case." He went on to discuss how they handpicked the Investigating Officer because she had "the right credentials" and that the Air Force's chief prosecutor himself would prosecute the case. [499] The right optics, the right credentials, and the (predetermined) right outcome, general?

About the time of Lt. Gen. Franklin's decision, Senators Kirsten Gillibrand, D-N.Y.; Barbara Boxer, D-Calif.; and Jeanne Shaheen, D-N.H., were holding hearings to "press top-ranking members of the military on widespread sexual assault in the armed services, demanding action to hold perpetrators accountable."[500] According to Gillibrand, "The issue of sexual violence in the military … has been allowed to go on in the shadows for far too long." The Senator went on to call "the military justice system dysfunctional, noting that less than one out of ten reported attackers are held accountable."[501] Speaking directly about Lt. Gen. Franklin's decision, Senator Gillibrand said: "The case is shocking, and the outcome should compel all of us to take the necessary action to ensure that justice is swift and certain, not rare and fleeting." Implied, of course, was that Lt. Col. Wilkerson was guilty and the general was wrong. It is doubtful Senator Gillibrand did research on the Wilkerson case to know any of the details discussed here. It is a clear trend that people associated with this case believe only what they are told and conduct no research on their own. Had the senator or her staff researched the Record of Trial, perhaps they would have chosen a different case to champion.

Secretary of Defense Chuck Hagel wrote in response to the senator's letter: "I believe this case does raise a significant question whether it is necessary or appropriate to place the Convening Authority in the position of having the responsibility to review the findings and sentence of a court-martial."[502] I also doubt that anyone in the Air Force who might have briefed the new Secretary of Defense (Hagel just moved into the job) would have briefed anything other than Col. Christensen's perspective. In other words, no one inside the Air Force supported Lt. Gen. Franklin's position, but rather they talked only of the conviction. Recall my discussion with some generals in the Pentagon who told me the Air Force blamed Lt. Col. Wilkerson and were going to continue to try to get him. Subsequently, an Air Force colonel, JAG, contacted Spinner and regurgitated the party line, admitting it was what he had heard and that he had done no research of his own. It appears the party line was swallowed by most without question. When some of these people learn the rest of the story, I hope they will reconsider blindly following the party line in the future.

Finally, even the president decided to weigh in on the issue of sexual assault in the military. President Barack Obama "expressed frustration with the Pentagon's struggles to cope with sex crimes in the military, saying he expected 'consequences' for sex offenders … The bottom line is, I have no tolerance for this … If we find out somebody's engaging in this stuff, they've got to be held accountable, prosecuted, stripped of their positions, court-martialed, fired, dishonorably discharged — period." Obama said he had instructed Defense Secretary Chuck Hagel "to step up our game exponentially."[503]

Our leaders might be well served to review the Justice Department's study on false imprisonment. Twenty-six percent of men convicted were wrongfully imprisoned. *Twenty-six percent!* And those are only the cases where DNA evidence was available for use later (after DNA technology was developed) to prove them innocent. And the Defense Department's own 2012 study said 17 percent of accusations inside the military were unfounded. Shouldn't that warrant concern? How many good Marines, soldiers, sailors, and Airmen have been wrongfully convicted?

Marine Corps Commandant General Amos' comments are likely to make it more difficult to successfully prosecute true criminals inside the Marine Corps. Judge Col. Daniel J. Daugherty, chief judge of the Navy-Marine Corps Trial Judiciary, issued a twenty-six-page ruling that the commandant's comments "raised the appearance of Unlawful Command Influence."

Texas-based attorney Brian Bouffard cited damning comments from Parris Island Marines to underscore the commandant's words. One officer acknowledged that in a close case, he'd side with the commandant, while a gunnery sergeant agreed with the commandant that eight out of ten sexual assault allegations are valid. "He (the Commandant) basically primed them to find people guilty and kick them out. ... What the commandant did was not in keeping with the presumption of innocence."[504] It appears the "presumption of innocence" is in danger in the Marine Corps as well as the Air Force.

Senator Claire McCaskill, D-Mo., sent a letter to senior Air Force officials "demanding" answers, while Senators Barbara Boxer, D-Calif., and Jeanne Shaheen, D-N.H., wrote to Defense Secretary Chuck Hagel, asking him to review the case.[505] "This is a travesty of justice," Senators Boxer and Shaheen wrote, noticeably, without first asking for any information about either the trial or Lt. Gen. Franklin's decision. Only after condemning the decision, when writing their letter to Secretary Hagel, did any of these Senators ask for "information on the basis for Franklin's decision." Senator McCaskill also wrote a letter to Air Force Secretary Michael Donley and Air Force Chief of Staff General Mark Welsh. In that letter, she wrote Franklin's decision "showed ignorance, at best, and malfeasance, at worst." [506] This letter was also written without the facts. We know this because her letter is the first request for information about the decision or the case. So she made her comments first and then asked for information.

"We're going to do a press conference on this case," said Rep. Jackie Speier, a California Democrat, who introduced a bill to require that sexual assault prosecutions be handled by military and civilian experts and remove commander authority. "That would inject professionalism into the process and remove commander conflicts of interest," she said. "It's a mockery of the UCMJ (Uniform Code of Military Justice) and the entire sense of military justice".[507] Her statement showed that Congresswoman Speier believes there was a lack of professionalism by commanders. Congresswoman Speier also assumed Lt. Gen. Franklin was wrong prior to asking for any information on the case or his decision. These Senators and Representatives ignored the possibility of a false allegation and a wrongful conviction.[508]

Senators Boxer, McCaskill and Gillibrand have accused Lt. Gen. Franklin of taking care of one of his own and asked the SECDEF to remove him and send Lt. Col. Wilkerson back to prison. "McCaskill is calling for the conviction to be reinstated, and for Lt. Gen. Craig A. Franklin to be removed from his post."[509] Of course, the conviction was not only overturned; all charges against Lt. Col. Wilkerson were dropped. Lt. Col. Wilkerson is innocent and, under American law and the Uniform Code of Military Justice, he cannot be placed back in prison. It is interesting, though, that some would clamor to put him back in prison and fire Lt. Gen. Franklin without knowing the actual evidence from the case.

Unfortunately, this rhetoric became the standard. In addition to members of Congress, several women's advocate groups, such as Protect Our Defenders and the Service Women's Action Network, railed against the decision. "It's atrocious. It's infuriating," "It's a perfect example of the due process system being overridden just at the whim of the commander. It's a real travesty of justice."[510] Of course, the Service Women's Action Network didn't have the Record of Trial either. There was a definitive rush to judgment. Information that might not fit with their agenda was not worthy of consideration, not wanted.

I reached out to several of these groups with an offer to show them some of the information from the Record of Trial and some of the probable rationale for Lt. Gen. Franklin's decision. They were not interested. In particular, Nancy Parrish of Protect Our Defenders engaged in some back and forth email. Her bottom line was, "It is nice you want to help your friend, but he's guilty." She, too, did not want information that might prove otherwise. It didn't fit with her agenda.

In a letter to Secretary Hagel after Lt. Gen. Franklin's decision, Parrish wrote: "In this attempt to justify his actions, Lt. Gen. Franklin repeatedly substituted his judgment for the judgment of the court members and the military judge. He offers nothing new. The only evidence Franklin viewed that the members did not was found baseless by the military judge."[511] Of course, Parrish has no idea what information Lt. Gen. Franklin had access to during his review. She just disagrees with the decision regardless of the evidence. In our email exchange, she insisted false accusations only occur 2 percent of the time and (as the Commandant said) most men are guilty.

Through April 25, 2013, and Lt. Col. Wilkerson arriving at his new assignment, Nancy Parrish refused to let the Wilkersons go back to a normal life. It became as if she had a personal grudge against the Wilkersons. She and her group organized a small (twenty-three-person) rally outside the base main gate where Lt. Col. Wilkerson was reassigned and held up a sign that said "Rapist — Lt. Col. Wilkerson." It also became common among the more radical groups like Protect Our Defenders to escalate the accusation to "rape," as Lt. Col. Watson did in the request for immunity letters.

Stars and Stripes reporter Nancy Montgomery having dinner with the Wilkerson case prosecution team the night the verdict was read. Photo by Bob Harvey

These types of attacks and negative reporting were far more prevalent than one might expect. From the beginning of this case, *Stars and Stripes* reporter Nancy Montgomery was on the side of the prosecution. Her coverage was biased toward guilt. Opposite is a photograph of her having dinner with the prosecution team at a local restaurant the night the verdict was read.

Montgomery's articles, after Lt. Gen. Franklin's decision, continued to be biased. She declined to interview Spinner after the trial and continued to share information — one-sided stories — with Parrish at Protect Our Defenders,. And like Parrish, Montgomery ignored the fact that false allegations and wrongful convictions happen.

Here are a few examples of how Montgomery embraced the prosecution's strategy of putting the pilot community on trial. Montgomery always pointed out that both Lt. Gen. Franklin and Lt. Col. Wilkerson are pilots: United States Air Forces Europe Commander, General "Breedlove and Franklin, like Wilkerson, are among 1,286 active duty *F-16 pilots* in the Air Force..."[512] "Franklin, the authority who convened Wilkerson's court-martial and a former commander of the 31st Fighter Wing who is *also an F-16 pilot...*"[513] and "In overruling the jury's verdict, Franklin, *himself a fighter pilot*, (emphasis added) had disregarded the recommendation of his staff lawyer, who had advised him that defense claims of legal errors in the court-martial were 'without merit.' "[514] This appears to be an attempt to capitalize on the cultural differences of the fighter pilot community — fighter pilot versus staff lawyer — using animosity toward the pilot community to enhance her articles.

Here is an example of Montgomery putting some spin on one of her reports. During the trial, the prosecution called the former wing director of staff, Col. Scott Cusimano, to testify. The prosecution's intent was for Col. Cusimano to testify that he thought Lt. Col. Wilkerson was unprofessional. This was to counter expected defense testimony supporting Lt. Col. Wilkerson's good military character. The testimony got out of hand when the assistant prosecutor, while questioning Col. Cusimano, stated that Brig. Gen. Zobrist had "fired" Lt. Col. Wilkerson. "Firing" Lt. Col. Wilkerson, as we have discussed, would have been an admission of Unlawful Command Influence. That statement is what prompted the defense to enter a motion for dismissal and to call Brig. Gen. Zobrist to the stand.

Defense attorneys asked Brig. Gen. Zobrist about firing Lt. Col. Wilkerson. The defense went on to clarify Col. Cusimano's opinion of Lt. Col. Wilkerson was an opinion he (Cusimano) had of all the wing leadership at that time; it was not limited to just Lt. Col. Wilkerson. To support their position, the defense got Col. Cusimano to testify that he Cusimano had filed an Inspector General complaint alleging Col. Ostovich had assaulted him Cusimano in the presence of Brig. Gen. Zobrist, but that Brig. Gen. Zobrist did nothing: "He did not address the issue, period." [515] The defense wanted to make the point that singling out Lt. Col. Wilkerson was taking Cusimano's negative comments out of context. Col. Cusimano was a disgruntled former employee with a grudge not only against Lt. Col. Wilkerson but also against Col. Ostovich and Brig. Gen. Zobrist.[516] Montgomery failed to report any of those facts.

Nancy Montgomery reported the reason for calling Brig. Gen. Zobrist to the stand differently: "Brig. Gen. Scott Zobrist, commander of 31st Fighter Wing, based at Aviano, was called unexpectedly by the defense lawyers for Lt. Col. James Wilkerson after a previous witness, the former base director of staff, told jurors he had found Wilkerson to be 'unprofessional' and 'exercising poor judgment at times.' "[517] Montgomery said the reason for calling Brig. Gen. Zobrist was because Cusimano said bad things about Lt. Col. Wilkerson. In truth, it was because of the testimony indicating Brig. Gen. Zobrist had committed Unlawful Command Influence. Montgomery, true to her record of prosecution bias, left out any reference to Unlawful Command Influence.

It is also clear from Montgomery's *Stars and Stripes* articles that she had almost immediate access to the OSI report and clemency letters. She quotes from the lead defense attorney's letter to Lt. Gen. Franklin in a March 11 article and from two clemency letters in an April 12 article critical of Lt. Gen. Franklin's decision.[518] She also quotes extensively from the video interrogation of Lt. Col. Wilkerson and repeatedly insists Lt. Col. Wilkerson "failed a polygraph test." She wrote the case "went forward in part, investigators said, because Wilkerson failed a polygraph" and that Lt. Gen. Franklin's decision was "despite the fact that Wilkerson had failed a polygraph test."[519] Someone inside the Aviano JAG office was feeding Montgomery insider information all along. There is no plausible explanation for her to have had so much detailed information without assistance from the prosecution. It is unprofessional and unethical conduct to provide information like this to the press. It is conduct unbecoming.

Lt. Col. Wilkerson voluntarily took a polygraph. However, polygraph exams are not admissible in court, and no mention was made during the trial about a polygraph. So how could Montgomery know about it unless the OSI or prosecution told her?

OSI agents asked Lt. Col. Wilkerson if he would take a polygraph exam. He willingly did so when he voluntarily returned for a second interview on April 26, 2012.[520] During his first interview, OSI investigators were vague about the allegations, suggesting that Lt. Col. Wilkerson inappropriately touched Hanks but nothing more. Just prior to conducting the polygraph, OSI agents notified Lt. Col. Wilkerson of Hanks' specific allegation against him — that he had groped and digitally penetrated her.[521]

As discussed earlier, Lt. Col. Wilkerson consistently denied ever leaving his own bed on the night in question. He continued denying wrongdoing throughout the interrogation and polygraph, even after OSI investigators told him he had failed the (entire) polygraph. They then switched their story and told Lt. Col. Wilkerson he only failed one question. Telling the accused he failed a polygraph is an often used and legal tactic. In the emails released on August 26, 2013, Col. Christensen admitted it was a "ruse" when writing to his superior officer: "The OSI used a ruse when they interviewed Lt. Col. Wilkerson ... I'm not exactly sure why, but I think they were just trying to get him to admit he was in bed with her."[522] None of this was reported by Montgomery.

Polygraphs are so unreliable their "results are not admissible in court."[523] OSI agents often tell the accused he "failed" or "lied" to see if he will change his story and confess to something. Lt. Col. Wilkerson did not.

If Lt. Col. Wilkerson had failed a polygraph and if polygraphs were reliable, those results would have been submitted in court. But they are not accurate or reliable and were not part of the Record of Trial in any manner. Of course, the OSI knew this. As Col. Christensen admitted, investigators told Lt. Col. Wilkerson he failed to try to get him to admit something. He did not. Montgomery's information was flawed, but she repeatedly included this information in her articles. This helped make the story more sensational. She was just selling newspapers.

As mentioned, either the OSI or the Aviano JAG office fed Montgomery with inside, confidential information. Our own Freedom of Information Act Request to the Air Force dated in November 2012 was not filled until August 26, 2013. So, who gave Montgomery the record of trial and the clemency package, and was it illegal to do so? There were so many unprofessional actions in this case that it is not surprising someone at Aviano leaked information to Montgomery. It is easy to think that someone in the prosecution was the source of the leaks. Montgomery's articles were not simply reporting the facts. Instead, they were reporting the prosecution perspective during the trial and both before and after the dismissal of charges. In any case, leaking information to a reporter to support your viewpoint is, if not illegal, unprofessional at least. The Air Force is investigating these series of leaks and, hopefully, they will stop them and provide clearer guidance concerning appropriate behavior.

The *Stars and Stripes* was not alone in their slanted and biased reporting. In fact, no major news outlet reported information or reasoning why the case might have been overturned. For various reasons, NBC, CBS, the *Air Force Times,* and the *Stars and Stripes*, along with several attorneys and various women's advocate websites, communicated with me directly in regard to the story. CBS, to its credit, was the only one that requested an interview to get the defense's side of the story. On advice of Lt. Col. Wilkerson's attorneys, the CBS request for an interview was not granted. I disagreed with that decision, and my feelings led to the writing of this book. The truth must be told. Most media outlets that carried the story simply went with the version that Lt. Gen. Franklin was wrong and Lt. Col. Wilkerson was guilty, without requesting any details of the case.

One particularly noteworthy event occurred during this media frenzy right after Lt. Gen. Franklin announced his decision. Interestingly, CBS, the only news outlet that made an effort to ask questions while reporting the story on Lt. Gen. Franklin's decision, posted Lt. Col. Wilkerson's social security number on its website.[524] Obviously, this was a violation of privacy laws, and when I contacted CBS to point this out, its people apologized and pulled it down. Still, that seems like a pretty basic thing to have overlooked accidently.

The *Air Force Times* also covered the story in depth. At one point, it gave Col. Christensen a full article to comment on the story. Again, Lt. Col. Wilkerson, on advice of counsel, has not yet spoken in public, but Col. Christensen had a lot to say. The following excerpts are from that *Air Force Times* article:

"Christensen was sitting next to a colleague when he got an email notifying him of Lt. Gen. Craig Franklin's Feb. 26 decision. 'I turned to [him] and said, "We just lost military justice." ' " The article said: "Colonel Christensen was clearly upset with General Franklin's dismissal of this case during clemency: 'Up until this point, I had never really given [the power to overturn a conviction] a lot of thought because I had never seen a Convening Authority do it.' "[525]

So, according to Col. Christensen, he had never had a Convening Authority overturn one of his cases before now, and he was okay with the legal process. But, now that one of his cases was dismissed, he had concluded that Convening Authorities should not have the right to review his work. He said: "This case brought it to the forefront. It makes sense that the Convening Authority doesn't need to be provided with that power."[526] In other words, as long as all Convening Authorities rubber-stamped his work, it was acceptable for them to review cases, but now that one disagreed with him, he had decided they should not have the right to do so.

Col. Christensen also said something unusual during his lengthy article in the *Air Force Times*. "From a prosecution point, the only thing unusual about this case is that there was an eyewitness."[527] In reality, the supposed "eyewitness" Col. Christensen was referring to is Beth Wilkerson, and she was a witness who provided an alibi for Lt. Col. Wilkerson. She was not an "eyewitness" as he is alluding to in the article. She is an "eyewitness" who said it never happened. He, of course, was insinuating an eyewitness who proves guilt, deliberately misleading the readers. Col. Christensen was clearly upset that the system reversed his case. It is important to point out that this was the one part of the process where he was unable to reach in and exert his influence or the influence of his office or position. It is the system he was so proud of earlier, but now that the process played out and went against him, he suggested a change was necessary.

Finally, the *Air Force Times* article sums it up by saying: Col. Christensen said he "was asked by the Aviano staff judge advocate to assist in the Wilkerson case because of the fighter pilot's rank and position..."[528] This article was published in the *Air Force Times* in April 2013. Two months after Lt. Gen. Franklin threw out the charges, Col. Christensen was still saying "fighter pilot." So was the case about fighter pilot culture or about sexual assault? Was a case against a "fighter pilot" just too juicy to turn down? If it was never about fighter pilots, why the constant use of the words?

28

A Toxic Atmosphere

"If you repeat a lie often enough, it becomes ~~truth~~ politics."
— *Unknown*

As a result of the media uproar and the senate hearings, Secretary of Defense Chuck Hagel agreed to support legislation to strip military commanders of their review authority to overturn verdicts and to mandate that commanders must provide written explanations for reducing sentences.[529]

Senator Lindsey Graham, R-S.C., also a JAG officer and Colonel in the U.S. Air Force Reserve, is the ranking member of the senate panel investigating sexual assault in the military. Graham argued for review authority to remain: "The commander shares the power to order troops into battle," he told the New York *Daily News*. "You don't want to take away the historical power of the commander to discipline the force."[530]

Frank Spinner, Lt. Col. Wilkerson's defense attorney, provided this comment to the senate:

> While it's important to address the problem of sexual assault, it's also important to make sure the military's criminal justice system has checks and balances that correspond as much as possible to those in the civilian system. We all know that people can be falsely accused and wrongly convicted. Just as civilian judges may set aside bad verdicts, the military system should allow for timely corrective oversight.[531] ... I am at a loss to understand what the senators are upset about, other than they believe any woman who claims she was sexually assaulted must be accepted as telling the truth.[532]

No doubt, there is a problem with sexual assault inside our military. The same problem also exists in our civilian society. The senators are pressuring only the military, perhaps because they can. They do not have the power to challenge any other organization, such as college campuses or corporate America. The fact is, there is a great deal of pressure on the Department of Defense to "do something" about sexual assault.

In response to that pressure, as we have seen, the previous Secretary of Defense and the Chairman of the Joint Chiefs of Staff released the memorandum that they admitted would lead to more prosecutions.[533] Clearly, Col. Christensen and the prosecution team took this guidance seriously. Remember, during the trial, he said: "If the boss made it clear he wants something to happen, we expect a good officer to salute and make sure those things happen, correct?"[534] Unfortunately, sometimes, when the boss says to do something, people get carried away and believe cutting corners or bending rules is acceptable as long as they are doing what the boss said.

The Air Force responded by increasing sexual assault awareness training with greater encouragement for women who thought they may have been harassed or assaulted to file complaints. Air Force training also claims that a woman who has had any alcohol to drink cannot legally consent to sexual relations.

Service members are taught that even just one drink makes a woman incapable of legally consenting to sex. While this is an easy thing to remember and draws a clear line — better safe than sorry — it is *legally inaccurate,* and many attorneys say it is a dangerous lesson for the courtroom. Defense Attorney Michael Waddington added, "It's not medically accurate."[535]

The impact of this type of training can be seen in these examples. Last year, a Marine Corps Staff Sergeant was charged with sexual assault and adultery for a brief affair with a 19-year-old female Marine. Potential jurors being questioned for jury duty reported that their training taught them that a woman cannot consent to sex if she has had even one drink — the same, incorrect training as the Air Force. The judge in the case told the potential jurors that was not true and instructed them to ignore their training. However, at least one potential juror stated he could not reconcile his training with the judge's instructions. He was dismissed as a juror, and the Navy tried the case anyway. The jury convicted the staff sergeant of adultery but not sexual assault.[536] In this case, it was a false allegation of sexual assault after a consensual affair. The man received a prison sentence even though there was no assault. Charges of adultery were dropped against the accuser, and she was later promoted.[537] She filed an unsubstantiated charge to cover up her own behavior and was rewarded for doing so.

In 2011, an Air Force enlisted man at Joint Base in New Jersey was accused of sexually assaulting an intoxicated woman. Potential Air Force jurors revealed that they, too, had been taught that a woman cannot legally consent to sex if she has had even one drink. "First of all, that's not the law," said the enlisted man's attorney, "and it's not medically accurate."[538] That Airman was lucky. He was eventually acquitted.

This misunderstanding, explicitly taught in sexual assault training as demonstrated by these two accounts, leads to false accusations of assault and confusion in the courtrooms. It encourages the services to prosecute more cases than should be tried. The truth is that sometimes, women drink and agree to sex with a man. It may be poor judgment, but it does not necessarily make the man a criminal.

UNRELIABLE NUMBERS

Much is made in the media and Congress about the number of sexual assaults in the military. The problem is, however, these numbers are highly contentious and all over the map. For example, in September 2012, the Commandant of the Marine Corps said "a survey of 2 percent of the military has yielded a widely quoted extrapolation that 19,000 service members are raped annually."[539] Democrat Congresswoman Jackie Speier of California also used that number in September 2012, citing what she called Pentagon estimates and calling it an "epidemic of rape and sexual assault."[540]

Further investigation of the report, however, shows that the definition of sexual assault includes any form of "unwanted sexual touching." This covers everything from a slap on the bottom to fondling to rape.[541] A civilian similarity is sexual harassment in the workplace. It might (should?) get a man fired, but it does not send him to prison, whereas in the military, particularly today, some form of criminal punishment is usually considered. Unwanted sexual touching is absolutely unacceptable, but it is not rape, and it may not be criminal. It certainly does not mean 19,000 service members are raped each year. The Congresswoman and others are hurting the validity and ability to successfully prosecute real cases with their wildly inflated claims. We all want criminals prosecuted. But we also want the truth.

The estimated number of sexual assaults used in the DoD report is based on a survey of only 2 percent of the military. Statistically, that is a very small sample and therefore vulnerable to significant error when extrapolating to the number of women in the entire DoD. David Segal, Director of the Center for Research on Military Organization at the University of Maryland and a professor of sociology, said: "The data are squishy, and I would be loath to infer trends from two or three data points."[542]

Later, in 2012, the Pentagon estimated the number of sexual assaults inside the military even higher: "An estimated 26,000 service members reported having experienced unwanted sexual contact last year."[543] But, again, according to polling experts, these numbers are highly questionable. These findings from the Pentagon survey on sexual assault are based on low response rates and broad definitions of what constitutes sexual assault.[544]

Paul Lavrakas, a pollster and president of the American Association for Public Opinion Research, said he's troubled that three years of survey data produced such different estimates: "When you see them jump around like that, the first thing that comes to mind is there's something wrong with the numbers."[545]

The surveys remain confidential to protect those who do not wish to publicly report; many victims fear retribution if they come forward. It is true, however, that more than ever before, women are encouraged to report anything and everything that can be construed as sexual assault, and this encouragement may have an impact on the increasing numbers. More reporting is a good step toward eliminating the problem and, hopefully, more and more women will report actual crimes.

The DoD said 17 percent of sexual assault allegations in 2012 were unfounded. These false allegations are harmful on many levels. They destroy the accused and many innocent families. They also diminish the credibility of true victims in real cases. Every allegation of sexual assault must be investigated fully, including an investigation of validity. When an allegation is determined to be false and the case is dismissed, other, true victims may hear only that the case was dropped and not understand why. The level of misinformation surrounding sexual assault is dramatic and, unfortunately, at this time, there is no discussion of false allegations in any of the military training. The military should add some level of education on false allegations to its sexual assault awareness programs.

Although the numbers of reports of sexual assault are increasing, many see this as a positive sign of awareness and reporting as opposed to increasing crime. In fact, a stated goal of the DoD sexual assault program is "to increase the number of victims who make a report of sexual assault. The Department strives to increase sexual assault reporting by improving Service members' confidence in the military justice process, creating a positive command climate, enhancing education and training about reporting options, and reducing stigma and other barriers that deter reporting."[546] There is no doubt some of the increase in numbers of accusations can be attributed to the effort to increase reporting. That is not to say sexual assault is not a real and significant problem. It does, however, prove the services are taking action to address the overall problem of sexual assault. They are trying to solve the problem. False allegations make success more challenging.

Greg Jacob, policy director for the Service Women's Action Network, a victims' advocacy group, admitted the numbers may have increased some due to awareness and better reporting and not solely due to an increase in actual crime. But at least one women's advocacy group claims the numbers are still artificially low. Nancy Parrish from Protect Our Defenders said the survey's numbers "are definitely not inflated. It has always been our concern that these surveys don't come near to capturing the extent of the crisis."[547] Again, Parrish cites no references to support her claim. We'll see in the next section that sexual assault inside the military is similar in scope and frequency to American civilian society, yet there is no effort by Parrish or the senators to affect the "crisis" outside the military.

The DoD estimate of 26,000 sexual assaults in 2012 is more than a 35 percent increase over the previous estimate, just two years earlier. This is, again, an estimate and demonstrates the difficulty in gaining any accuracy by using estimates from small sample sizes. On the other hand, in actual reports of sexual assault, the numbers are factually identified and are a far better indicator of crime. The number of actual reports of sexual assault increased 14 percent from 2006 to 2010.[548] There were 3,374 reports of sexual assault recorded in 2012.[549] The DoD also states 17 percent of those reports are false or unfounded. Nevertheless, this increase is seen as a positive sign that more victims are coming forward. It is a sign of increased reporting and not that there is an increase in the actual number of crimes.

Politicians and women's advocate groups help create hysteria over sexual assault in the military as if it were out of control and far worse than anything experienced elsewhere. In truth, sexual assault is about the same inside the military as it is in civilian society. The bottom line is sexual assault is a problem, both inside and outside the Department of Defense. The military is a reflection of our society, but at least the military is attempting to aggressively address the problem.

There are more than 1.4 million personnel on active duty and an additional 1.2 million in the reserve armed forces.[550] According to City-Data.com, in 2011, there were 1,092 rapes per 100,000 people in New York City. This rape rate would equate to more than 15,300 rapes in the current active forces and 13,000 in the reserves each year — more than 28,000 total rapes. Given the more strict definitions of sexual assault inside the military, it is clear the armed forces are doing far better than the city of New York.[551]

From the Department of Defense 2012 annual report on sexual assault: "The risk of sexual violence for military and civilian women is the same. With few exceptions, the (occurrence) of sexual violence in the civilian and military populations are quite similar."[552] Additionally, the percentage of women who report sexual assault in the military is about the same as in the civilian population — about 16 percent.[553] Non-military studies cited by the National Institute of Justice indicate approximately 20 percent of college women say they were raped or sexually assaulted during college. The National Intimate Partner and Sexual Violence Survey results indicate almost 20 percent of U.S. women have experienced rape or attempted rape at some point in their lives, with approximately 65 percent of sexual assault victims not reporting to police.[554] The bottom line is there is no significant difference between the percentages of sexual assaults inside the military as compared to outside the military. In short, there is no "crisis" or "dramatic increase" in sexual assaults inside the military. The statistics simply do not support either claim. There is inside the military, however, an aggressive effort to deal with the problem of sexual assaults.

OVERZEALOUS PROSECUTION

Is "nothing being done," or are we overreacting to make the services "look good"?

Congresswoman Speier said there was an "epidemic of rape and sexual assault in the military" and claimed the military is "indifferent." "We have done nothing about it," she said.[555]

But McClatchy Newspapers, which covered the sexual assault issue in depth, reported that "contrary to public and political impression, an extensive review of military sexual assault finds plenty of Pentagon and congressional action. Some (action) works. Some falls short. Some goes too far, in a legal arena that's notorious for its complications."[556]

Michael Waddington, a former Army judge advocate who now defends sexual assault cases, said: "In the media and on Capitol Hill, there's this myth that the military doesn't take sexual assault seriously. But the reality is they're charging more and more people with bogus cases just to show that they do take it seriously."[557] A McClatchy Newspaper review of nearly 4,000 sexual assault allegations showed that the military has taken an aggressive stance against sexual assault. In 2011, which the review studied, military commanders sent 70 percent more cases to courts-martial than in 2009.[558]

Psychologist David Lisak, a forensic consultant to the military and expert on sexual violence, said the military now does more to deal with sexual assault than other segments of society.[559] As Judge Waddington said, the services are prosecuting more cases, not with more evidence, but because they are reacting to political pressure to get more convictions.[560] So, the services are getting more convictions — doing "what the boss wants" as Col. Christensen said in court — with no additional evidence. To some, this effort makes the Air Force "look good," but to others, particularly those falsely accused, it is unbelievable.

Defense lawyers who represent military members accused of sexual assault say the prosecution rate has increased dramatically, and they question why. "There are a lot of non-meritorious cases being brought," said Neal Puckett, a former Marine lawyer and judge who now represents service members for sexual assault. "I think that the pendulum has swung towards, if someone makes an allegation, she has her day in court. I've got to tell you, this whole concept that the system is broken (for victims) is a flawed proposition."[561]

False allegations disrupt the system, lead to false convictions and make it more difficult to prosecute true crimes. One Navy prosecutor, who asked to remain anonymous because she feared retaliation for speaking out, told McClatchy News: "Because there is this spin-up of 'we have to take cases seriously even though they're crap,' there is a pressure to prosecute, prosecute, prosecute. When you get (a case) that's actually real, there's a lot of skepticism. You hear it routinely: 'Is this a rape case or is this a Navy rape case?'"[562] The most important point she brought out is that there is pressure to prosecute, prosecute, prosecute even when cases don't warrant prosecution, when they are "crap." Why would the military bow to political-correctness pressure and take questionable cases to court-martial? Is it willingly accusing (and possibly convicting) innocent men?

As mentioned, these unsubstantiated trials hurt "real" cases. They convict innocent men for the sake of looking good for purely political reasons. And this trend is not likely to change soon.

Charles Feldmann, a former military and civilian prosecutor who's now a defense attorney, said: "Most of the rape cases that I've defended in the military system never would have gone to trial in a civilian system because the prosecutor would say, 'There's no way I'm taking that to trial because I'm not going to get a conviction.' But in the military, the decision-maker is an admiral or a general who is not going to put his career at risk on an iffy rape case by not prosecuting it. It's easy for him to say, 'Prosecute it.' If a jury acquits or convicts, then he can say justice was done either way… If a military commander dismisses a case and there's political backlash, he's going to take some real career heat over that dismissal."[563]

Under the Uniform Code of Military Justice, the military's justice system, the commander, similar to the district attorney in the civilian justice system, makes the decision whether to proceed to a court martial. Attorney Feldman said, "At times, the commanders disregard their legal advisors' recommendations and pursue allegations of sexual assault, raising concerns that the anti-rape campaign of advocacy groups and Congress is influencing them."[564]

Feldmann is right. The trend now, of which the Wilkerson case is just one example, is that defendants are being charged and prosecuted despite a lack of evidence and questionable accusers.[565] Besides the Wilkerson case, another example is the case against Marine Staff Sergeant Jamie Walton, who was court-martialed for rape. Like Hanks' account, Walton's accuser's story had also changed several times. A military lawyer who evaluated the case advised Walton's commander there was not enough evidence to proceed to court martial. Even the prosecuting JAG attorney agreed, also recommending against court-martial. Finally, the Article 32 Investigating Officer also recommended against court-martial. Nonetheless, the Marine commander ignored all of their advice and sent the young Marine to a court-martial anyway.[566]

Staff Sergeant Walton said, "Everyone knew I didn't rape her, but they went ahead with the trial anyway."[567] Walton and his accuser were both married to others. She initially denied having any sex, consensual or otherwise, with Walton, but when he confessed to adultery, she admitted having an affair with him. At that time, she wrote a sworn statement admitting to consensual sex in a hotel room and denied drinking any alcohol at all. However, three months later, she changed her story. She claimed then that "Walton had plied her with hard liquor before taking her to the hotel," and while they were watching TV on the bed, she said, "he all of a sudden rolled on top of me."[568]

The Article 32 Investigating Officer recommended the Marines drop the aggravated sexual assault charge. Like Hanks' story, the accuser's story had changed. The accuser's friends testified she told them the sex was consensual and she would consider doing it again to get even with her own cheating spouse. But later, Walton's accuser said she "realized she'd been raped" after she attended the Marine's anti-sexual assault training classes, at which time she told her own attorney, who was defending her against adultery charges, that she wanted to change her story to one of being raped. She only "realized she'd been raped after she attended the Marine's anti-sexual assault training classes..."[569] Despite the overwhelming evidence that the sex was consensual, the Marine commander went against all recommendations and pushed the case to court-martial.[570] Perhaps he or she did not want to be accused of being soft on sexual assault.

The accuser in the Walton case changed her story after attending sexual assault training. If it was consensual sex to get back at her own cheating husband, then there is something wrong with the military's training that would encourage her to claim a sexual assault, or it was a good defense for the charges against her. In any event, it worked.

Several defense attorneys contend the military's sexual assault training provides "a roadmap on how to make a false complaint."[571] Sexual assault training classes do encourage women to report sexual assault and rightfully so. But there must also be some responsibility taught in that training as well. There should be some balance with the counseling that helps individual women understand the difference between a bad decision and an assault and help them take responsibility for a consensual act. The jury in the Walton case did not believe his accuser was assaulted. It was clear, she was trying to cover up her own wrongdoing after drinking and having consensual sex to get even with a cheating spouse — which are two of Defense Attorney John Floyd's five reasons for falsely crying rape: the need to deny a consensual tryst and an alcohol-fueled encounter.[572]

The military services should use some criteria to help them identify false allegations — possibly Floyd's research. In their sexual assault training, they should incorporate counseling for women as to what constitutes a true assault versus a false allegation. They have a duty to protect the accused equal to the accuser and should protect men (who are also military members) from women who are willing to make a false accusation.

Investigators should be trained to get all the facts and supporting evidence and avoid making judgment calls and pursuing only one side. They should be better trained to detect false allegations. Unfortunately, in this politically charged atmosphere, to even hint that you might believe an accused is innocent can cost you your career. That is a powerful motivation to go along with the crowd, and the military has an obligation to change that. Justice should be blind, not politically poisoned.

It appears many in the military have given up the truth in order to "look good" to the politicians. Certainly, commanders are under political pressure to be, just like Brig. Gen. Zobrist said in his *Stars and Stripes* interview, "tough on sexual assault." As Captain Beliles, the assistant trial counsel in the Wilkerson court-martial, said during sentencing: "It must not be said. It must not be said that we as an Air Force did not take this crime seriously."[573]

Given the overwhelming political pressure, many commanders defer to a trial as their best way to avoid criticism. They don't want to be seen as weak on sexual assault. That can get them fired. A case in point: Recently, the Army fired a major general because someone else didn't believe he was tough enough on sexual assault. Major General Michael Harrison, the Commander of Army Forces in Japan, was "suspended from his duties on suspicion of failing to properly investigate an allegation of sexual assault."[574] Is it no wonder then that commanders are fearful of losing their careers for not proceeding to court-martial for each allegation. The political pressure to "do something" is taking a toll on commanders and establishing a dangerous precedent. They should be concerned about the truth. They should protect the accused equally as they do the accuser. An accusation is not evidence of an assault. Innocent until proven guilty must remain the standard, and commanders must have moral courage enough to uphold justice.

Think of this case against Sergeant Walton: The accuser signed a sworn statement saying there was no alcohol and the sex was consensual. Only when she was being investigated for and charged with adultery did she create the accusation of sexual assault. One has to wonder why the commander continued to court martial in this case. There were plenty of red flags indicating a false accusation. Was this commander so afraid of political correctness, he or she decided to put the young marine though a full court martial rather than risk his or her own career? Unfortunately, commanders are not only encouraged to follow this commander's example; they may be punished if they don't.

Once Sergeant Walton's accuser made the rape accusation, the adultery charges against her were dropped. The rape case against Walton went to trial; he was acquitted of rape but found guilty of adultery and given a bad conduct discharge. The accuser was never punished. Rather, she was later promoted. After thirteen years in the Marine Corp, Sergeant Walton has lost his retirement, his veteran's benefits, and the ability to attend college for free. He also worries even an acquittal will be seen as a mark of guilt. "A lot of people aren't going to like me because I made a stupid decision and I cheated on my wife," he said. "But I don't deserve to be seen as a rapist."[575] No, he doesn't. And women who make false allegations should not be rewarded. But that is the reality of the toxic atmosphere inside the military services today. Political correctness overrules right vs. wrong.

The high-profile case against Lt. Col. Wilkerson was too good for the Air Force to pass up. Here officials could try a lieutenant colonel that had been selected for promotion to full colonel, and as Col. Christensen made so clear in the trial, a fighter pilot. In this case, win or lose, they could say the Air Force takes this crime seriously. Even if they didn't get a conviction, they could say they tried the case in court. That "looks good" to the politicians and would help the Air Force image. Ironically, had they done a professional, honest and ethical job in the investigation, and determined there was not enough evidence to go to trial, the Air Force would not be in the middle of the media and political turmoil in which it finds itself embroiled.

Captain Lindsay L. Rodman, a Marine Corps Judge Advocate, wrote for *Joint Forces Quarterly Magazine* in January 2013: "The accusation that commanders do not take these cases seriously is completely unfounded. The truth is quite the opposite; commanders feel hamstrung to prosecute sexual assaults to the fullest, regardless of the possibility of success at trial. Political pressure from victims' rights groups have created an environment in which Service members are no longer presumed innocent until proven guilty beyond a reasonable doubt, which is a constitutional travesty. Public complaints that the military does not take sexual assault seriously have prompted over-prosecution in cases that would likely not go to trial in the civilian world."[576]

Could a wrongful conviction happen again? Could other Airmen, soldiers, Marines and seamen find themselves wrongfully accused and wrongfully convicted of a crime they did not commit? Marine Staff Sergeant Walton will tell you yes. Lt. Col. James Wilkerson will tell you yes, and, unfortunately, they are not alone.

So far, the Air Force has failed to take any steps to find out what went wrong in the Wilkerson case; how the investigators failed to properly investigate motive for a false allegation; why Lt. Col. Wilkerson was wrongly convicted; or how they might prevent future injustices perpetrated against innocent men simply because "she has no *apparent* motive to lie."

He-said, she-said now equals guilt in the poisoned atmosphere inside the Military Services. A commander must press with a vigorous investigation and push for a full court-martial or risk losing his or her job, and many defense attorneys are now raising the issue that it is unlikely someone accused of sexual assault can get a fair trial inside the military. The burden of proof has shifted to the defense — the accused now has to prove he did not do something (that never happened). Prove you are not a witch, or you get burned at the stake.

ACTUAL NUMBERS

By all accounts, rapes and sexual assaults remain underreported. While sexual assault surveys conducted in the military services yield estimated total numbers of sexual assaults, those numbers are only as reliable as the methodology used to estimate them. One often-quoted survey was from such a small sample of participants that the numbers have been challenged. The Department of Defense does, however, have some firm, fact-based numbers. Actual reports are a matter of record and provide much information on sexual assault inside the military.

In 2012, the United States military received 3,158 reports of sexual assault. Of that number, rape accounted for about 25 percent of the total. Remember, the term sexual assault is defined by the Air Force as any intentional unwanted and inappropriate touching. That is why rape is only one-quarter of the reported assaults. If the rape rates are about the same as reported in civilian society, i.e., 20 percent of the reports, then the number of rapes inside the Department of Defense last year was about 3,900.[577] There is no question, that number is far too high, and that is why the DoD is aggressively attacking the issue.

The Department of Defense report also indicates approximately 17 percent of the 3,158 reported rapes in 2012 were "unfounded." Unfounded means once the allegations were investigated, it was likely the accused did not commit the offense. The allegation was baseless or false.[578] So, the DoD's own report says 17 percent of the allegations of sexual assault last year were false. It seems many politicians and, perhaps, the OSI ignore this fact.

Other highlights from the Department of Defense Fiscal Year 2012 report on sexual assault:

• Sexual assault includes rape, sexual assault, nonconsensual sodomy, aggravated sexual contact, abusive sexual contact and attempts to commit these offenses.

• The Army had 2.3 reported sexual assaults per 1,000 service members, the highest of the services. The Navy's rate was 2.1, the Air Force's 2.0 and the Marine Corps' 1.7 per 1,000.

• Of the 2,558 *unrestricted* reports of sexual assault, 62 percent involved service members as the attacker and the victim, and 22 percent alleged a service member attacked a civilian.

• Of the *unrestricted* reports, 61 percent were rape, nonconsensual sodomy, aggravated sexual assault or sexual assault.

• Of the *unrestricted* reports, 88 percent of the victims were female. Slightly more than half were 20 to 24 years old.

• Of the 1,714 accused attackers who could be considered for action by military commanders, court-martial charges were preferred against 594 (34 percent). In those cases, the charges were dismissed against 88 people, and 70 were allowed to resign or were discharged instead of court-martial. Cases went to trial against 302 people, and 64 were acquitted (a 79 percent conviction rate).

• There were 239 reports of sexual assault in combat areas, including 23 in Iraq and 132 in Afghanistan.

• The 2012 Workplace and Gender Relations Survey of Active Duty Members found that 30 percent of women and 6 percent of men reported experiencing unwanted sexual contact *prior to entering the military*. The survey also found that 23 percent of women and 4 percent of men said they had experienced it since joining the military.[579]

29

THE INSPECTOR GENERAL COMPLAINTS

"Only two things are infinite, the universe and human stupidity, and I'm not sure about the former."
— *Albert Einstein*

In the aftermath of Lt. Gen. Franklin's decision, the media circus and political uproar raged on. In May 2013, during a phone call with some Air Force general officers in the Pentagon, the generals informed me, "The Air Force thinks (this media circus and political pressure) is all Wilkerson's fault, and they are out to get him." Shortly thereafter, Brig. Gen. Zobrist gave Lt. Col. Wilkerson what is called a "referral Officer Performance Report" (OPR). This was a clear attempt to keep Lt. Col. Wilkerson from pinning on the rank he had earned prior to the trial — that of full colonel. What is truly disappointing on Brig. Gen. Zobrist's part is the rationale he used for the negative report:

"Ratee did not meet standards in Leadership Skills, Professional Qualities, and Judgment & Decisions. As 31 FW/IG, failed to set/meet/enforce standards when he participated in and enabled an unsafe driving situation where 7 people who had been drinking rode in a car with seatbelts for 5; poor judgment put 7 people at serious risk. Despite doing many good things as 31 FW/IG, his behavior/judgment were unacceptable for a senior leader and IG."[580]

This is a clear attempt at retribution and reprisal against Lt. Col. Wilkerson. Clearly stated, there is no guidance as to what an Air Force member should do when other passengers in someone else's car do not wear seatbelts. There is guidance for the driver of the car and the individual passenger, but not for others in the car who are properly restrained by a seatbelt. There is no policy, guidance, memorandum, directive, or anything else written or otherwise that states Lt. Col. Wilkerson, as a passenger wearing a seatbelt, had any other duty in that situation. This was a made-up violation of non-existent guidance. It is petty and highlights Brig. Gen. Zobrist's feelings that Lt. Col. Wilkerson was guilty. It also suggests that Brig. Gen. Zobrist took his many Unlawful Command Influence actions against Lt. Col. Wilkerson intentionally.

As of this writing, there are a minimum of five Inspector General Complaints filed against the prosecution team, the Aviano Judge Advocate General's office, and now Major General Scott Zobrist for Unlawful Command Influence and reprisal actions against Lt. Col. Wilkerson. In short, the Air Force, as an institution, prosecuted an innocent man, wrongfully convicted him and put him in prison for four months before one reasonable man with great moral courage dismissed the charges, and yet the Air Force still refuses to admit it did anything wrong. And it is still persecuting Lt. Col. Wilkerson. Its actions are petty and disgusting and do not bode well for other Airmen falsely accused.

The main points of these various inspector general complaints are:

- Unlawful Command Influence by Brig. Gen. Zobrist as outlined earlier in this book.
- That the Aviano JAG office:
    ◊ Falsified the two letters of request for immunity to the 3rd Air Force Commander by inflating the charges to rape when they clearly never included rape.
    ◊ Violated privacy laws when they released the clemency package to Hanks (she has no legal right to these letters except through the FOIA process).
    ◊ Threatened witnesses.
    ◊ Violated privacy laws when they leaked (and continue to leak) Lt. Col. Wilkerson's personal private information, including his assignment, personal emails he sent while at Aviano, etc.
- That Colonel Christensen:
    ◊ Performed unprofessional actions.

◊ Threatened two witnesses and intimidated others.

◊ May have influenced the Article 32 Investigating Officer to recommend a court-martial against her first inclination.

◊ Delayed proper and legal discovery of phone records.

Lt. Col. Wilkerson filed a Department of Defense Inspector General complaint against Brig. Gen. Zobrist for the referral performance report — the made-up standard — because it is an illegal reprisal action against Lt. Col. Wilkerson. In accordance with Inspector General policy, the IG was supposed to decide if there was merit to the complaint prior to opening an investigation of Brig. Gen. Zobrist. They decided that, yes, there was merit to the complaint. However, in yet another unbelievable and unconscionable action, the leadership at the DoD IG deviated from policy and investigated Lt. Col. Wilkerson instead. Then the leadership, despite the action officer recommendation to investigate Brig. Gen. Zobrist, overrode the decision and refused to investigate. Brig. Gen. Zobrist had been promoted by the Air Force to Major General. An appeal has been filed with the acting Director of the DoD Inspector General, citing the violation of policy. Unfortunately, it appears even the DoD IG is unwilling to follow the rules when it comes to this case.

It is sad, but due to the failures the Air Force has demonstrated to date, its trustworthiness and integrity are now directly called into question. Some of these IG complaints were therefore filed with the Department of Defense Inspector General (DoD IG), whose own integrity has now been compromised. The honor of the Air Force is at risk. If officials want to do the right thing and correct these errors, ethics violations and unprofessional behavior, they have the opportunity to do so with the Inspector General complaints and a set of lessons learned provided to them. The Air Force has the opportunity, given the amount of information provided in these Inspector General complaints, to revisit the case to learn from it and make systemic improvements in training to prevent these errors from happening again. Only time will tell if the Air Force will continue to railroad other men into prison or reset the course back toward the truth. Given the poisoned atmosphere inside all the services right now, it is doubtful the pendulum will swing back toward justice anytime soon.

It may be difficult to turn the tide of prosecutions that has developed inside our military. The pendulum has swung, and many innocent men will pay the price before it swings back. The lucky ones will be released on appeal and maybe even get their careers back. No longer will convening authorities have the right to dismiss wrongful convictions. My sincere hope is that the Air Force will use the lessons learned from the failure to do a professional job in the Wilkerson case to, hopefully, help avoid sending other innocent men to prison.

3 0

THE SINS
OF THE PAST

"Man is the cruelest animal."
— *Friedrich Nietzsche*

The adverse actions and punishment continued for Lt. Col. Wilkerson.

A woman in Utah read about Lt. Col. Wilkerson's release. She said she was upset with Lt. Gen. Franklin's decision because she had had a consensual sexual relationship with Lt. Col. Wilkerson nine years earlier, and she had a child as a result of that relationship. The woman contacted Nancy Montgomery of the *Stars and Stripes*. Nancy Montgomery contacted the Air Force and wrote another story about the relationship.[581] The Air Force conducted a Commander Directed Investigation (CDI) in which Lt. Col. Wilkerson again cooperated fully.

The Air Force CDI report states "during this time the Wilkersons were experiencing marital problems and were physically separated." However, adultery is a crime under the UCMJ, regardless of separation. Therefore, the Air Force punished Lt. Col. Wilkerson again. Punishment, this time, was for an unprofessional relationship and conduct unbecoming of an officer. The statute of limitations had expired on adultery.[582]

On June 27, 2013, Air Force officials released information from the Commander Directed Investigation to news organizations. They did not release the part about the Wilkersons being separated and living apart.[583] This was another attempt to "look good" in response to political pressure, a motivation that seemed to drive much of their action.

The "Ferris Doctrine" prevents a military member, or dependent of a military member, from suing the United States or any of the military services. In 1950, the United States Supreme Court ruled, "The United States is not liable under the Federal Tort Claims Act for injuries to members of the armed forces sustained while on active duty and not on furlough and resulting from the negligence of others in the armed forces."[584] The result of this doctrine is that Lt. Col. Wilkerson has no opportunity to retrieve compensation for being maliciously prosecuted and wrongfully imprisoned for four months. He cannot sue the Air Force.

Lt. Col. Wilkerson did four months in prison for a crime he did not commit — a crime that never happened. The Air Force is unwilling to admit its mistake and corporately is doing everything possible to punish Lt. Col. Wilkerson further.

One might think four months of wrongful imprisonment would mitigate the egregious actions of the Air Force, but it appears it has no conscience when it comes to wrongful convictions. No matter what else he may have done, nothing justifies putting an innocent man in prison. To date, the Air Force, corporately, has demonstrated a lack of moral courage to admit a wrongful conviction and, in my opinion, a lack of decency.

One reason for its continued actions is its mistaken belief that Lt. Col. Wilkerson is a "bad guy." One colonel JAG officer said to Frank Spinner, who continues to represent Lt. Col. Wilkerson: "Hell, he's a bad guy. He peeks over bathroom stalls at women." This statement shows that those inside the Air Force associated with this case have not reviewed the case before passing judgment. They haven't read Lt. Gen. Franklin's letter either, evidently. They choose rather to believe hearsay without verifying facts for themselves. In short, they are just like Protect Our Defenders and the senators who push an agenda prior to (if ever) asking for the facts. It is disappointing that individual service members pass on what they hear rather than taking the time to do research themselves.

While the Air Force was not willing to admit wrongdoing, the Secretary of Defense took a step in the right direction when he released the following memorandum to all Department of Defense personnel on August 6, 2013:

SUBJECT: Integrity of the Military Justice Process

This memorandum reiterates my expectations and those of the President regarding the integrity of the military justice process. Every military officer and enlisted member of the Department of Defense is to be made aware of its contents.

Military justice is an essential element of good order and discipline, the indispensable ingredient that allows our Armed Forces to be the best in the world. Central to military justice is the trust that those involved in the process base their decisions on their independent judgment. Their judgment, in turn, must be based purely on the facts of each individual case, not personal interest, career advancement, or an effort to produce what is thought to be the outcome desired by senior officials, military or civilian.

Service members and the American people must be confident that the military justice system is inherently fair and adheres to the fundamental principle of due process of law. Everyone who exercises discretionary authority in the military justice process must apply his or her independent judgment. Military judges, commanders, convening authorities, criminal and administrative investigators, staff judge advocates, supervisors, Article 32 investigating officers, trial counsel, defense counsel, members of court-martial panels, and witnesses in military justice cases are among those included in this mandate.

Senior military and civilian leaders in the Department have an obligation to establish the standards of conduct expected of all military personnel. Drug abuse, sexual assault, hazing, and other criminal misconduct are not acceptable; senior leaders have made that clear and will continue to do so. But those comments are not made with the intent to indicate in any way what should or should not occur in any case. As Kathryn Ruemmler, the Counsel to the President, emphasized, "The President expects all military personnel who are involved in any way in the military justice process to exercise their independent professional judgment."

To be clear, each military justice case must be resolved on its own facts. Those who exercise discretionary authority in the military justice process must exercise their independent judgment, consistent with applicable law and regulation. There are not expected or required dispositions, outcomes, or sentences in any military justice case, other than what result from the individual facts and merits of a case and the application to the case of the fundamentals of due process of law.

Please ensure that this message is widely and immediately disseminated throughout your organizations. The integrity of the military justice process is too important to risk misunderstanding of what the President and I expect from those involved in it.

Thank you

//Signed//

Chuck Hagel[585]

Military personnel are specifically taught right from wrong, which orders they must follow and how to follow them. Training and education specify no rules should be broken to follow an order but that an order must, rather, be challenged if in itself it can result in questionable behavior. Subsequent to the actions surrounding this case, the Secretary of Defense felt the need to publish the above guidance. Acknowledging that need speaks for itself. The Wilkerson case garnered so much political attention and highlighted such a number of other current cases that the military was forced to look inside itself for wrongdoing. This guidance is an admission of excesses and an attempt to ensure they do not continue as well as an attempt to cover for the excesses of the past. This memorandum appears to be the secretary telling DoD personnel to do the right thing. I said this was a step in the right direction. Others think it was an effort to cover up for past misdeeds and alleviate the backlash against Unlawful Command Influence. I leave it to the reader to decide. In any event, I hope the military services will take the secretary at his word.

IT IS NOT OVER

Lt. Col. Wilkerson thought the Commander Directed Investigation and subsequent non-judicial punishment was the end of the Air Force's efforts to hurt him; however, on September 8, 2013, the Air Force announced it intended to persecute him further by convening a Board of Inquiry to force him out of the Air Force. In lieu of another trial before the Board of Inquiry, Lt. Col. Wilkerson submitted his resignation. Subsequently, the Air Force, at the behest of the acting Secretary of The Air Force, Eric Fanning, made the determination that Lt. Col. Wilkerson be retired at the rank of Major. Mr. Fanning, under direct pressure from Congresswoman Speier, and despite a full, legal acquittal, stated two reasons. He claims Lt. Col. Wilkerson 1) sexually assaulted a woman, and 2) committed adultery. The law says Lt. Col. Wilkerson did not assault anyone, but that didn't stop the acting secretary from doing the congresswoman's bidding. He simply ignored and abused the law. In this case, that did not come as a surprise.

Forcing Lt. Col. Wilkerson to retire at the rank of major is a reduction in rank of two grades from full colonel, to which he is legally entitled. This is a significant loss of pension benefits. Most Americans understand if one completes a military career, he or she retires with a pension. The difference between a colonel's pension and that of a major with twenty years of service is approximately $900 per month.[586] That is a considerable level of punishment, as it is a monthly amount for the remainder of his life. It is an unprecedented level of punishment considering Lt. Col. Wilkerson's four months in prison and the fact that he is innocent. His only recourse is to appeal this reduction in grade through what is called the Board of Corrections of Military Records. I hope the board sees the illegality of this action and returns the rank Lt. Col. Wilkerson earned.

Lt. Col. Wilkerson had been selected for promotion to full colonel, which the Air Force refused to give him after his acquittal. Further, Lt. Col. Wilkerson had been given commander-directed punishment for conduct unbecoming of an officer as a result of the child out of wedlock. This lower grade determination disregarded both his acquittal and previous punishment. And, of course, the Air Force completely ignored the fact that they put Lt. Col. Wilkerson in prison for four months for a crime that did not happen. Four months in prison and only one grade reduction in rank was not enough for the politically motivated Air Force.

31

LESSONS LEARNED

"The wise man learns from the mistakes of others.
The fool has to learn from his own."
— *The Book of Proverbs*

Fighter pilots train for combat. After every training event, sortie or simulator, we debrief the mission and learn lessons — why something didn't work and how to fix it so that it works next time. What follows here are lessons for the Air Force to help avoid wrongful convictions in the future, and for anyone accused of sexual assault.

First and foremost, the lesson everyone should already know is don't do anything that can be interpreted or misunderstood as sexual assault. Be very, very careful with whom you socialize, date, hook up with — whatever you want to call it. What often begins as typical, consensual, social interaction, such as time spent at the club, a party or whatever, mixed with alcohol, can have devastating consequences, particularly now inside the military. Don't mix alcohol with a woman you do not know. If sex is a factor, you have opened yourself up to a claim of sexual assault — right or wrong — and you are vulnerable. Years later, she can claim rape; if the Democratic senators have their way, an unlimited number of years later. Don't put yourself in a situation. Period.

A lesson for those in law enforcement is to do one's job in a professional and unbiased manner and let the facts take the investigation in the right direction. With the current political atmosphere of overwhelming pressure to "do something" about sexual assault, it is tempting and easy to ignore the possibility of innocence. But if you do the right thing and follow the evidence; you can always look yourself in the mirror without regret.

OSI investigators must be, and in fact are supposed to be, independent of the prosecution. They must follow the evidence, no matter where it goes. That may mean collecting evidence when it might not yield results. It may mean taking photos weeks after an allegation, and it may mean questioning the validity of an accuser's statements. Follow the evidence and let the case determine the outcome. Avoid a presumption of guilt, and never rationalize or accept poor behavior.

JAG officers and commanders, if there is no case, don't prosecute for the sake of prosecutions. There was no evidence in the Wilkerson case. Zero. Several attorneys suggested this case would never have gone to trial in civilian court. Why did it go to court in the Air Force? Analyze the decision to go to trial. Are we going to trial simply to get our numbers up? Are we punishing commanders who aren't aggressive enough? Why?

We don't have to bow to political pressure. With the Secretary of Defense's new guidance, everyone associated with the military justice system now has top cover to do a professional job and should be held accountable when they don't.

Make no mistake, the intent here is not to further victimize a victim; my recommendation is to fully investigate both sides of every accusation and to follow where the evidence takes the investigation without predetermined bias. The accused has a right to equal protection and investigation under the law. He or she is also a military member and has earned the support of our system equal to the accuser — innocent until proven guilty.

Investigating Officers must also have the moral courage to stand by their convictions. Changing a recommendation to send a man to court-martial based on "the absence of any *apparent* motive" on the part of the accuser, without bothering to investigate whether there was apparent motive, is criminal in and of itself.

The composition of the jury must be representative of the service, not slanted toward representing the accuser or the accused. Justice should be blind, with no stovepipe bias built in.

Sexual awareness training inside the military must change. Training must become more than simply a blueprint for filing complaints. The services must acknowledge the existence of false allegations. They must learn to recognize warning signs like *The Rape Investigation Handbook*'s nine "red flags" and investigate accordingly. They must admit wrongful convictions also happen. Wrongful convictions are mistakes that must be overcome and corrected within our military justice system, not demonized by our leadership. The services have an obligation to the accused as much as to the accuser. Treat both equally under the law.

Unlawful Command Influence must be better explained and taught to military leaders, including general officers. Commanders must not give the perception of influencing the case, wittingly or unwittingly, and must be held accountable when they do. Innocent until proven guilty is not just a saying. It must be reflected in our actions and the actions of every military leader.

Our system of justice is designed to allow a guilty person to go free rather than incarcerate an innocent person. The truth must remain the focus. Focus on the truth, and the outcome will be the right one.

Those lessons are for the Air Force and Air Force personnel involved with the justice system. For those ever accused of sexual assault, the most important lesson learned is never to talk with investigators without legal counsel present. Lt. Col. and Mrs. Wilkerson voluntarily met with the OSI, twice. Lt. Col. Wilkerson voluntarily took a polygraph. The OSI ignored any of his statements that did not fit with Hanks' version of events. They focused solely on convicting him and twisted everything he said to that end. This story is a cautionary tale of what can happen. It is a no-win situation. Don't talk with investigators without an attorney.

Never take a polygraph — never. Polygraphs are only tools. They are subject to interpretation depending on the person reading them. You may be honestly innocent and trying to help prove that, but the sad truth is, polygraphs are never helpful. OSI investigators, as Col. Christensen said, will use a ruse against accused persons in an attempt to confuse them and get them to incriminate themselves. Polygraph results are inadmissible and will not help your case. Volunteering to take one gains nothing.

The tough lesson to accept is that, once accused, a military member will lose his career. Even if found not guilty, there will be people who say he did it and just didn't get convicted. In today's military, to be accused is a lose-lose situation. In today's environment, one cannot expect the Air

Force, or any other military service, to treat the accused as innocent. They will end his or her career as soon as they can. It is an unsettling fact.

People lie. Not only do some women lie, but investigators, prosecutors, attorneys and witnesses sometimes lie as well. It is a sad commentary on human nature, but it is a fact, something that must be considered in any investigation and trial. Many of us associated with this case are shocked at the process, the investigation, the testimony and the rationalization of bad behavior. It awakened us to the fact that, for various motivations, some people are untruthful. That is a tough lesson to accept, but it is reality.

The final lesson is that there are still good people in the military. Try to find them. Lt. Gen. Franklin did the right thing. He displayed remarkable moral courage by reversing a wrongful conviction. All members of the Air Force should follow his example. Have moral courage.

Epilogue

The Truth Is
Not Welcome
in This Debate

"The only thing necessary for the triumph of evil is for
good men to do nothing."
— *Edmund Burke*

Lieutenant Colonel James Wilkerson is one of the lucky ones, relatively speaking. The charges against him were dismissed. He was acquitted, completely, as if it never happened. Unfortunately, Air Force leaders continue to bow to political pressure and persecute Lt. Col. Wilkerson. While at least he is not in prison, zealots in congress supported by Protect Our Defenders have demonstrated they want to continue to harm Lt. Col. Wilkerson. Four months in prison was not enough for them. They also want to harm Lt. Gen. Franklin. Senator McCaskill put a hold on a different general officer's promotion as a result of overturning one sexual assault conviction, and that general retired.[587] In short, McCaskill ended an otherwise exceptional career to further her own agenda. It is likely Senator McCaskill will stop Lt. Gen. Franklin from continuing in the Air Force as well. Too bad, since he seems to be in a minority as a leader with moral courage associated with this case.

The reprisal actions by Brig. Gen. (now Major General) Scott Zobrist continue. There is the made-up standard for seat belts for which only Lt. Col. Wilkerson was punished, and there are reprisal actions against at least two supporters of Lt. Col. Wilkerson. In the emails released in late August 2013, Col. Christensen told his superior how Brig. Gen. Zobrist would punish some of the supporters. Col. Christensen said: "I talked with Brig. Gen. Zobrist about this after the trial, and I know he intends to address it. I am confident (name redacted) will ensure it is done in a way that does not involve UCI" (Unlawful Command Influence).[588] The name of the person or persons in the email who would "ensure it is done in a way that does not involve UCI" were redacted by the Air Force. My guess as to who would ensure it was done in a way that does not involve UCI is the Aviano JAG office, which would advise Brig. Gen. Zobrist on how to cover up his reprisal actions to make sure they don't "involve UCI." Basically, someone (the JAG office at Aviano?) would advise Brig. Gen. Zobrist how to take illegal reprisal actions against Lt. Col. Wilkerson supporters without it appearing to be unlawful. It would be hard to believe if it were not in writing. Also in writing is that the senior litigator and the senior attorney in the United States Air Force acknowledged this action would happen and that it must be made to look like it was not unlawful. Rather than put a stop to what they acknowledged as Unlawful Command Influence, they condoned and conspired to accomplish it without repercussion. It is disappointing to all Americans that senior Air Force leaders behaved in this manner.

As this book went to press, on December 18, 2013, I received an official reply from the Air Force on several Inspector General complaints filed as a result of the conduct in this case.

The official position of the United States Air Force is this:

> We have finished our review of your concerns of the actions of people involved in the prosecution of the Wilkerson case ... three separate organizations — The Judge Advocate General's Professional Responsibility Administrator (HAF/JAA-PR); the Office of Special Investigations (AFOSI) 5th Field Investigations Region; and my Senior Official Inquiries Directorate (SAF/IGS) investigated the issues contained in your complaints. Applying a "preponderance of the evidence" standard of proof ... [the Air Force] determined there were no violations on the part of personnel assigned to the JAG Corps or AFOSI. [The Air Force] also ... determined Brig Gen Zobrist's verbal and written communications did not unlawfully influence the court-martial and were not otherwise in violation of any AF standards.

It is a shame the Air Force condones the behavior of the prosecutors, commander, and investigators in this case. It is a warning to
those accused and their defense attorneys. Threatening and intimidating
witnesses, misleading the Convening Authority, reprisal actions against
those who testify for the defendant and hiding information from defense
attorneys should never be tolerated. But the official position of the Air
Force is that the actions in the Wilkerson case, all of those detailed with
facts here in this book, were not violations of any Air Force policy or
regulation. They were acceptable behavior.

Also at this time, the Air Force removed Lt. Gen. Franklin as the
Convening Authority in another sexual assault case. This time, Lt. Gen.
Franklin agreed with the IO, who recommended against a court-martial.
Rather than drop the sexual assault charges in this latest case, the Air
Force removed Lt. Gen. Franklin from the case and found another
general officer who would push the case to court-martial.[589] If a general
won't go to court-martial, get another general who will. Simple.

Senator McCaskill went even further. She pushed through a new law
stripping commanders of the ability to overturn sexual assault cases (they
can only rubber stamp the findings), and if a commander ever decides
not to proceed to court-martial, that decision must be reviewed by a
civilian oversight panel.[590] The message is clear: All sexual assault
allegations will go to court-martial regardless of the evidence, or lack
thereof, and regardless of the Investigating Officer recommendation or
Convening Authority decision.

Others have been, and will continue to be, wrongfully convicted of
crimes that didn't happen under a system twisted to accommodate
political correctness. How many, no one knows. The world has never
been fair, but the U.S. justice system (of the past) was the closest thing we
had to fair. Now, who knows?

The military services are trying cases that civilian prosecutors refuse
to prosecute. The services have virtually unlimited budgets to prosecute,
and when commanders do not push for trial, they risk losing careers. U.S.
vs. Wilkerson was a case about pressure to get a conviction, to "do
something" about sexual assault.

Commanders send sexual assault cases to trial without merit because they fear they will be "perceived as taking the accusations lightly" and will be relieved of command.[591] In yet another case against a Marine, the local district attorney said he would not press charges, and the Marine Reserve colonel, the Investigating Officer, who himself is a former military judge, agreed, saying he would not recommend continuing to trial. He stated for the record: "The allegations were baseless."[592] Yet, the commander (Convening Authority) overrode both recommendations. Political correctness has created a witch hunt; the odds are, once accused, you will go to trial. How many defendants will get unlucky and have a jury who cannot reconcile what they have been taught with reasonable doubt? How many innocent men — volunteers who defend our nation — are in prison?

Eugene Fidell, who teaches military law at Yale Law School, said: "If you send the case to trial against the recommendation (of the investigating officer), people will complain that you're being too hard and politically correct. If you refuse to send the case to trial against a recommendation, then it means you're unwilling to bite the bullet and make the difficult decision. So most convening authorities right now are probably scratching their heads. The commander is 'traversing a minefield,' "[593] a minefield in which neither the commander nor an innocent man can win.

The military is a reflection of our society. Sexual assault is a problem in our society. Sexual assault is a problem inside the military. But that is no excuse for a wrongful conviction. People lie. Women lie about assault sometimes. Some estimates indicate false accusations are as high as 45 percent. The Justice Department proved wrongful convictions run as high as 25 percent. Our system was designed to allow a guilty person to go free rather than convict an innocent person. Sometimes our system gets it wrong. The Air Force gave in under the pressure and pushed a shaky case with no evidence to a jury of officers biased by daily propaganda to "do something." When an accused makes it to court, jurors have a predisposition to believe guilt. When the defendant does not take the stand on his own behalf, jurors have another predisposition to believe he is guilty. Most defendants come into court with two strikes against them. Stacking the deck with the poisoned atmosphere of political correctness today, it is entirely possible no man accused of sexual assault can get a fair trial inside the military. This is the case despite proof that last year alone, 17 percent of all allegations of sexual assault inside the military were unfounded.

One of the major problems with false allegations in the military is that there are no repercussions. Women who falsely accuse, as we have seen, are not only not prosecuted, but often charges are dropped against them for other crimes, and some continue their military career and continue to advance. The pendulum is indeed fully extended in the direction where a woman can do no wrong and speak no falsehood.

As a retired military officer and a citizen of the United States, the current condition inside our military is depressing to me. The military has a duty to both the accuser and the accused; to the military member and his/her family on both sides of the allegation. Until proven guilty, the accused is innocent. Reasonable doubt is just that — reasonable. Investigators, JAG officers, commanders and jurors should remain impartial and professional and follow the evidence. Court-martials are reserved for when there is evidence to support the conviction, not because "she has no obvious reason to lie." All services should have the decency and professionalism to investigate the accuser's reasons to lie before making an assumption that she didn't and risk sending an innocent man to prison. Research proves false accusations are far more common than some senators and women's advocacy groups admit or want the public to know. They, along with an unwitting media, ignore these studies. We've proven there are false allegations and that the rate, unfortunately, is quite high. Everyone associated with investigating and prosecuting sexual assault should understand this fact.

Current military sexual assault training is a blueprint for how to file a sexual assault allegation with not a single word or caution concerning false allegations. It's as one-sided as it gets. The scales of law are supposed to be balanced, not one-sided. Training should be balanced. Training should include awareness and investigative techniques used to discover false allegations for those assigned to investigate allegations. Women who are proven to have lied should be punished. Perjury is a crime, just like assault. False allegations hurt real cases, and they hurt our military.

Col. Christensen's closing argument focused on convicting a fighter pilot: "He's a fighter pilot. Fighter pilots, as Mrs. Wilkerson told you, parties all the time." *We can rely on our knowledge of the world...* He successfully convinced a panel of non-pilots that a pilot was guilty, but of what? Singing songs with dirty words? Dormitory antics? Burning a couch? Condemnation of fighter-pilot traditions is no reason to so grievously harm an innocent officer and his wife and son, not even a fighter pilot. Not even in today's environment poisoned by political correctness. Innocent men do not belong in prison.

The evidence in this case, when examined in total, not only proves reasonable doubt; it strongly suggests beyond a reasonable doubt that Hanks may have committed perjury. It also casts a shadow on the entire military effort to address sexual assault. Military service is difficult enough. We don't need to live in fear that someone somewhere might make a false allegation against us and send us to a court-martial for a crime that did not happen. We have enough to contend with in fighting real sexual assaults.

In the Wilkerson trial, as is now coming to light in other trials, the court-martial panel had been indoctrinated with the idea that most (if not all) men accused of sexual assault are guilty. From General Amos' comments to sexual assault training, they had heard that a woman cannot consent and that most men are guilty. Add in the natural bias against any accused that gets to trial, and that of a jury against a defendant who does not take the stand in his own defense, and it becomes easy to rationalize guilt. As mentioned, we later heard through the grapevine the five members of the Wilkerson court-martial panel unanimously agreed on the verdict. They said Hanks' story never changed and that Beth Wilkerson's story was "all over the map." How could they hear that? Just like the potential juror who "could not reconcile his training with the judge's instructions," perhaps these panel members could not overcome the training and bias of an entire career. They had been subjected to years' worth of programming: We "must do something to stop sexual assault," and each had been briefed on the SECDEF's new guidance to be more aggressive. They all had been exposed to the prejudice that if a defendant gets to trial, he must be guilty, and it was a jury completely comprised of non-pilots, heavy with medical personnel. Add on, and make a big deal out of, a bias against fighter pilots, and there is the recipe for a guilty verdict without any evidence. This jury deliberated for only three and a half hours, during which time they ate lunch. Did they really look at Hanks' versions of her story for inconsistencies? They clearly did not watch Lt. Col. Wilkerson's OSI interview as Lt. Gen. Franklin did. It was four hours long. They could not possibly have watched it. Why they would not want to hear his side is interesting, but we will never know. Did they really discuss Hanks' statements about how she exited the house and compare them to the layout of the house to see they didn't matched? Did they do their job in a professional manner? All of my points are backed up with facts printed in the Record of Trial and available for verification. So, you, the reader, can conduct your own research and form your own opinion.

My personal opinion of these jurors is that they failed to do their duty. A he-said, she-said case has reasonable doubt to begin with. Without evidence to support Hanks' story, that is all it is — a story. Our system of justice is designed so that innocent men are not imprisoned. The burden of proof is on the prosecution. These jurors ignored that. There was no evidence to support a conviction. In fact, if they listened to or read Hanks' testimony, they would have seen what I have written here, that Hanks could not possibly have been where she says she was based on the physical attributes of the house. She did not have her cell phone on the counter if she was texting from the bedroom, she did not have a bright overhead light come on if she herself claims the only light in the room was a lamp by the bed, and she repeatedly provided statements of her concern over an alcohol-related incident. It was not hard to see *THE WHOLE TRUTH*, if they would have listened and read with open minds.

Credit, if you can call it that, must be given to the prosecution. Clearly, the prosecuting attorneys were better at convincing the jurors that the Wilkersons' story had changes, that Kim Hanks "had no reason to lie," and that despite the many changes in her story, somehow it never really changed. The defense must have failed to emphasize adequately the multiple inconsistencies we've documented, or the jurors must have ignored them. Spinner failed to attack the details of the case as aggressively as hindsight now shows he might have. Spinner had thirty-five-plus years of experience at these types of cases in the military. He was confident that with no evidence, this "he-said, she-said" case had plenty of reasonable doubt. He felt he didn't need to attack Hanks in court. Unfortunately, the current atmosphere in the military is a whole new ballgame. Political pressure has changed the rules, and what Spinner thought was an open and shut case that never should have come to trial was really the hunting of a fighter pilot looking for an excuse to convict.

As we have documented, the intimidation of witnesses, leadership creating the perception of guilt and publishing it with the help of an overzealous newspaper writer, a less than professional OSI investigation, and, dare we say, a biased "dream jury" combined to create an entirely different court than Spinner had ever seen. The new standard of guilt — simply that the accuser "has no obvious reason to lie" — is damning to defendants. The burden of proof is now squarely on the defense to prove either she is lying or someone else is guilty of the assault. Col. Christensen was aggressive, smug and arrogant in the courtroom, and Judge Brown, for some inexplicable reason, allowed unusual and aggressive behavior from the prosecutor, who works closely with the judge's boss. Spinner was, in hindsight, too much of a gentleman for Col. Christensen, who didn't mind raising his voice at witnesses and sensationalizing hearsay and fighter-pilot, frat-boy antics.

According to the Innocence Project, "based on studies, some 47,000 American men are falsely accused of rape each year."[594] Some men are wrongly convicted and imprisoned. Even if they aren't convicted, being accused of sexual assault can often "emotionally, socially, and economically destroy a person."[595] Of course, wrongful accusations and wrongful convictions are not excluded from the military justice system.

The damage to the Wilkerson family certainly has been extensive. Lt. Col. Wilkerson spent four months of his life in prison because of an overzealous JAG officer, an unprofessional OSI investigation, the overwhelming political pressure and the Air Force's blind desire to "look good." He has been ridiculed and slandered by politicians and others to further their own agendas without even a cursory look at the evidence. The Wilkersons' son had to find out his father was accused of sexual assault in a newspaper with one-sided coverage that judged him guilty from the first article by Brig. Gen. Zobrist.

The continued attacks against Lt. Col. Wilkerson, such as the fabricated new standard for seatbelt wear, are disappointing. After four months in prison, how much more punishment should Lt. Col. Wilkerson be given to cover up the Air Force's mistake?

The reprisal actions against witnesses who testified for Lt. Col. Wilkerson are simply disgusting. Who in the Air Force can trust that the military justice system is just? Who in the Air Force will not fear the reprisals of a vindictive and prejudicial commander? There are no repercussions for false allegations and, evidently, there are no repercussions for reprisals either.

I wrote this book because the story needed to be told. It is a story of how otherwise good people such as investigators, attorneys and witnesses can go wrong; how otherwise professional military service members can turn a blind eye under pressure; how political correctness and the overwhelming pressure to "do something" led to a corrupt system that willingly sent an innocent man to prison. Unfortunately, in my research, it became a story of how some people lie and how an entire system became so corrupted by a political agenda that it tolerates such bad behavior. This is a story not limited to one person or one service that demonstrates how the United States military is willing to sacrifice the truth in the name of political correctness. It is a sad commentary on human nature when so many willingly bow to such pressure at the expense of others.

Suzanne Berrong, a virtual outsider to the military, said: "I was expecting more on the side of honor, integrity to be in play. ...This was not about the truth, but going after the rank and person."[596]

Remember the excerpt from lead defense attorney Spinner's email asking for clemency letters: "Given the political climate, we do not believe Lt. Gen. Franklin would disapprove the findings of the court or remove the dismissal." The *political climate* should have nothing to do with the justice system. Equal justice under the law; that should be the goal.

As I said in the beginning of this project and, in fact, right after the trial, this is my Air Force, and the way these men and women behaved is upsetting and disappointing. We in the military are held to a higher standard than the politicians who clamor about wrongs. It is not acceptable for us to commit wrongs, such as convicting innocent men, simply to please politicians. We used to be above that, and we should be again. It is my hope this book in some small way will help others in uniform remember that doing right may not always be easy, but it is always right.

The point of justice is to, as much as is humanly possible, achieve the right, correct, just outcome. Lt. Col. James H. Wilkerson did not assault Hanks. Evidence shows she falsely accused him of assault to cover up her alcohol-related behavior and protect her job. The proof may not have been properly vetted or exposed during the trial, but the truth did come out, and the right, final outcome was achieved. Lt. Col. Wilkerson spent four months in prison and has already endured a year's worth of character assassination by a group of biased political leaders and agenda-driven special interest groups not interested in the truth.

Unfortunately, many people don't trouble themselves to seek the truth; they simply repeat hearsay. Google Lt. Col. Wilkerson, and everything is negative; most of it untrue. But it's on the Internet, and that is what people see. He and his family face many challenges trying to put their life back together. The sad truth — THE WHOLE TRUTH — is that the Air Force doesn't really care. In fact, it demonstrated consistently throughout this entire case, from the early email by Brig. Gen. Zobrist to his reprisal actions and the continued attacks against Lt. Col. Wilkerson, that what the Air Force cares about is looking good for vocal politicians.

Despite the pain the Air Force put the Wilkersons through, the truth did prevail. There is one man, Lt. Gen. Franklin, with exceptional moral courage to thank for that. Moral courage like that displayed by Lt. Gen. Franklin is rare indeed. But it should not be rare in the military. We are held to a higher standard because we can uphold that higher standard. I hope others will follow General Franklin's example and do the right thing.

Finally, out of all of this, one thing struck me as both particularly hurtful and telling. Suzanne Berrong, formerly Kim Hanks' close friend, participated in the entire military justice system process. The summary of her experience leaves me haunted and fearful that our justice system is so deeply, negatively affected by political correctness that many more innocent men will face prison for crimes that didn't happen. Berrong said this experience was "rather eye opening and disappointing... as an outsider, I was expecting more on the side of honor and integrity."[597] I have to admit, I was expecting more honor and integrity as well. I am hopeful this book will prompt others inside the military to expect both honor and integrity as well and to demand both in the future.

The Truth must still count. The goal must be the truth ... *THE WHOLE TRUTH..*

ACKNOWLEDGMENTS

First and foremost, I want to thank James H. (Jay) "Roscoe" Wilkerson, Beth Wilkerson, and their son and to apologize, on behalf of my Air Force and my country. What we did to you was an injustice too great to describe. How you handled yourselves under this atrocity was professional and dignified at every moment. The frustration level and stress must have been tremendous at times, and I thank you for your strength of character and your forgiveness. And I thank you for your twenty-plus years of honorable service to our country.

Thank you to my wonderful bride, Connie Harvey, for understanding and supporting me. On the first day of the trial, I received an email from my CEO saying not to return to work. My company in Florida had gone out of business. When Jay was found guilty, I felt, as did Connie, that my being unemployed was meant to be. That gave me the time to review and research the record of trial and to help Jay. I often believe in a higher power or fate, whatever you want to call it, and I do believe the unemployment was meant to be. I am therefore also grateful to God for giving me the strength to help the Wilkersons, and for Jay's release.

Thank you JP and Nancy Reilly, who read the entire Record of Trial and were a constant support toward setting the record straight.

Thanks also to Congressman Mick Mulvaney and his Chief of Staff, Al Simpson. Sexual assault in the military is an incredibly sensitive subject, and being on the side of an accused was, in Washington, on the wrong political side of the issue. I applaud Congressman Mulvaney and Congressmen Jeff Duncan and Joe Wilson of South Carolina for their courage in the face of political correctness.

Thank you to authors and friends Nick Wynne, Bob McCarty, and Dan Hampton for advice and friendship. Bob's book, *Three Days in August,* describes the wrongful conviction of another military member and inspired me to tell this story.

I could not have completed this, my first book, without the assistance of my editor and friend Chris Kridler. I am forever in her debt. She rescued me when I was stalled near the finish line. Without her assistance, publishing this would likely have taken significantly longer and cost far more. Many, many thanks.

Finally, I would like to offer a special salute to Lieutenant General Craig Franklin: Thank you, sir, for being the calmer head that prevailed. It was refreshing to find someone in the Air Force who saw this for what it was. It is a true failure of leadership that the Air Force allowed you to take the brunt of criticism from politicians who didn't want the truth because it hurt their agenda. You showed true courage. We sincerely hope others inside our military will follow your example to do the right thing.

A P P E N D I X 1

From the Secretary of Defense
and the Chairman of the Joint Chiefs of Staff
17 April 2012

INITIATIVES TO COMBAT SEXUAL ASSAULT IN THE MILITARY

The men and women of the U.S. military deserve an environment that is free from the threat of sexual assault. Service members and their families must feel secure enough to report this crime without fear of retribution and commanders must hold offenders appropriately accountable. Under the leadership of Secretary of Defense Leon E. Panetta and General Martin Dempsey, the Chairman of the Joint Chiefs of Staff, the Department is actively pursuing additional policy and training changes to help address this challenging issue.

At a meeting with interested members of Congress, Secretary Panetta announced today additional steps to combat sexual assault in the military. These new initiatives include:

- Elevating disposition authority for the most serious sexual assault offenses (rape, sexual assault, forcible sodomy, and attempts to commit those offenses) so that, at a minimum, these cases are addressed by a "Special Court-martial Convening Authority" who is an officer at the Colonel (or Navy Captain) level.
    - This will ensure that cases of sexual assault receive a high level of command attention, given the seriousness of those offenses.
    - This will also ensure that these cases remain within the chain of command, so that our leaders retain responsibility and accountability for the problem of sexual assault.
- Establishing "Special Victim's Unit" capabilities within each of the Services, to ensure that specially trained investigators, prosecutors and victim-witness assistance personnel are available to assist with sexual assault cases.
    - This will provide specially-trained experts in evidence collection, interviewing, and interacting with survivors of sexual assault.

- <u>Requiring that sexual assault policies be explained to all service members within 14 days</u> of their entrance on active duty.
  - o This will educate our newest members right away, so that they enter the military knowing that our culture will not tolerate sexual assault, and understand what to do in the event an offense occurs.
- <u>Allowing Reserve and National Guard personnel who have been sexually assaulted while on active duty to remain in their active duty status</u> in order to obtain the treatment and support afforded to active duty members.
- <u>Requiring a record of the outcome of disciplinary and administrative proceedings</u> related to sexual assault, and requiring that copies of those records be centrally retained.
  - o This will allow the Department to better track our progress in combating sexual assault in the military, and will help better identify potential patterns of misconduct and systemic issues.
- <u>Requiring commanders to conduct annual organizational climate assessments.</u>
  - o This will allow commanders to measure whether they are meeting the Department's goal of a culture of professionalism and respect and zero-tolerance of sexual assault.
- <u>Mandating wider public dissemination of available sexual assault resources, like the DoD "Safe Helpline."</u> The helpline is available 24 hours a day via web, phone, or text message and is operated by the nonprofit Rape, Abuse, and Incest National Network through a contractual agreement with the department. Between its launch in April 2011 through Sept. 2011, the Safe Helpline assisted more than 770 individuals. The helpline can be reached at 877-995-5247 or http://www.safehelpline.org
- <u>Enhancing training programs for sexual assault prevention, including training for new military commanders in handling sexual assault matters.</u>

The initiatives announced today build on new victim-focused policies that have been implemented in the past year, these initiatives include:

- Assignment of a two star general as the Director of our Sexual Assault Prevention and Response Office.
- Expansion of legal assistance for military spouses and adult military dependents, so they can file confidential reports and receive the services of a victim advocate and a sexual assault response coordinator.

- Expedited transfers of victims who report a sexual assault to protect them from possible harassment and remove them from proximity to the alleged perpetrator.
- Extended retention of forensic examination and investigative reports.
- Establishment of a sexual assault advocate credentialing and certification program.
- Expansion of sexual assault support services to military spouses and adult military dependents.
- Expansion of emergency care and support services to DoD civilians stationed abroad and DoD U.S. citizen contractors in combat areas.
- Increased funding for investigators and judge advocates to receive additional specialized training.
- Implementation of an integrated data system for tracking sexual assault reports and managing cases.
- Assessment of how the department trains commanding officers and senior enlisted leaders on sexual assault prevention and response.

For media inquiries, please call OSD/PA at (703) 697-5135.

For congressional inquiries, please call OSD/LA at (703) 697-6210.[dxcviii]

A P P E N D I X   2

This is the article by Colonel Christensen posted on the Ramstein
Air Base website for more than two months prior to the trial. The jurors
all came from Ramstein.

My job is prosecuting sexual assault
Commentary by Col. Don M. Christensen,
Chief, Government Trial and Appellate Counsel

Posted 7/19/2012 at: **http://www.af.mil/news/story.asp?id=123310611**.
That link was taken down; here is the new link:
http://www.af.mil/News/Commentaries/Display/tabid/271/Article/14131
7/my-job-is-prosecuting-sexual-asault.aspx

7/19/2012 — WASHINGTON (AFNS) — Here's a simple truth ...
sexual offenders reject our core values of integrity, service and excellence,
in favor of following their own base, undisciplined, criminal desires.
Most sexual assaults committed by Airmen are "blue on blue," or Airmen
victimizing other Airmen. So in addition to rejecting our core values,
these undisciplined Airmen reject the Wingman concept that we prize in
the Air Force. They represent a direct threat to unit morale, good order,
and discipline. They degrade combat readiness but with the combined
efforts of command, law enforcement, and our team of prosecutors, they
will be held accountable. Together, as a team, we will protect other
Airmen and protect our strength and combat readiness as the world's
greatest Air Force.

Detecting and prosecuting sexual assault is our priority. Recently,
we posted on the internet significant Air Force sexual assault
prosecutions. The posting may be found here: http://www.afjag.af.mil/
sexualassaultprosecution/index.asp. As you can tell from a quick review
of this information, we will prosecute sexual offenders anywhere they are

found. From reviewing these cases, you can see sexual assault in the Air Force carries substantial penalties.

Our partners in AFOSI thoroughly investigate each allegation to provide commanders with timely, accurate, and prosecutable evidence. They pass the ball to commanders, who call upon my team to prosecute the offender to the maximum extent allowed under law.

Our team of prosecutors is better than any you will see in the civilian community or on TV. I have 17 highly skilled senior trial prosecutors, who are selected from among hundreds of judge advocates for their top notch trial skills. They have the very best trial skills in the Air Force JAG Corps. They prosecute the Air Force's most serious courts-martial. Seven of my senior trial prosecutors have been identified as "Special Victim Unit (SVU)" prosecutors, due to their training and experience in combating sexual assault. They are dedicated to bringing justice to victims of sexual assault and ensuring commanders are able to appropriately hold offenders accountable.

In the typical case we prosecute, the accused Airman exploits his victim's intoxicated state to commit the sexual assault. We are very effective in prosecuting these offenders, and the law encourages us to prosecute Airmen who use alcohol to facilitate sexual assault of substantially incapacitated victims. Prosecuting this kind of case is one of our core specialties.

The Air Force has done a great job training Airmen about respecting other Airmen and not sexually abusing their fellow Airmen. Training can reach many Airmen who might be tempted to commit this crime. For others, who cannot be persuaded by training, my team, the Senior Trial Prosecutors — Special Victims Unit, stands at the ready to vindicate the victims.

ABOUT THE AUTHOR

Robert "Bob" Harvey is a retired U.S. Air Force Colonel with more than thirty-three years of service. He has flown more than 3100 hours in the F-16, including combat in DESERT STORM. His combat decorations include five Air Medals, the Distinguished Flying Cross with valor and the Bronze Star. He commanded a Fighter Squadron and is a National Defense Fellow and a graduate of the USAF Fighter Weapons School. During his career, Col. Harvey witnessed four military sexual assault cases as commander and court-martial panel member. He lives in Cocoa, Florida, with his wife, Connie.

ENDNOTES

The complete Record of Trial for U.S. vs. James H. Wilkerson is on the U.S. Air Force Freedom of Information website at: http://www.foia.af.mil/reading/thewilkersonfoiacase.asp

---

[1] TODAY SHOW, NBC News: http://www.today.com/video/today/51159896#51159896

[2] USO, downloaded from their website, July 24, 2013, at: http://www.uso.org/the-organization.aspx

[3] "Band of Brothers in History and Literature," downloaded August 19, 2013, from: http://www.indepthinfo.com/band-of-brothers/henry-v.shtml

[4] Cheryl Pone, summarized Article 32 testimony, U.S. v Wilkerson, Record of Trial, IO exhibit 31

[5] Kim Hanks, statement April 17, 2012, U.S. v Wilkerson, Record of Trial, IO exhibit 3

[6] Col. Don Christensen, affidavit to Lt. Gen. Franklin, January 24, 2013, Air Force Freedom of Information website, pg 71/134, downloaded April 25, 2013, from: http://www.foia.af.mil/shared/media/document/AFD-130404-224.pdf

[7] Colonel Don Christensen, Prosecutor, U.S v Wilkerson, Record of Trial, pg 187

[8] Beth Wilkerson, testimony, U.S. v Wilkerson, Record of Trial, pg 740

[9] Colonel Don Christensen, U.S v Wilkerson, Record of Trial, pg 477

[10] Colonel Don Christensen, U.S v Wilkerson, Record of Trial, pg 484

[11] Captain Benjamin Beliles, Assistant Trial Counsel, U.S. v Wilkerson, Record of Trial, pg 522

[12] Colonel Don Christensen, Prosecution Closing Argument, U.S. v Wilkerson, Record of Trial pg 943

[13] U.S. v Wilkerson, Record of Trial, defense exhibits 7

[14] U.S. v Wilkerson, Record of Trial, defense exhibits 7, June 30, 1998 performance report

[15] U.S. v Wilkerson, Record of Trial, defense exhibits 7, June 2000, training report

[16] Doyle, Michael and Taylor, Marisa, "Bureaucracy has blossomed in military's war on rape," McClatchy Newspapers, November 28, 2011, downloaded June 4, 2013, from: http://www.mcclatchydc.com/2011/11/28/131524/bureaucracy-has-blossomed-in-militarys.html#.UauEKZzD-M9

[17] Kim Hanks, testimony, U.S. v Wilkerson, Record of Trial, pg 262

[18] Kim Hanks, statement April 17, 2012, U.S. v Wilkerson, Record of Trial, IO exhibit 3

[19] Kim Hanks, summarized Article 32 testimony, U.S. v Wilkerson, Record of Trial, IO exhibit 24

[20] Kim Hanks, summarized Article 32 testimony, U.S. v Wilkerson, Record of Trial, IO exhibit 24

[21] Kim Hanks, statement April 17, 2012, U.S. v Wilkerson, Record of Trial, IO exhibit 3

[22] Kim Hanks, statement April 17, 2012, U.S. v Wilkerson, Record of Trial, IO exhibit 3

[23] MSgt. Danielle Dunnivant, statement April 20, 2012, U.S. v Wilkerson, Record of Trial, IO exhibit 6

[24] Major Michael O'Keefe, statement, April 25, 2012, U.S. v Wilkerson, Record of Trial, IO exhibit 20

[25] Lt. Col. James Wilkerson, videotaped interrogation, on the Air Force Freedom of Information website at:
http://www.foia.af.mil/reading/thewilkersonfoiacase.asp

[26] Beth Wilkerson, testimony, U.S. v Wilkerson, Record of Trial, pg 707

[27] Beth Wilkerson, summarized Article 32 testimony, U.S. v Wilkerson, Record of Trial, IO exhibit 29

[28] Beth Wilkerson, summarized Article 32 testimony, U.S. v Wilkerson, Record of Trial, IO exhibit 29

[29] Kim Hanks, testimony, U.S. v Wilkerson, Record of Trial, pg 263

[30] Beth Wilkerson, summarized Article 32 testimony, U.S. v Wilkerson, Record of Trial, IO exhibit 29

[31] Frank Spinner, Defense Attorney, opening remarks, U.S. v Wilkerson, Record of Trial pg 205, and Beth Wilkerson, interview with author, February 24, 2013

[32] Rodman, Lindsay L., "Fostering Constructive Dialogue on Military Sexual Assault," April 2013, Joint Forces Quarterly on line, downloaded April 3, 2013, from: **http://www.ndu.edu/press/military-sexual-assault.html**

[33] Powers, Rod, Punitive Articles of the UCMJ, Article 120, Rape, sexual assault, and other sexual misconduct, About.com, downloaded April 25, 2013 from: **http://usmilitary.about.com/od/justicelawlegislation/a/art120new.htm**

[34] Powers, Rod, Punitive Articles of the UCMJ, Article 133, Conduct unbecoming an officer and gentleman, About.com, downloaded April 25, 2013, from: **http://usmilitary.about.com/od/punitivearticles/a/mcm133.htm**

[35] The Free Dictionary, downloaded July 24, 2013, from: **http://legal-dictionary.thefreedictionary.com/Reasonable+Doubt**

[36] Cave, Philip, "UCMJ Clemency & Parole," downloaded March 19, 2013, from: **http://court-martial.com/ucmj-clemency-parole/**

[37] Captain Benjamin Beliles, Assistant Trial Counsel, U.S. v Wilkerson, Record of Trial, pg 191

[38] Kim Hanks, statement April 17, 2012, U.S. v Wilkerson, Record of Trial, IO exhibit 3

[39] Kim Hanks, testimony, U.S. v Wilkerson, Record of Trial, pg 242

[40] Kim Hanks, testimony, U.S. v Wilkerson, Record of Trial, pg 262

[41] Kim Hanks, summarized Article 32 testimony, U.S. v Wilkerson, Record of Trial, IO exhibit 24

[42] Suzanne Berrong, statement, April 20, 2012, U.S. v Wilkerson, Record of Trial, IO exhibit 7

[43] Kim Hanks, testimony, U.S. v Wilkerson, Record of Trial, pg 239

[44] Kim Hanks, testimony, U.S. v Wilkerson, Record of Trial, pg 264

[45] Kim Hanks, statement April 17, 2012, U.S. v Wilkerson, Record of Trial, IO exhibit 3

[46] Kim Hanks, statement April 17, 2012, U.S. v Wilkerson, Record of Trial, IO exhibit 3

[47] Kim Hanks, statement April 17, U.S. v Wilkerson, Record of Trial, IO exhibit 3

[48] Kim Hanks, summarized Article 32 testimony, U.S. v Wilkerson, Record of Trial, IO exhibit 24

[49] Kim Hanks, testimony, U.S. v Wilkerson, Record of Trial, pg 244
[50] Suzanne Berrong, statement, April 20, 2012, U.S. v Wilkerson, Record of Trial, IO exhibit 7
[51] Major Michael O'Keefe, statement, April 25, 2012, U.S. v Wilkerson, Record of Trial, IO exhibit 20
[52] Beth Wilkerson, summarized Article 32 testimony, U.S. v Wilkerson, Record of Trial, IO exhibit 29
[53] Kim Hanks, testimony, U.S. v Wilkerson, Record of Trial, pg 234
[54] Beth Wilkerson, testimony, U.S. v Wilkerson, Record of Trial, pg 731
[55] Kim Hanks, summarized Article 32 testimony, U.S. v Wilkerson, Record of Trial, IO exhibit 24
[56] Major Tanya Manning, testimony, U.S. v Wilkerson, Record of Trial, pg 364
[57] Kim Hanks testimony, U.S. v Wilkerson, Record of Trial, pg 235
[58] Major Gerremy Goldsberry, testimony, U.S. v Wilkerson, Record of Trial, pg 586
[59] Major Gerremy Goldsberry, testimony, U.S. v Wilkerson, Record of Trial, pg 586
[60] Kim Hanks, testimony, U.S. v Wilkerson, Record of Trial, pg 285
[61] Kim Hanks, testimony, U.S. v Wilkerson, Record of Trial, pg 286
[62] Kim Hanks, testimony, U.S. v Wilkerson, Record of Trial, pg 286
[63] Kim Hanks, testimony, U.S. v Wilkerson, Record of Trial, pg 237
[64] Kim Hanks, summarized Article 32 testimony, U.S. v Wilkerson, Record of Trial, IO exhibit 24
[65] Kim Hanks, summarized Article 32 testimony, U.S. v Wilkerson, Record of Trial, IO exhibit 24
[66] Kim Hanks, testimony, U.S. v Wilkerson, Record of Trial, pg 236
[67] Kim Hanks, testimony, U.S. v Wilkerson, Record of Trial, pg 236
[68] Suzanne Berrong, summarized Article 32 testimony, U.S. v Wilkerson, Record of Trial, IO exhibit 26
[69] Investigating Officer's report, U.S. v Wilkerson, Record of Trial, pg 3
[70] Kim Hanks, statement April 17, 2012, U.S. v Wilkerson, Record of Trial, IO exhibit 3
[71] Kim Hanks, testimony, U.S. v Wilkerson, Record of Trial, pg 237
[72] Beth Wilkerson, statement, U.S. v Wilkerson, Record of Trial, IO exhibit 13
[73] Beth Wilkerson, summarized Article 32 testimony, U.S. v Wilkerson, Record of Trial, IO exhibit 29
[74] MSgt. Danielle Dunnivant, Summarized Article 32 testimony, U.S. v Wilkerson, Record of Trial, IO exhibit 25
[75] MSgt. Danielle Dunnivant, testimony, U.S. v Wilkerson, Record of Trial, pg 311
[76] Kim Hanks, testimony, U.S. v Wilkerson, Record of Trial, pg 240
[77] Major Michael O'Keefe, statement, April 25, 2012, U.S. v Wilkerson, Record of Trial, IO exhibit 20
[78] Kim Hanks, statement April 17, 2012, U.S. v Wilkerson, Record of Trial, IO exhibit 3
[79] Letter to Lt. Gen. Franklin, November 27, 2012, downloaded April 23, 2013 from: **http://www.foia.af.mil/shared/media/document/AFD-130404-223.pdf**
[80] Suzanne Berrong, statement, April 19, 2012, U.S. v Wilkerson, Record of Trial, IO exhibit 8
[81] Kim Hanks, testimony, U.S. v Wilkerson, Record of Trial, pg 253
[82] Kim Hanks, statement April 17, 2012, U.S. v Wilkerson, Record of Trial, IO exhibit 3

[83] Kim Hanks, summarized Article 32 testimony, U.S. v Wilkerson, Record of Trial, IO exhibit 24

[84] Wilcox, Robert K., 2008, *Target Patton,* Washington, D.C., Regnery Publishing, Inc., pg 326

[85] MSgt. Danielle Dunnivant, testimony, U.S. v Wilkerson, Record of Trial, pg 320

[86] Suzanne Berrong, statement, April 19, 2012, U.S. v Wilkerson, Record of Trial, IO exhibit 8

[87] U.S. v Wilkerson, Record of Trial, appellate exhibit XLII, pg 2, downloaded July 29, 2013, from: **http://www.foia.af.mil/shared/media/document/AFD-130404-049.pdf**

[88] Kim Hanks, statement April 17, 2012, U.S. v Wilkerson, Record of Trial, IO exhibit 3

[89] Kim Hanks, summarized Article 32 testimony, U.S. v Wilkerson, Record of Trial, IO exhibit 24

[90] Kim Hanks, summarized Article 32 testimony, U.S. v Wilkerson, Record of Trial, IO exhibit 24

[91] Kim Hanks, testimony, U.S. v Wilkerson, Record of Trial, pg 270

[92] Kim Hanks, summarized Article 32 testimony, U.S. v Wilkerson, Record of Trial, IO exhibit 24, pg 4

[93] Clemency package, part 2, Air Force Freedom of Information web site, Wilkerson Trial, pg 111/134, downloaded May 2, 2013, from: **http://www.foia.af.mil/shared/media/document/AFD-130404-224.pdf**

[94] Letter to Lt. Gen. Franklin, November 27, 2012, **http://www.foia.af.mil/shared/media/document/AFD-130404-223.pdf**

[95] Kim Hanks, statement April 17, 2012, U.S. v Wilkerson, Record of Trial, IO exhibit 3

[96] Kim Hanks, summarized Article 32 testimony, U.S. v Wilkerson, Record of Trial, IO exhibit 24

[97] Kim Hanks, testimony, U.S. v Wilkerson, Record of Trial, pg 242

[98] MSgt. Danielle Dunnivant, summarized Article 32 testimony, U.S. v Wilkerson, Record of Trial, IO exhibit 25

[99] Kim Hanks, testimony, U.S. v Wilkerson, Record of Trial, pg 243

[100] Kim Hanks, statement April 17, 2012, U.S. v Wilkerson, Record of Trial, IO exhibit 3

[101] Beth Wilkerson, summarized Article 32 testimony, U.S. v Wilkerson, Record of Trial, IO exhibit 29

[102] MSgt. Danielle Dunnivant, testimony, U.S. v Wilkerson, Record of Trial, pg 309

[103] MSgt. Danielle Dunnivant, testimony, U.S. v Wilkerson, Record of Trial, pg 309

[104] MSgt. Danielle Dunnivant, summarized Article 32 testimony, U.S. v Wilkerson, Record of Trial, IO exhibit 25

[105] MSgt. Danielle Dunnivant, summarized Article 32 testimony, U.S. v Wilkerson, Record of Trial, IO exhibit 25

[106] US v Wilkerson, OSI report, pg 14/34 at **http://www.foia.af.mil/shared/media/document/AFD-130403-029.pdf**

[107] MSgt. Danielle Dunnivant, testimony, U.S. v Wilkerson, Record of Trial, pg 309

[108] Suzanne Berrong, statement, April 19, 2012, U.S. v Wilkerson, Record of Trial, IO exhibit 8

[109] Suzanne Berrong, statement, April 19, 2012, U.S. v Wilkerson, Record of Trial, IO exhibit 8

[110] Major Michael O'Keefe, statement, April 25, 2012, U.S. v Wilkerson, Record of Trial, IO exhibit 20

[111] Kim Hanks, statement April 17, 2012, U.S. v Wilkerson, Record of Trial, IO exhibit 3

[112] Suzanne Berrong, statement, April 19, 2012, U.S. v Wilkerson, Record of Trial, IO exhibit 8

[113] Major Michael O'Keefe, statement, April 25, 2012, U.S. v Wilkerson, Record of Trial, IO exhibit 20

[114] Major Michael O'Keefe, testimony, U.S. v Wilkerson, Record of Trial, pg 374

[115] Kim Hanks, testimony, U.S. v Wilkerson, Record of Trial, pg 275

[116] Beth Wilkerson, summarized Article 32 testimony, U.S. v Wilkerson, Record of Trial, IO exhibit 29

[117] Kim Hanks, testimony, U.S. v Wilkerson, Record of Trial, pg 275

[118] Lt. Col. James Wilkerson, statement, April 19, 2012, U.S. v Wilkerson, Record of Trial, IO exhibit 21

[119] Beth Wilkerson, summarized Article 32 testimony, U.S. v Wilkerson, Record of Trial, IO exhibit 29

[120] Major Albert Lowe, summarized Article 32 testimony, U.S. v Wilkerson, Record of Trial, IO exhibit 28

[121] Major Gerremy Goldsberry, summarized Article 32 testimony, U.S. v Wilkerson, Record of Trial, IO exhibit 32

[122] Kim Hanks, testimony, U.S. v Wilkerson, Record of Trial, pg 275-276

[123] Letter to Lt. Gen. Franklin, from co-worker of Ms. Hanks; redacted version at **http://www.foia.af.mil/shared/media/document/AFD-130404-224.pdf. number 10/134**; The Air Force redacted the portion concerning complaints to Medical Group leadership about Ms. Hanks not wearing shoes while seeing patients

[124] Kim Hanks, testimony, U.S. v Wilkerson, Record of Trial, pg 234

[125] Kim Hanks, testimony, U.S. v Wilkerson, Record of Trial, pg 241

[126] Kim Hanks, testimony, U.S. v Wilkerson, Record of Trial, pg 277

[127] Kim Hanks, testimony, U.S. v Wilkerson, Record of Trial, pg 289

[128] U.S. v Wilkerson, Record of Trial, pg 113-129

[129] Kim Hanks, testimony, U.S. v Wilkerson, Record of Trial, pg 241

[130] Kim Hanks, testimony, U.S. v Wilkerson, Record of Trial, pg 238

[131] Kim Hanks, testimony, U.S. v Wilkerson, Record of Trial, pg 219-294

[132] Beth Wilkerson, summarized Article 32 testimony, U.S. v Wilkerson, Record of Trial, IO exhibit 29

[133] Kim Hanks, summarized Article 32 testimony, U.S. v Wilkerson, Record of Trial, IO exhibit 24

[134] Kim Hanks, testimony, U.S. v Wilkerson, Record of Trial, pg 241

[135] U.S. v Wilkerson, Record of Trial, stipulation of fact, Prosecution exhibit 4, October 30, 2012

[136] Kim Hanks, testimony, U.S. v Wilkerson, Record of Trial, pg 908

[137] Kim Hanks, testimony, U.S. v Wilkerson, Record of Trial, pg 908

[138] Colonel Don Christensen, Prosecutor, US v Wilkerson, Record of Trial, pg 952

[139] US v Wilkerson, Prosecutor closing argument, Rebuttal, Record of Trial, pg 1013

[140] US v Wilkerson, OSI report, pg 7/34 at **http://www.foia.af.mil/shared/media/document/AFD-130403-029.pdf**

[141] Kim Hanks, summarized Article 32 testimony, U.S. v Wilkerson, Record of Trial, IO exhibit 24

[142] Kim Hanks, summarized Article 32 testimony, U.S. v Wilkerson, Record of Trial, IO exhibit 24

[143] Kim Hanks, summarized Article 32 testimony, U.S. v Wilkerson, Record of Trial, IO exhibit 24

[144] Major Gerremy Goldsberry, testimony, U.S. v Wilkerson, Record of Trial, pg 586

[145] Lt. Col. Paula McCarron, Investigating Officer's report, U.S. v Wilkerson, Record of Trial, June 26, 2012, pg 2

[146] Clemency letter, addressed to Lt. Gen. Franklin, Air Force Freedom of Information website, pg 45/134, downloaded April 25, 2013, from: **http://www.foia.af.mil/shared/media/document/AFD-130404-224.pdf**

[147] Kim Hanks, testimony, U.S. v Wilkerson, Record of Trial, pg 277

[148] Kim Hanks, testimony, U.S. v Wilkerson, Record of Trial, pg 289

[149] U.S. v Wilkerson, Record of Trial, U.S. Air Force Freedom of Information website at: **http://www.foia.af.mil/reading/thewilkersonfoiacase.asp**

[150] Kim Hanks, testimony, U.S. v Wilkerson, Record of Trial, pg 223

[151] Major Tanya Manning, testimony, U.S. v Wilkerson, Record of Trial, pg 366

[152] Kim Hanks, testimony, U.S. v Wilkerson, Record of Trial, pg 223

[153] Kim Hanks, testimony, U.S. v Wilkerson, Record of Trial, pg 261

[154] Suzanne Berrong, testimony, U.S. v Wilkerson, Record of Trial, pg 617

[155] MSgt. Danielle Dunnivant, statement April 20, 2012, U.S. v Wilkerson, Record of Trial, IO exhibit 6

[156] Clemency letter, addressed to Lt. Gen. Franklin, Air Force Freedom of Information website, pg 60/134 , downloaded May 5, 2013, from: **http://www.foia.af.mil/shared/media/document/AFD-130404-224.pdf**

[157] Major Michael O'Keefe, statement, April 25, 2012, U.S. v Wilkerson, Record of Trial, IO exhibit 20

[158] Major Michael O'Keefe, testimony, U.S. v Wilkerson, Record of Trial, pg 373

[159] Major Michael O'Keefe, testimony, U.S. v Wilkerson, Record of Trial, pg 373

[160] Major Michael O'Keefe, testimony, U.S. v Wilkerson, Record of Trial, pg 373

[161] Dr. Howard Taylor, testimony, U.S. v Wilkerson, Record of Trial, pg 634

[162] Kim Hanks, testimony, U.S. v Wilkerson, Record of Trial, pg 262

[163] Suzanne Berrong, statement, April 20, 2012, U.S. v Wilkerson, Record of Trial, IO exhibit 7

[164] U.S. v Wilkerson, Record of Trial, Pg 292

[165] Suzanne Berrong, statement, April 20, 2012, U.S. v Wilkerson, Record of Trial, IO exhibit 7

[166] Kim Hanks, testimony, U.S. v Wilkerson, Record of Trial, pg 264

[167] Beth Wilkerson, summarized Article 32 testimony, U.S. v Wilkerson, Record of Trial, IO exhibit 29

[168] Kim Hanks, statement April 17, 2012, U.S. v Wilkerson, Record of Trial, IO exhibit 3

[169] Beth Wilkerson, testimony, U.S. v Wilkerson, Record of Trial, pg 731

[170] Kim Hanks, statement April 17, 2012, U.S. v Wilkerson, Record of Trial, IO exhibit 3

[171] Kim Hanks, statement April 17, 2012, U.S. v Wilkerson, Record of Trial, IO exhibit 3

[172] Kim Hanks, testimony, U.S. v Wilkerson, Record of Trial, pg 223

[173] MSgt. Danielle Dunnivant, testimony, U.S. v Wilkerson, Record of Trial, pg 304

[174] US v Wilkerson, OSI report pg 22/34 at **http://www.foia.af.mil/shared/media/document/AFD-130403-029.pdf**

[175] Major Tanya Manning, testimony, U.S. v Wilkerson, Record of Trial, pg 366

[176] US v Wilkerson, OSI report, pg 22/34 at
http://www.foia.af.mil/shared/media/document/AFD-130403-029.pdf
[177] Kim Hanks, summarized Article 32 testimony, U.S. v Wilkerson, Record of Trial, IO exhibit 24
[178] Kim Hanks, testimony, U.S. v Wilkerson, Record of Trial, pg 224-225
[179] Major Tanya Manning, statement, April 18, 2012, U.S. v Wilkerson, Record of Trial, IO exhibit 2
[180] MSgt. Danielle Dunnivant, testimony, U.S. v Wilkerson, Record of Trial, pg 312
[181] MSgt. Danielle Dunnivant, Summarized Article 32 testimony, U.S. v Wilkerson, Record of Trial, IO exhibit 25
[182] MSgt. Danielle Dunnivant, testimony, U.S. v Wilkerson, Record of Trial, pg 306
[183] Kim Hanks, summarized Article 32 testimony, IO exhibit 24, and trial testimony pg 228, U.S. v Wilkerson, Record of Trial
[184] US v Wilkerson, OSI report, pg 11/34 at
http://www.foia.af.mil/shared/media/document/AFD-130403-029.pdf
[185] Suzanne Berrong, statement, April 20, 2012, U.S. v Wilkerson, Record of Trial, IO exhibit 7
[186] Suzanne Berrong, summarized Article 32 testimony, U.S. v Wilkerson, Record of Trial, IO exhibit 26
[187] Suzanne Berrong, summarized Article 32 testimony, U.S. v Wilkerson, Record of Trial, IO exhibit 26
[188] US v Wilkerson, OSI report, pg 7/34 at
http://www.foia.af.mil/shared/media/document/AFD-130403-029.pdf
[189] US v Wilkerson, OSI report, pg 10/34 at
http://www.foia.af.mil/shared/media/document/AFD-130403-029.pdf
[190] Major Tanya Manning, summarized Article 32 testimony, U.S. v Wilkerson, Record of Trial, IO exhibit 23
[191] US v Wilkerson, OSI report, pg 14/34 at
http://www.foia.af.mil/shared/media/document/AFD-130403-029.pdf
[192] Kim Hanks, summarized Article 32 testimony, U.S. v Wilkerson, Record of Trial, IO exhibit 24
[193] Major Tanya Manning, statement, April 18, 2012, U.S. v Wilkerson, Record of Trial, IO exhibit 2
[194] Suzanne Berrong, statement, April 20, 2012, U.S. v Wilkerson, Record of Trial, IO exhibit 7
[195] Major Michael O'Keefe, statement, April 25, 2012, U.S. v Wilkerson, Record of Trial, IO exhibit 20
[196] Beth Wilkerson, testimony, U.S. v Wilkerson, Record of Trial, pg 718
[197] Kim Hanks, testimony, U.S. v Wilkerson, Record of Trial, pg 251-278
[198] Colonel Stentz, court-martial panel member, question to MSgt. Dunnivant, U.S. v Wilkerson, Record of Trial, pg 321
[199] Collymore, Joy, "Red Bull & Vodka gives you wings… and death," October 1, 2008, downloaded May 10, 2013, from: http://www.examiner.com/article/red-bull-vodka-gives-you-wings-and-death and Hsu, Christine, "Clubbers Downing 'Red Bull and Vodka' Are 600% More Likely to Suffer Heart Palpitations," August 16, 2012, downloaded May 10, 2013, from: http://www.medicaldaily.com/articles/11548/20120816/red-bull-alcohol-monster-energy-drinks-club-heart-palpitations.htm
[200] Collymore, Joy, "Red Bull & Vodka gives you wings… and death," October 1, 2008, downloaded May 10, 2013, from: http://www.examiner.com/article/red-bull-vodka-gives-you-wings-and-death

[201] Hsu, Christine, "Clubbers Downing 'Red Bull and Vodka' Are 600% More Likely to Suffer Heart Palpitations," Aug 16, 2012, downloaded May 10, 2013, from: http://www.medicaldaily.com/articles/11548/20120816/red-bull-alcohol-monster-energy-drinks-club-heart-palpitations.htm

[202] Hsu, Christine, "Clubbers Downing 'Red Bull and Vodka' Are 600% More Likely to Suffer Heart Palpitations," August 16, 2012, downloaded May 10, 2013, from: http://www.medicaldaily.com/articles/11548/20120816/red-bull-alcohol-monster-energy-drinks-club-heart-palpitations.htm

[203] Beth Wilkerson, summarized Article 32 testimony, U.S. v Wilkerson, Record of Trial, IO exhibit 29

[204] Suzanne Berrong, testimony, U.S. v Wilkerson, Record of Trial, pg 621

[205] Hsu, Christine, "Clubbers Downing 'Red Bull and Vodka' Are 600% More Likely to Suffer Heart Palpitations," August 16, 2012, downloaded May 10, 2013, from: http://www.medicaldaily.com/articles/11548/20120816/red-bull-alcohol-monster-energy-drinks-club-heart-palpitations.htm

[206] US v Wilkerson, OSI report, pg 14/34 at http://www.foia.af.mil/shared/media/document/AFD-130403-029.pdf

[207] Suzanne Berrong, statement, April 20, 2012, U.S. v Wilkerson, Record of Trial, IO exhibit 7

[208] Major Michael O'Keefe, statement, April 25, 2012, U.S. v Wilkerson, Record of Trial, IO exhibit 20

[209] Sexual Assault reporting options, Wright Patterson Air Force Base, web site, downloaded April 25, 2013 from: http://www.wpafb.af.mil/units/sarc/

[210] Kim Hanks, summarized Article 32 testimony, U.S. v Wilkerson, Record of Trial, IO exhibit 24

[211] Rodman, Lindsay L., "Fostering Constructive Dialogue on Military Sexual Assault," April 2013, Joint Forces Quarterly on line, downloaded April 3, 2013, from: http://www.ndu.edu/press/military-sexual-assault.html

[212] Rodman, Lindsay L., "Fostering Constructive Dialogue on Military Sexual Assault," April 2013, Joint Forces Quarterly on line, downloaded April 3, 2013, from: http://www.ndu.edu/press/military-sexual-assault.html

[213] Rodman, Lindsay L., "Fostering Constructive Dialogue on Military Sexual Assault," April 2013, Joint Forces Quarterly on line, downloaded April 3, 2013, from: http://www.ndu.edu/press/military-sexual-assault.html

[214] Kim Hanks, summarized Article 32 testimony, U.S. v Wilkerson, Record of Trial, IO exhibit 24

[215] Major Michael O'Keefe, statement, April 25, 2012, U.S. v Wilkerson, Record of Trial, IO exhibit 20

[216] Beth Wilkerson, interview with author, January 24, 2013, and Frank Spinner, defense counsel, interview with the author October 28, 2012

[217] Kim Hanks, summarized Article 32 testimony, U.S. v Wilkerson, Record of Trial, IO exhibit 24

[218] Beth Wilkerson, interview with author, January 24, 2013, and Frank Spinner, defense counsel, interview with the author October 28, 2012

[219] Department of Defense Instruction 6495.02, March 28, 2013, downloaded July 24, 2013, from: http://www.afpc.af.mil/shared/media/document/AFD-130416-049.pdf

[220] Major Michael O'Keefe, statement, April 25, 2012, U.S. v Wilkerson, Record of Trial, IO exhibit 20

[221] White and Meeks, LLP., downloaded August 24, 2013, from: http://www.militarylawyers.com/Article-32-Investigation.html

[222] Karns, Stephen P. ,US Military Lawyer, http://www.usmilitarylawyer.com/military-article-32-investigations.asp

[223] Investigating Officer's report, U.S. v Wilkerson, Record of Trial, pg 6
[224] Investigating Officer's report, U.S. v Wilkerson, Record of Trial, pg 6
[225] Investigating Officer's report, U.S. v Wilkerson, Record of Trial, pg 3
[226] Investigating Officer's report, U.S. v Wilkerson, Record of Trial, pg 3
[227] Investigating Officer's report, U.S. v Wilkerson, Record of Trial, pg 2
[228] Suzanne Berrong, summarized Article 32 testimony, U.S. v Wilkerson, Record of Trial, IO exhibit 26
[229] US v Wilkerson, OSI report, pg 14/34 at http://www.foia.af.mil/shared/media/document/AFD-130403-029.pdf
[230] Suzanne Berrong, summarized Article 32 testimony, U.S. v Wilkerson, Record of Trial, IO exhibit 26
[231] Beth Wilkerson, summarized Article 32 testimony, U.S. v Wilkerson, Record of Trial, IO exhibit 29
[232] Lt. Col. Paula McCarron, Investigating Officer's report, U.S. v Wilkerson, Record of Trial, pg 6
[233] Kim Hanks, summarized Article 32 testimony, U.S. v Wilkerson, Record of Trial, IO exhibit 24
[234] Investigating Officer's report, U.S. v Wilkerson, Record of Trial, pg 6
[235] Interviews with author, with two separate attorneys not associated with the case. Both request to remain unnamed in this book.
[236] Beth Wilkerson, interview with author, January 24, 2013
[237] Email from Brigadier General Zobrist to Lieutenant General Franklin, dated June 3, 2012, FOIA release, August 26, 2013, downloaded, August 26, 2013, from: http://www.foia.af.mil/reading/thewilkersonfoiacase.asp
[238] U.S. v Wilkerson, Record of Trial, Prosecutor closing argument, pg 967
[239] Suzanne Berrong statement, April 20, 2012, U.S. v Wilkerson, Record of Trial, IO exhibit 7
[240] Suzanne Berrong, statement, April 20, 2012, U.S. v Wilkerson, Record of Trial, IO exhibit 7
[241] Suzanne Berrong, statement, April 20, 2012, U.S. v Wilkerson, Record of Trial, IO exhibit 7
[242] US v Wilkerson, Record of Trial, Prosecutor closing argument, pg 943
[243] Fraternization, Militarytriallawyers.com, downloaded July 24, 2013, from: http://www.militarytriallawyers.com/fraternization.asp
[244] Colonel Dean Ostovich, testimony, U.S. v Wilkerson, US v Wilkerson, Record of Trial, pg 476
[245] Colonel Dean Ostovich, testimony, U.S. v Wilkerson, US v Wilkerson, Record of Trial, pg 486-487
[246] U.S. v Wilkerson, US v Wilkerson, Record of Trial, Prosecutor closing argument, pg 943
[247] Colonel Don Christensen, US v Wilkerson, Record of Trial, Prosecutor closing argument, pg 943
[248] US v Wilkerson, OSI report, pg 20/34 at http://www.foia.af.mil/shared/media/document/AFD-130403-029.pdf
[249] Cheryl Pone, testimony, U.S. v Wilkerson, Record of Trial, pg 574
[250] Angela Newbill, summarized Article 32 testimony, U.S. v Wilkerson, Record of Trial, IO exhibit 30
[251] Cheryl Pone, testimony, U.S. v Wilkerson, Record of Trial, pg 574
[252] Angela Newbill, interview with author, October 29, 2012
[253] Angela Newbill and Emily Ozgul, interview with author, October 29, 2012
[254] Name withheld, (spouse of military member stationed at Aviano) interview with author, November 1, 2012
[255] Emily Ozgul, testimony, U.S. v Wilkerson, Record of Trial, pg 797

[256] Lt. Col. Paula McCarron, Investigating Officer's report, U.S. v Wilkerson, Record of Trial, pg 6
[257] Beth Wilkerson, testimony, U.S. v Wilkerson, Record of Trial, pg 748-749
[258] Colonel Don Christensen, US v Wilkerson, Record of Trial, Prosecutor closing argument, pg 956-957
[259] Colonel Don Christensen, US v Wilkerson, Record of Trial, Prosecutor closing argument, pg 955-960
[260] US v Wilkerson, Record of Trial, Prosecutor closing argument, pg 967
[261] Beth Wilkerson, testimony, U.S. v Wilkerson, Record of Trial, pg 748-49 and Lt. Col. James Wilkerson, statement, April 19, 2012, U.S. v Wilkerson, Record of Trial, IO exhibit 21
[262] Beth Wilkerson, summarized Article 32 testimony, U.S. v Wilkerson, Record of Trial, IO exhibit 29, and Lt. Col. James Wilkerson, statement, April 19, 2012, U.S. v Wilkerson, Record of Trial, IO exhibit 21
[263] Colonel Don Christensen, US v Wilkerson, Record of Trial, Prosecutor closing argument, pg 955-960
[264] US v Wilkerson, Record of Trial, Prosecutor closing argument, pg 953
[265] Letter to Lt. Gen. Franklin, December 10, 2012, pg 60/134 downloaded June 29, 2013, from: **http://www.foia.af.mil/shared/media/document/AFD-130404-224.pdf**
[266] Colonel Don Christensen, US v Wilkerson, Record of Trial, Prosecutor closing argument, pg 957
[267] Colonel Don Christensen, US v Wilkerson, Record of Trial, Prosecutor closing argument, pg 957
[268] Colonel Don Christensen, US v Wilkerson, Record of Trial, Prosecutor closing argument rebuttal, pg 1014
[269] Major Dawn Brock, testimony, US v Wilkerson, Record of Trial, pg 324
[270] Major Dawn Brock, testimony, US v Wilkerson, Record of Trial, pg 340; Major Gerremy Goldsberry, testimony, US v Wilkerson, Record of Trial, pg 584; Beth Wilkerson, testimony, US v Wilkerson, Record of Trial, pg 705
[271] Major Dawn Brock, testimony, US v Wilkerson, Record of Trial, pg 341
[272] Beth Wilkerson, testimony, U.S. v Wilkerson, Record of Trial, pg 703
[273] Major Dawn Brock, testimony, US v Wilkerson, Record of Trial, pg 342
[274] Beth Wilkerson, testimony, US v Wilkerson, Record of Trial, pg 705
[275] Major Dawn Brock, testimony, US v Wilkerson, Record of Trial, pg 342
[276] Major Dawn Brock, testimony, US v Wilkerson, Record of Trial, pg 343-350
[277] Kim Hanks, testimony, U.S. v Wilkerson, Record of Trial, pg 232 and pg 255
[278] Major Dawn Brock, testimony, US v Wilkerson, Record of Trial, pg 348
[279] Major Tanya Manning, testimony, US v Wilkerson, Record of Trial, pg 367
[280] Major Tanya Manning, testimony, US v Wilkerson, Record of Trial, pg 363
[281] US v Wilkerson, Record of Trial, OSI interview with Lt. Col. Wilkerson from the Air Force Freedom of Information web site at: **http://www.foia.af.mil/reading/thewilkersonfoiacase.asp**
[282] Major Dawn Brock, testimony, US v Wilkerson, Record of Trial, pg 342
[283] Major Gerremy Goldsberry, US v Wilkerson, Record of Trial, Summarized Article 32 testimony, IO exhibit 32
[284] Major Albert Lowe, US v Wilkerson, Record of Trial, Summarized Article 32 testimony, IO exhibit 28
[285] Colonel Don Christensen, US v Wilkerson, Record of Trial, Prosecutor closing argument, pg 954
[286] Colonel Don Christensen, US v Wilkerson, Record of Trial, Prosecutor closing argument, pg 1020

[287] Colonel Don Christensen, US v Wilkerson, Record of Trial, Prosecutor closing argument, pg 964

[288] Colonel Don Christensen, US v Wilkerson, Record of Trial, Prosecutor closing argument, pg 943

[289] Colonel Don Christensen, U.S. v Wilkerson, Record of Trial, closing argument, pg 938

[290] Colonel Don Christensen, U.S. v Wilkerson, Record of Trial, closing argument, pg 956

[291] Colonel Don Christensen, U.S. v Wilkerson, Record of Trial, closing argument, pg 966

[292] Colonel Don Christensen, U.S. v Wilkerson, Record of Trial, closing argument, pg 938-967

[293] The person at Mannheim prison requests to remain anonymous for fear of retribution.

[294] U.S. v Wilkerson, Record of Trial, appellate exhibit XLII, pg 2, downloaded July 29, 2013, from: **http://www.foia.af.mil/shared/media/document/AFD-130404-049.pdf**

[295] Montgomery, Nancy, November 2, 2012, "Former Aviano IG is found guilty in sexual assault case," *Stars and Stripes,* downloaded June 4, 2013, from: **http://www.stripes.com/news/former-aviano-ig-is-found-guilty-in-sexual-assault-case-1.195656**

[296] Montgomery, Nancy, November 2, 2012, "Former Aviano IG is found guilty in sexual assault case," *Stars and Stripes,* downloaded June 4, 2013, from: **http://www.stripes.com/news/former-aviano-ig-is-found-guilty-in-sexual-assault-case-1.195656**

[297] Letter to Lt. Gen. Franklin, dated December 19, 2012, pg 119/134, downloaded May 28, 2013, from: **http://www.foia.af.mil/shared/media/document/AFD-130404-224.pdf**

[298] Bazelon, Emily and Larimore, Rachael; Oct. 1, 2009, "How Often Do Women Falsely Cry Rape? The question the Hofstra disaster left dangling," Slate.com, downloaded, May 28, 2013, from: **http://www.slate.com/articles/news_and_politics/jurisprudence/2009/10/how_often_do_women_falsely_cry_rape.html**

[299] McElroy, Wendy, "False Rape Accusations May Be More Common Than Thought," May 2, 2006, downloaded March 21, 2013, from: **http://www.foxnews.com/story/0,2933,194032,00.html**

[300] Nancy Parrish, Protect Our Defenders, email to author, March 5, 2013

[301] Angelucci, Marc, and Sacks, Glenn, 2012, "Research shows false allegations of rape common," *Los Angeles Daily Journal,* September 15, 2004, downloaded June 30, 2013, from: **http://www.glennsacks.com/research_shows_false.htm**

[302] Silverman, Craig, February 2, 2004, "Craig's Court: I Call Them As I See Them," downloaded June 2, 2013 from: **http://web.archive.org/web/20050404230831/http://www.thedenverchannel.com/kobebryanttrial/2812198/detail.html**

[303] Gross, Bruce, PhD, JD, MBA, "False Rape Allegations: An Assault On Justice," downloaded March 15, 2013, from: **http://www.theforensicexaminer.com/archive/spring09/15/**;

[304] Gross, Bruce, PhD, JD, MBA, "False Rape Allegations: An Assault On Justice," downloaded March 15, 2013, from: **http://www.theforensicexaminer.com/archive/spring09/15/**;

[305] McElroy, Wendy, "False Rape Accusations May Be More Common Than Thought," May 2, 2006, downloaded March 21, 2013, from: **http://www.foxnews.com/story/0,2933,194032,00.html**

[306] McElroy, Wendy, "False Rape Accusations May Be More Common Than Thought," May 2, 2006, downloaded March 21, 2013, from: http://www.foxnews.com/story/0,2933,194032,00.html

[307] McElroy, Wendy, "False Rape Accusations May Be More Common Than Thought," May 2, 2006, downloaded March 21, 2013, from: http://www.foxnews.com/story/0,2933,194032,00.html

[308] Department of Defense Annual Report on Sexual Assault in the Military, Volume 1, Fiscal Year 2012, exhibit 16, pg 80, downloaded May 30, 2013, from: http://www.sapr.mil/media/pdf/reports/FY12_DoD_SAPRO_Annual_Report_on_Sexual_Assault-VOLUME_ONE.pdf

[309] Bazelon, Emily and Larimore, Rachael, October 1, 2009, "How Often Do Women Falsely Cry Rape? The question the Hofstra disaster left dangling," Slate.com, downloaded March 21, 2013, from: http://www.slate.com/articles/news_and_politics/jurisprudence/2009/10/how_often_do_women_falsely_cry_rape.html

[310] McElroy, Wendy, "False Rape Accusations May Be More Common Than Thought," May 2, 2006, downloaded March 21, 2013, from: http://www.foxnews.com/story/0,2933,194032,00.html

[311] Floyd, John and Sinclair, Billy August 25, 2012, "Cry Rape: False Allegations Destroy Lives," downloaded March 21, 2013, from: http://www.johntfloyd.com/blog/2012/08/cry-rape-false-allegations-destroy-lives/

[312] Grisham, John, The Innocent Man; 2006, Doubleday, Random House, Inc. http://www.innocenceproject.org/Content/Ron_Williamson.php

[313] US v Wilkerson, Record of Trial, Investigating Officer's report, pg 6

[314] Colonel Don Christensen, US v Wilkerson, Record of Trial, closing argument, pg 966

[315] MSgt. Daniel Dunnivant, statement to OSI, U.S. v Wilkerson, Record of Trial, IO exhibit 5

[316] MSgt. Daniel Dunnivant, statement to OSI, U.S. v Wilkerson, Record of Trial, IO exhibit 5

[317] US v Wilkerson, OSI report, pg 14/34, downloaded April 23, 2013, from: http://www.foia.af.mil/shared/media/document/AFD-130403-029.pdf

[318] Dr. Howard Taylor, testimony, U.S. v Wilkerson, Record of Trial, pg 634

[319] Suzanne Berrong, statement, April 20, 2012, US v Wilkerson, Record of Trial, IO exhibit 7

[320] Suzanne Berrong, summarized Article 32 testimony, US v Wilkerson, Record of Trial, IO exhibit 26

[321] Letter to Lt. Gen. Franklin, dated December 19, 2012, pg 18/134, downloaded May 28, 2013, from: http://www.foia.af.mil/shared/media/document/AFD-130404-224.pdf; note: although the Air Force redacted the name on this letter, it is clear this is Major Manning writing by her details of the evening as confirmed by her written statement, Article 32 and trial testimony in the Record of Trial.

[322] US v Wilkerson, OSI report, pg 14/34 at http://www.foia.af.mil/shared/media/document/AFD-130403-029.pdf, and Suzanne Berrong, summarized Article 32 testimony, US v Wilkerson, Record of Trial, IO exhibit 26

[323] Letter to Lt. Gen. Franklin, dated December 15, 2012, pg 20/134, downloaded May 28, 2013, from: http://www.foia.af.mil/shared/media/document/AFD-130404-224.pdf

[324] Floyd, John and Sinclair, Billy, August 25, 2012, "Cry Rape: False Allegations Destroy Lives," downloaded March 21, 2013, from:
http://www.johntfloyd.com/blog/2012/08/cry-rape-false-allegations-destroy-lives/

[325] Floyd, John and Sinclair, Billy, August 25, 2012, "Cry Rape: False Allegations Destroy Lives," downloaded March 21, 2013 from:
http://www.johntfloyd.com/blog/2012/08/cry-rape-false-allegations-destroy-lives/

[326] "How to Avoid a False Rape Claim, A Voice for Men," downloaded March 24, 2013, from **http://www.avoiceformen.com/miscellaneous/how-to-avoid-a-false-rape-claim/**

[327] Gross, Bruce, PhD, JD, MBA, "False Rape Allegations: An Assault On Justice," downloaded March 15, 2013, from:
http://www.theforensicexaminer.com/archive/spring09/15/

[328] Kim Hanks' summarized Article 32 testimony, US v Wilkerson, Record of Trial, IO exhibit 24

[329] Gross, Bruce, PhD, JD, MBA, "False Rape Allegations: An Assault On Justice," downloaded March 15, 2013, from:
http://www.theforensicexaminer.com/archive/spring09/15/

[330] Gross, Bruce, PhD, JD, MBA, "False Rape Allegations: An Assault On Justice," downloaded March 15, 2013, from:
http://www.theforensicexaminer.com/archive/spring09/15/

[331] Gross, Bruce, PhD, JD, MBA, "False Rape Allegations: An Assault On Justice," downloaded March 15, 2013, from:
http://www.theforensicexaminer.com/archive/spring09/15/

[332] Gross, Bruce, PhD, JD, MBA, "False Rape Allegations: An Assault On Justice," downloaded March 15, 2013, from:
http://www.theforensicexaminer.com/archive/spring09/15/

[333] Gross, Bruce, PhD, JD, MBA, "False Rape Allegations: An Assault On Justice," downloaded March 15, 2013, from:
http://www.theforensicexaminer.com/archive/spring09/15/

[334] Kim Hanks, summarized Article 32 testimony, US v Wilkerson, Record of Trial, IO exhibit 24

[335] Gross, Bruce, PhD, JD, MBA, "False Rape Allegations: An Assault On Justice," downloaded March 15, 2013, from:
http://www.theforensicexaminer.com/archive/spring09/15/

[336] "Why RADAR Finds McDowell's Research and Kanin's Research Credible," downloaded May 31, 2013, from:
http://www.mediaradar.org/mcdowell_kanin_credible.php

[337] Savino, John O. and Turvey, Brent E., (2011), *The Rape Investigation Handbook*, Waltham, Mass., Academic Press, Elsevier

[338] MSgt. Daniel Dunnivant, statement, IO exhibit 5, Suzanne Berrong statement, IO exhibit 7, and Kim Hanks' summarized Article 32 testimony, IO exhibit 24, pg 3, U.S. v Wilkerson, Record of Trial

[339] Savino, John O. and Turvey, Brent E., (2011), *The Rape Investigation Handbook*, Waltham, Mass., Academic Press, Elsevier

[340] Kim Hanks, testimony, U.S. v Wilkerson, Record of Trial, pg 908

[341] Savino, John O. and Turvey, Brent E., (2011), *The Rape Investigation Handbook*, Waltham, Mass., Academic Press, Elsevier

[342] Kim Hanks, summarized Article 32 testimony, U.S. v Wilkerson, Record of Trial, IO exhibit 24

[343] Savino, John O. and Turvey, Brent E., (2011), *The Rape Investigation Handbook*, Waltham, Mass., Academic Press, Elsevier

[344] MSgt. Dunnivant, Summarized Article 32 testimony, U.S. v Wilkerson, Record of Trial, IO exhibit 25

[345] US v Wilkerson, OSI report, pg 14/34 at **http://www.foia.af.mil/shared/media/document/AFD-130403-029.pdf**

[346] U.S. v Wilkerson, Record of Trial, Investigating Officer's report, pg 6

[347] Major Tanya Manning, summarized Article 32 testimony, U.S. v Wilkerson, Record of Trial, IO exhibit 23

[348] Savino, John O. and Turvey, Brent E., (2011), *The Rape Investigation Handbook*, Waltham, Mass., Academic Press, Elsevier

[349] U.S. v Wilkerson, Record of Trial, Investigating Officer's report, pg 6

[350] Major Tanya Manning, summarized Article 32 testimony, U.S. v Wilkerson, Record of Trial, IO exhibit 23

[351] Savino, John O. and Turvey, Brent E., (2011), *The Rape Investigation Handbook*, Waltham, Mass., Academic Press, Elsevier

[352] Savino, John O. and Turvey, Brent E., (2011), *The Rape Investigation Handbook*, Waltham, Mass., Academic Press, Elsevier

[353] Kim Hanks, statement April 17, 2012, U.S. v Wilkerson, Record of Trial, IO exhibit 3

[354] Kim Hanks, summarized Article 32 testimony, U.S. v Wilkerson, Record of Trial, IO exhibit 24

[355] U.S. v Wilkerson, Record of Trial, USAF Freedom of Information website, exhibit pgs 201-225, downloaded May 31, 2013, from: **http://www.foia.af.mil/shared/media/document/AFD-130404-038.pdf**

[356] Savino, John O. and Turvey, Brent E., (2011), *The Rape Investigation Handbook*, Waltham, Mass., Academic Press, Elsevier

[357] Savino, John O. and Turvey, Brent E., (2011), *The Rape Investigation Handbook*, Waltham, Mass., Academic Press, Elsevier

[358] Gross, Bruce, PhD, JD, MBA, "False Rape Allegations: An Assault On Justice," downloaded March 15, 2013, from: **http://www.theforensicexaminer.com/archive/spring09/15/**

[359] Kim Hanks, testimony, U.S. v Wilkerson, Record of Trial, pg 236

[360] US v Wilkerson, OSI report, pg 14/34 at **http://www.foia.af.mil/shared/media/document/AFD-130403-029.pdf**

[361] Hsu, Christine, "Clubbers Downing 'Red Bull and Vodka' Are 600% More Likely to Suffer Heart Palpitations," August 16, 2012, downloaded May 10, 2013, from: **http://www.medicaldaily.com/articles/11548/20120816/red-bull-alcohol-monster-energy-drinks-club-heart-palpitations.htm**

[362] "The dangers of vodka red bull. Red bull cocktails," downloaded July 31, 2013, from: **http://recoveringaddict.hubpages.com/hub/dangers-of-vodka-red-bull-**

[363] Kim Hanks, summarized Article 32 testimony, U.S. v Wilkerson, Record of Trial, IO exhibit 24, pg 2

[364] Email from Brigadier General Zobrist to Lieutenant General Franklin, dated June 3, 2012, FOIA release, August 26, 2013, downloaded August 26, 2013 from: **http://www.foia.af.mil/reading/thewilkersonfoiacase.asp**

[365] Suzanne Berrong, email on prosecution threats, February 5, 2013; Sent to this author and Lt. Gen. Franklin

[366] Gross, Bruce, PhD, JD, MBA, False Rape Allegations: An Assault On Justice; downloaded March 15, 2013, from: **http://www.theforensicexaminer.com/archive/spring09/15/**

[367] Gross, Bruce, PhD, JD, MBA, False Rape Allegations: An Assault On Justice; downloaded March 15, 2013, from: **http://www.theforensicexaminer.com/archive/spring09/15/**

[368] Cave, Philip, "UCMJ Clemency & Parole," downloaded March 19, 2013, from: **http://court-martial.com/ucmj-clemency-parole/**

[369] Captain Jeffrey Martin, Area Defense Counsel, U.S. v Wilkerson, email dated November 19, 2012

[370] Captain Jeffrey Martin, Area Defense Counsel, U.S. v Wilkerson, letter dated November 19, 2012

[371] Bob Harvey, email to Wilkerson support group, November 19, 2012. Provided by author.

[372] Letter to Lt. Gen. Franklin, dated December 19, 2012, pg 18/134, downloaded May 28, 2013, from: **http://www.foia.af.mil/shared/media/document/AFD-130404-224.pdf**; note: although the Air Force redacted the name on this letter, it is clear this is Major Manning writing by her details of the evening as confirmed by her written statement, Article 32 and trial testimony in the Record of Trial

[373] Letter to Lt. Gen. Franklin, dated December 19, 2012, pg 62/134, downloaded May 28, 2013, from: **http://www.foia.af.mil/shared/media/document/AFD-130404-224.pdf**; note: although the Air Force redacted the name on this letter, it is clear this is Suzanne Berrong writing by her details of the evening as confirmed by her written statement, Article 32 and trial testimony in the Record of Trial

[374] Suzanne Berrong summarized Article 32 testimony, U.S. v Wilkerson, Record of Trial, IO exhibit 26

[375] Letter to Lt. Gen. Franklin, dated December 15, 2012, pg 20/134, downloaded May 28, 2013, from: **http://www.foia.af.mil/shared/media/document/AFD-130404-224.pdf**

[376] Letter to Lt. Gen. Franklin, dated December 20, 2012, pg 60/134, downloaded May 28, 2013, from: **http://www.foia.af.mil/shared/media/document/AFD-130404-224.pdf**

[377] Colonel Joseph Bialke, Addendum to Addendum to Staff Judge Advocate's Recommendation – United States v. Lieutenant colonel James H. Wilkerson, February 25, 2013, pg 93/134, downloaded May 28, 2013, from: **http://www.foia.af.mil/shared/media/document/AFD-130404-224.pdf**

[378] Colonel Joseph Bialke, Addendum to Addendum to Staff Judge Advocate's Recommendation – United States v. Lieutenant Colonel James H. Wilkerson, February 25, 2013, pg 93/134, downloaded May 28, 2013, from: **http://www.foia.af.mil/shared/media/document/AFD-130404-224.pdf**

[379] Lieutenant Colonel James Wilkerson, letter to Lt. Gen. Franklin, February 21, 2013, pg 101/134, downloaded May 28, 2013, from: **http://www.foia.af.mil/shared/media/document/AFD-130404-224.pdf**

[380] Colonel Joseph Bialke, Addendum to Addendum to Staff Judge Advocate's Recommendation – United States v. Lieutenant Colonel James H. Wilkerson, February 25, 2013, pg 93/134, downloaded May 28, 2013, from: **http://www.foia.af.mil/shared/media/document/AFD-130404-224.pdf**

[381] Colonel Don Christensen, Prosecuting Attorney, U.S. v Wilkerson, pg 71/134, downloaded July 29, 2013, from: **http://www.foia.af.mil/shared/media/document/AFD-130404-224.pdf**

[382] Colonel Don Christensen, Affidavit dated January 24, 2013, pg 71/134, downloaded May 28, 2013, from: **http://www.foia.af.mil/shared/media/document/AFD-130404-224.pdf**

[383] Colonel Don Christensen, Prosecuting Attorney, U.S. v Wilkerson, pg 71/134, downloaded July 29, 2013, from: **http://www.foia.af.mil/shared/media/document/AFD-130404-224.pdf**

[384] Colonel Don Christensen, Prosecuting Attorney, U.S. v Wilkerson, pg 71/134, downloaded July 29, 2013, from:
http://www.foia.af.mil/shared/media/document/AFD-130404-224.pdf
[385] Captain Jeffrey Martin, Letter to Lt. Gen. Franklin, dated February 22, 2013, pg 96/134, downloaded May 28, 2013, from:
http://www.foia.af.mil/shared/media/document/AFD-130404-224.pdf
[386] Letter to Lt. Gen. Franklin, dated January 29, 2013, pg 84/134, downloaded May 28, 2013, from: **http://www.foia.af.mil/shared/media/document/AFD-130404-224.pdf**; note: although the Air Force redacted the name on this letter, it is clear this is Ms Hanks writing by her details of the evening as confirmed by her written statement, Article 32 and trial testimony in the Record of Trial.
[387] Letter to Lt. Gen. Franklin, dated January 29, 2013, pg 84/134, downloaded May 28, 2013, from: **http://www.foia.af.mil/shared/media/document/AFD-130404-224.pdf**; note: although the Air Force redacted the name on this letter, it is clear this is Ms Hanks writing by her details of the evening as confirmed by her written statement, Article 32 and trial testimony in the Record of Trial.
[388] Sex Assault Clemency Surprised Prosecutor, April 22, 2013, downloaded May 19, 2013, from:
http://www.airforcetimes.com/article/20130422/NEWS/304220007/Sex-assault-clemency-surprised-prosecutor
[389] General Franklin's memo the Secretary of the Air Force, March 12, 2013, downloaded May 31, 2013, from:
http://www.foia.af.mil/shared/media/document/AFD-130403-022.pdf
[390] Montgomery, Nancy, April 12, 2013, "Overturning verdict was right decision, general says," *Stars and Stripes*, downloaded June 3, 2013, from:
http://www.stripes.com/news/overturning-verdict-was-right-decision-general-says-1.216406
[391] Kim Hanks, summarized Article 32 testimony, U.S. v Wilkerson, Record of Trial, IO exhibit 24
[392] Dao, James, April 17, 2012, "Panetta Proposes New Sexual Assault Rules for the Military," *The New York Times online*, downloaded June 2, 2013, from:
http://atwar.blogs.nytimes.com/2012/04/17/panetta-proposes-new-sexual-assault-rules-for-the-military/ and Doyle, Michael, "Tough talk by Marine Commandant James Amos complicates sexual-assault cases," McClatchy Newspapers, downloaded June 2, 2013, from:
http://www.mcclatchydc.com/2012/09/13/168410/tough-talk-by-marine-commandant.html
[393] Doyle, Michael, "Tough talk by Marine Commandant James Amos complicates sexual-assault cases," McClatchy Newspapers, downloaded June 2, 2013, from:
http://www.mcclatchydc.com/2012/09/13/168410/tough-talk-by-marine-commandant.html
[394] Colonel Don Christensen, U.S. v Wilkerson, Record of Trial, pg 533
[395] Klimas, Jacqueline, May 29, 2013, "Annapolis rape trial: Alleged victim takes the stand," *Navy Times online*, downloaded June 2, 2013, from:
http://www.navytimes.com/article/20130529/NEWS/305290025/Annapolis-rape-trial-Alleged-victim-takes-stand
[396] Klimas, Jacqueline, June 1, 2013, "Marine major found not guilty of raping mid," *The Marine Corps Times online,* downloaded June 2, 2013, from:
http://www.marinecorpstimes.com/article/20130601/NEWS06/306010004/Marine-major-found-not-guilty-raping-mid
[397] Kim Hanks, summarized Article 32 testimony, U.S. v Wilkerson, Record of Trial, IO exhibit 24, pg 2

[398] Klimas, Jacqueline, May 29, 2013, "Annapolis rape trial: Alleged victim takes the stand," *Navy Times online,* downloaded June 2, 2013, from: **http://www.navytimes.com/article/20130529/NEWS/305290025/Annapolis-rape-trial-Alleged-victim-takes-stand**

[399] Cave, Philip, D., "UCMJ and Sexual Assault Accusations, It could happen to you," downloaded June 2, 2013, from: **http://www.court-martial.com/Practice-Areas/Under-Investigation/UCMJ-And-Sexual-Assault-Accusations.shtml**

[400] Cave, Philip, D., "UCMJ and Sexual Assault Accusations, It could happen to you," downloaded June 2, 2013, from: **http://www.court-martial.com/Practice-Areas/Under-Investigation/UCMJ-And-Sexual-Assault-Accusations.shtml**

[401] Cave, Philip, D., "UCMJ and Sexual Assault Accusations, It could happen to you," downloaded June 2, 2013, from: **http://www.court-martial.com/Practice-Areas/Under-Investigation/UCMJ-And-Sexual-Assault-Accusations.shtml**

[402] Grisham, John, *The Innocent Man,* 2006, **http://www.innocenceproject.org/Content/Ron_Williamson.php**

[403] List of sexual assault articles, downloaded June 2, 2013, from: **http://www.stripes.com/search-7.269?q=sexual+assault&x=0&y=0** and **http://www.afneurope.net/**

[404] Frank Spinner, Defense Attorney, U.S. v Wilkerson, interview with author, October 29, 2012

[405] TSgt Jameon Speed, U.S. v Wilkerson, Record of Trial, pg 864

[406] Colonel Don Christensen, U.S. v Wilkerson, Record of Trial, closing argument, pg 966

[407] Montgomery, Nancy, "Air Force strengthens sex assault prosecutions with new measures," January 9, 2013, *Stars and Stripes,* downloaded January 10, 2013, from: **http://www.stripes.com/news/air-force-strengthens-sex-assault-prosecutions-with-new-measures-1.203291**

[408] Doyle, Michael and Taylor, Marisa, "Bureaucracy has blossomed in military's war on rape," McClatchy Newspapers, **http://www.mcclatchydc.com/2011/11/28/131524/bureaucracy-has-blossomed-in-militarys.html**

[409] Captain Benjamin Beliles, U.S. v Wilkerson, Record of Trial, pg 1077

[410] Letter to Lt. Gen. Franklin, December 10, 2012, pg 45/134 downloaded June 29, 2013, from: **http://www.foia.af.mil/shared/media/document/AFD-130404-224.pdf**

[411] Brigadier General Scott Zobrist, email to Lt. Gen. Franklin, June 3, 2012, downloaded September 3, 2013, from: **http://www.foia.af.mil/shared/media/document/AFD-130821-017.pdf**

[412] Frank Spinner, Defense Counsel, closing argument, U.S. v Wilkerson, Record of Trial, pg 1000-1001

[413] Air Force Office of Special Investigations, Printable Fact Sheet, *Posted 5/9/2011,* downloaded April 28, 2013, from: **http://www.osi.af.mil/library/factsheets/factsheet.asp?id=4848**

[414] These general officers I spoke with request to remain unidentified. Even at the General Officer level, there is fear of repercussions if one is associated with this case.

[415] U.S. v Wilkerson, Record of Trial, OSI report, pg 6, downloaded, April 23, 2013, from: **http://www.foia.af.mil/shared/media/document/AFD-130403-029.pdf**

[416] Special Agent Derrick Neives, testimony, US v Wilkerson, Record of Trial, pg 820

[417] US v Wilkerson, Record of Trial, OSI interview with Lt. Col. Wilkerson from the Air Force Freedom of Information web site at: **http://www.foia.af.mil/reading/thewilkersonfoiacase.asp**

[418] U.S. v Wilkerson, Record of Trial, OSI report, pg 32, downloaded April 23, 2013, from: **http://www.foia.af.mil/shared/media/document/AFD-130403-029.pdf**

[419] U.S. v Wilkerson, Record of Trial, OSI report, pg 32, downloaded, April 23, 2013, from: **http://www.foia.af.mil/shared/media/document/AFD-130403-029.pdf**

[420] American Psychological Association, "The Truth About Lie Detectors (aka Polygraph Tests)," downloaded November 11, 2013, from: http://www.apa.org/research/action/polygraph.aspx

[421] American Psychological Association, "The Truth About Lie Detectors (aka Polygraph Tests)," downloaded, November 11, 2013, from: http://www.apa.org/research/action/polygraph.aspx

[422] US v Wilkerson, Record of Trial, OSI interview with Lt. Col. Wilkerson from the Air Force Freedom of Information web site at: **http://www.foia.af.mil/reading/thewilkersonfoiacase.asp**

[423] American Psychological Association, "The Truth About Lie Detectors (aka Polygraph Tests)," downloaded, November 11, 2013, from: http://www.apa.org/research/action/polygraph.aspx

[424] U.S. v Wilkerson, OSI interview with Lt. Col. Wilkerson from the Air Force Freedom of Information web site at: **http://www.foia.af.mil/reading/thewilkersonfoiacase.asp**

[425] I have personally seen the OSI use this technique to gain additional information. Additionally, in interviews with the Wilkersons and four other witnesses in this case, each said the OSI used the same technique.

[426] Special Agent Derrick Neives, testimony, US v Wilkerson, Record of Trial, pg 819

[427] Beth Wilkerson, testimony, US v Wilkerson, Record of Trial, pg 759

[428] Dao, James, posted April 17, 2012, "Panetta Proposes New Sexual Assault Rules for the Military," *New York Times* website, downloaded April 29, 2013, from: **http://atwar.blogs.nytimes.com/2012/04/17/panetta-proposes-new-sexual-assault-rules-for-the-military/**

[429] "Sex Assault Clemency Surprised Prosecutor," April 22, 2013, downloaded May, 19, 2013, from: **http://www.airforcetimes.com/article/20130422/NEWS/304220007/Sex-assault-clemency-surprised-prosecutor**

[430] Waddington, Michael, "Courts Martial Trial Practice & Procedure," Ezine Articles, downloaded July 28, 2013, from: **http://ezinearticles.com/?Courts-Martial-Trial-Practice-and-Procedure&id=875540**

[431] U.S. v Wilkerson, US v Wilkerson, Record of Trial, pg 859

[432] Author's personal observation during jury selection

[433] Colonel Don Christensen was overheard to say this by several witnesses in the hallway during jury selection

[434] Letter to Lt. Gen. Franklin, December 10, 2012, pg 45/134 downloaded June 29, 2013 from: **http://www.foia.af.mil/shared/media/document/AFD-130404-224.pdf**

[435] "Sex Assault Clemency Surprised Prosecutor," April 22, 2013, downloaded May 19, 2013, from: **http://www.airforcetimes.com/article/20130422/NEWS/304220007/Sex-assault-clemency-surprised-prosecutor**

[436] Letter to Gen.Franklin about Col. Christensen's behavior, dated December 11, 2012, pg 7/134 from the Air Force Freedom of Information website, downloaded May 20, 2013, from:
http://www.foia.af.mil/shared/media/document/AFD-130404-224.pdf

[437] Letter to Gen.Franklin about Col. Christensen's behavior, dated February 23, 2013, pg 130/134 from the Air Force Freedom of Information website, downloaded May 20, 2013, from:
http://www.foia.af.mil/shared/media/document/AFD-130404-224.pdf

[438] Letter to Gen.Franklin about Col. Christensen's behavior, dated February 20, 2013, pg 125/134 from the Air Force Freedom of Information website, downloaded May 20, 2013, from:
http://www.foia.af.mil/shared/media/document/AFD-130404-224.pdf. Note, this letter was followed with another. The author wishes to remain unidentified.

[439] Air Force Instruction 36-703, downloaded April 23, 2013, from:
http://www.e-publishing.af.mil/shared/media/epubs/AFI36-703.pdf.

[440] Colonel Don Christensen, US v Wilkerson, Record of Trial, Prosecutor closing argument, pg 1020

[441] Suzanne Berrong email on prosecution threats, February 5, 2013; sent to this author and Lt. Gen. Franklin.

[442] U.S. Court of Appeals for the Armed Forces. UNITED STATES, v. Adam D. DOUGLAS, Senior Airman, U.S. Air Force, Appellant. 68 M.J. 349, downloaded September 2, 2013, from:
http://webcache.googleusercontent.com/search?q=cache:4G6BHmPG8kQJ:w ww.armfor.uscourts.gov/opinions/2009SepTerm/09-0466.pdf+U.S.+Court+of+Appeals+for+the+Armed+Forces.+UNITED+STA TES,+v.+Adam+D.+DOUGLAS,+Senior+Airman,+U.S.+Air+Force,+Appella nt.+68+M.J.+349.&cd=1&hl=en&ct=clnk&gl=us

[443] Brigadier General Pamela Milligan, email to author, April 22, 2013

[444] Letter to Gen. Franklin about Col. Christensen's behavior, dated Dec. 15, 2012, pg 19/134 from the Air Force Freedom of Information website, downloaded May 20, 2013, from:
http://www.foia.af.mil/shared/media/document/AFD-130404-224.pdf

[445] Email to author, February 2, 2013. Writer wishes to remain unnamed due to his active duty status and fear of retribution.

[446] Sex Assault Clemency Surprised Prosecutor, April 22, 2013, downloaded May 19, 2013, from:
http://www.airforcetimes.com/article/20130422/NEWS/304220007/Sex-assault-clemency-surprised-prosecutor

[447] Cornell University Law School's Legal Information Institute says, "It is customary in many courts during direct or cross-examination for an attorney to ask the presiding judge for permission before approaching the witness on the stand." **http://www.law.cornell.edu/wex/permission_to_approach_the_witnes s**; The Rules of Practice Before Army Courts-Martial, March 26, 2012, says "Counsel will not first approach a witness without asking prior permission of the judge."
https://www.jagcnet.army.mil/Portals/USArmyTJ.nsf/(JAGCNetDocID)/122 A45612911AD2B852571F8006A5487/$FILE/Army%20Judiciary%20Rules%2 0of%20Court%20(26%20March%202012)%20FINAL.pdf ; and the New York State Unified Court System rule is "Do not approach a witness without permission of the Court."
http://www.nycourts.gov/courts/11jd/supreme/civilterm/partrules/civil_part rules_35.shtml

[448] Letter to Gen.Franklin about Col. Christensen's behavior, dated February 20, 2013, pg 45/134 from the Air Force Freedom of Information website, downloaded May 20, 2013, from: **http://www.foia.af.mil/shared/media/document/AFD-130404-224.pdf**.

[449] "Sex Assault Clemency Surprised Prosecutor," April 22, 2013, downloaded May 19, 2013, from: **http://www.airforcetimes.com/article/20130422/NEWS/304220007/Sex-assault-clemency-surprised-prosecutor**

[450] Letter to Gen.Franklin about Col. Christensen's behavior, dated February 20, 2013, pg 45/134 from the Air Force Freedom of Information website, downloaded May 20, 2013, from: **http://www.foia.af.mil/shared/media/document/AFD-130404-224.pdf**.

[451] Kim Hanks, summarized Article 32 testimony, U.S. v Wilkerson, Record of Trial, IO exhibit 24

[452] Beth Wilkerson, statement, U.S. v Wilkerson, Record of Trial, IO exhibit 13and Lt. Col. James Wilkerson, statement, April 19, 2012, U.S. v Wilkerson, Record of Trial, IO exhibit 21

[453] US v Wilkerson, OSI report, pg 14/34 at **http://www.foia.af.mil/shared/media/document/AFD-130403-029.pdf**

[454] Colonel Don Christensen, US v Wilkerson, Record of Trial, Prosecutor closing argument, pg 952

[455] Kim Hanks, testimony, U.S. v Wilkerson, Record of Trial, pg 238

[456] What's a JAG? Downloaded May 20, 2013, from: **http://www.rcfp.org/reporters-guide-military-justice/whats-jag**

[457] Colonel Jefferson Brown, Trial Judge, U.S. v Wilkerson, Record of Trial, pg 557

[458] U.S. v Wilkerson, Record of Trial, pg 558-567

[459] Lt. Col. Paula McCarron, Investigating Officer's report, U.S. v Wilkerson, Record of Trial, pg 6

[460] U.S. v Wilkerson, Record of Trial, pg 505-508

[461] Captain Jeffrey Martin, letter to Lt. Gen. Franklin, February 23, 2013, pg 96/134 downloaded May 20, 2013, from **http://www.foia.af.mil/shared/media/document/AFD-130404-224.pdf**

[462] Colonel Jefferson Brown, Trial Judge, U.S. v Wilkerson, Record of Trial, pg 129

[463] Colonel Jefferson Brown, Trial Judge, U.S. v Wilkerson, Record of Trial, pg 1037

[464] Williams, Tech. Sgt. Richard A. Jr., "CSAF nominee testifies before Senate committee," Air Force Public Affairs Agency, July 20, 2012, downloaded May 21, 2013, from: **http://www.af.mil/news/story.asp?id=123310764**

[465] Dao, James, April 17, 2012, "Panetta Proposes New Sexual Assault Rules for the Military," *The New York Times* online, downloaded June 2, 2013, from: **http://atwar.blogs.nytimes.com/2012/04/17/panetta-proposes-new-sexual-assault-rules-for-the-military/**

[466] U.S. v Wilkerson, Record of Trial, Investigating Officer's report, pg 7

[467] U.S. v Wilkerson, Record of Trial, pg 130-134

[468] U.S. v Wilkerson, Record of Trial, pg 208

[469] U.S. v Wilkerson, Record of Trial, pg 991

[470] Cornell University Law School's Legal Information Institute says, "It is customary in many courts during direct or cross-examination for an attorney to ask the presiding judge for permission before approaching the witness on the stand." **http://www.law.cornell.edu/wex/permission_to_approach_the_witnes s**; The Rules of Practice Before Army Courts-Martial, March 26, 2012, says "Counsel will not first approach a witness without asking prior permission of the judge." **https://www.jagcnet.army.mil/Portals/USArmyTJ.nsf/(JAGCNetDocID)/122 A45612911AD2B852571F8006A5487/$FILE/Army%20Judiciary%20Rules%2 0of%20Court%20(26%20March%202012)%20FINAL.pdf** ; and the New York State Unified Court System rule is "Do not approach a witness without permission of the Court." **http://www.nycourts.gov/courts/11jd/supreme/civilterm/partrules/civil_part rules_35.shtml**

[471] Letter to Gen.Franklin about Col. Christensen's behavior, dated February 20, 2013, pg 45/134 from the Air Force Freedom of Information website, downloaded May 20, 2013, from: **http://www.foia.af.mil/shared/media/document/AFD-130404-224.pdf** and Beth Wilkerson, interview with author January 24, 2013

[472] Military Justice 101, The Court-Martial Process, Unlawful Command Influence, About.com US Military, downloaded May 21, 2013, from: **http://usmilitary.about.com/library/weekly/aa103000d.htm**, and the Uniform Code of Military Justice, at: http://www.au.af.mil/au/awc/awcgate/ucmj.htm#837.%20ART.%2037.%20UNL AWFULLY%20INFLUENCING%20ACTION%20OF%20COURT

[473] Brigadier General Scott Zobrist, email to Lt. Gen. Franklin, May 25, 2012, downloaded September 3, 2013, from: **http://www.foia.af.mil/shared/media/document/AFD-130821-017.pdf**

[474]Brigadier General Scott Zobrist, email to Lt. Gen. Franklin, June 3, 2012, downloaded September 3, 2013, from: **http://www.foia.af.mil/shared/media/document/AFD-130821-017.pdf**

[475] Kim Hanks statement April 17, 2012, U.S. v Wilkerson, Record of Trial, IO exhibit 3

[476] Kim Hanks' summarized Article 32 testimony, U.S. v Wilkerson, Record of Trial, IO exhibit 24

[477] U.S. v Wilkerson, Record of Trial, pg 489

[478] Initiatives to Combat Sexual Assault in the Military, **www.defense.gov**, downloaded April 23, 2013, from: **http://www.defense.gov/home/features/department_messages/DoD_Initiativ es_to_Combat_Sexual_Assault.pdf**

[479] Kim Hanks statement April 17, 2012, U.S. v Wilkerson, Record of Trial, IO exhibit 3

[480] U.S. v Wilkerson, Record of Trial, OSI report, downloaded, April 23, 2013, from: **http://www.foia.af.mil/shared/media/document/AFD-130403-029.pdf**

[481] U.S. v Wilkerson, Record of Trial, OSI report, at **http://www.foia.af.mil/shared/media/document/AFD-130403-029.pdf**, and U.S. v Wilkerson, Record of Trial, pg 758, and Beth Wilkerson, interview with author, February 24, 2013

[482] Lieutenant Colonel James H. Wilkerson, telephone interview with author, from Mannheim Prison, December 15, 2012

[483] Email from Interim Inspector General (name withheld); Original Message dated Monday, May 14, 2012, 09:59 PM, From: (name withheld) LtCol. USAF USAFE 31 FW/IGQ, To: Squadron Commanders - Aviano

Cc: Zobrist, Scott J BrigGen.USAF USAFE 31 FW/CC; Group/Deputy
Commanders - Aviano; Subject: IG change
[484] Lieutenant Colonel James H. Wilkerson, telephone interview with author,
from Mannheim Prison, December 15, 2013
[485] Air Force instruction 36-6001, 29 SEPTEMBER 2008, Sexual Assault
Prevention and Response (SAPR) program, pg 41, downloaded June 29, 2013,
from: **http://www.afpc.af.mil/shared/media/document/AFD-130510-040.pdf**
[486] Email from Interim Inspector General (name withheld) Original Message
dated Monday, May 14, 2012, 09:59 PM, From: (name withheld) LtCol. USAF
USAFE 31 FW/IGQ, To: Squadron Commanders - Aviano
Cc: Zobrist, Scott J BrigGen.USAF USAFE 31 FW/CC; Group/Deputy
Commanders - Aviano; Subject: IG change
[487] U.S. v Wilkerson, Record of Trial, pg 859
[488] Lieutenant Colonel James H. Wilkerson, telephone interview with author,
from Mannheim Prison, December 15, 2013
[489] "Former IG for 31st Fighter Wing charged with sexual assault," *Stars and
Stripes,* By Nancy Montgomery, August 16, 2012, downloaded April 15, 2013,
from: **http://www.stripes.com/news/former-ig-for-31st-fighter-wing-charged-
with-sexual-assault-1.185915**
[490] Lieutenant Colonel James H. Wilkerson, telephone interview with author,
from Mannheim Prison, December 15, 2013
[491] U.S. v Wilkerson, Record of Trial, pg 838
[492] U.S. v Wilkerson, Record of Trial, pg 876
[493] Colonel Don Christensen, US v Wilkerson, Record of Trial, pg 854
[494] Dictionary.com, downloaded May 25, 2013, from:
http://dictionary.reference.com/browse/removed?s=t.
[495] Colonel (retired) Scott Cusimano, U.S. v Wilkerson, Record of Trial, pg 832
[496] Colonel (retired) Scott Cusimano, U.S. v Wilkerson, Record of Trial, pg 838
[497] Stepman, Jarrett, May 6, 2013, "3rd AF commander victim of politically-
correct witch hunt," HumanEvents.com, downloaded June 4, 2013, from:
**http://www.humanevents.com/2013/05/06/commander-of-3rd-air-force-
victim-of-politically-correct-witch-hunt-2/**
[498] Lawrence, Chris, CNN, June 29, 2012, "31 victims identified in widening Air
Force sex scandal," downloaded September 19, 2013, from:
http://www.cnn.com/2012/06/28/justice/texas-air-force-scandal/index.html
[499] Brigadier General Scott Zobrist, email to Lt. Gen. Franklin, June 3, 2012,
downloaded September 3, 2013, from:
http://www.foia.af.mil/shared/media/document/AFD-130821-017.pdf
[500] Dao, James, July, 20, 2012, "Instructor for Air Force is Convicted in Sex
Assaults," *New York Times* online, downloaded August 3, 2013, from:
**http://www.nytimes.com/2012/07/21/us/lackland-air-force-base-instructor-
guilty-of-sex-assaults.html?pagewanted=all&_r=0** and O'Toole, Molly, March
13, 2013, "Senate Hearing On Sexual Assault In The Military Takes On Justice
System," *The Huffington Post online,* downloaded June 4, 2013, from:
**http://www.huffingtonpost.com/2013/03/13/senate-sexual-assault-military-
hearing_n_2865363.html**
[501] O'Toole, Molly, March 13, 2013, "Senate Hearing On Sexual Assault In The
Military Takes On Justice System," *The Huffington Post online*, downloaded June
4, 2013, from: **http://www.huffingtonpost.com/2013/03/13/senate-sexual-
assault-military-hearing_n_2865363.html**
[502] O'Toole, Molly, March 13, 2013, "Senate Hearing On Sexual Assault In The
Military Takes On Justice System," *The Huffington Post online*, downloaded June

4, 2013, from: http://www.huffingtonpost.com/2013/03/13/senate-sexual-assault-military-hearing_n_2865363.html
[503] Whitlock, Craig, May 8, 2013, "President Obama frustrated by Pentagon's struggle to prosecute, prevent military sex assaults," *The Washington Post*, downloaded June 2, 2013, from:
http://bangordailynews.com/2013/05/08/politics/president-obama-frustrated-by-pentagons-struggle-to-prosecute-prevent-military-sex-assaults/
[504] Doyle, Michael, "Tough talk by Marine Commandant James Amos complicates sexual-assault cases," McClatchy Newspapers, downloaded June 2, 2013, from:
http://www.mcclatchydc.com/2012/09/13/168410/tough-talk-by-marine-commandant.html
[505] Cassata, Donna, March 5, 2013, "Senators outraged by dismissal of assault case," Associated Press, downloaded June 3, 2013, from:
http://www.beaumontenterprise.com/news/crime/article/Senators-outraged-by-dismissal-of-assault-case-4330393.php and Montgomery Nancy, April 25, 2013, "Air Force plans to investigate new allegations against Wilkerson," *Stars and Stripes*, downloaded June 3, 2013, from: http://www.stripes.com/news/air-force/air-force-plans-to-investigate-new-allegations-against-wilkerson-1.218182
[506] Cassata, Donna, March 5, 2013, "Senators outraged by dismissal of assault case," Associated Press, downloaded June 3, 2013, from:
http://www.beaumontenterprise.com/news/crime/article/Senators-outraged-by-dismissal-of-assault-case-4330393.php
[507] Montgomery, Nancy, "Air Force pilot's sex assault dismissal sparks cries for reform," March 3, 2013, *Stars and Stripes*, downloaded June 4, 2013, from:
http://www.stripes.com/news/air-force-pilot-s-sex-assault-dismissal-sparks-cries-for-reform-1.210371
[508] Montgomery, Nancy, "Air Force pilot's sex assault dismissal sparks cries for reform," March 3, 2013, *Stars and Stripes,* downloaded June 4, 2013, from:
http://www.stripes.com/news/air-force-pilot-s-sex-assault-dismissal-sparks-cries-for-reform-1.210371
[509] Mims, Alisha, March 11, 2013, "Sex Offender Acquitted By Air Force General," Ringoffireradio.com, downloaded, June 6, 2013, from:
http://www.ringoffireradio.com/2013/03/11/sex-offender-acquitted-by-air-force-general/
[510] Montgomery, Nancy, "Air Force pilot's sex assault dismissal sparks cries for reform," March 3, 2013, *Stars and Stripes*, downloaded June 4, 2013, from:
http://www.stripes.com/news/air-force-pilot-s-sex-assault-dismissal-sparks-cries-for-reform-1.210371
[511] Stepman, Jarrett, May 6, 2013, "3rd AF commander victim of politically-correct witch hunt," HumanEvents.com, downloaded June 4, 2013, from:
http://www.humanevents.com/2013/05/06/commander-of-3rd-air-force-victim-of-politically-correct-witch-hunt-2/
[512] Montgomery, Nancy, March 7, 2013, "Reinstated Air Force pilot unlikely to get promoted any time soon," *Stars and Stripes*, downloaded June 4, 2013, from:
http://www.stripes.com/news/reinstated-air-force-pilot-unlikely-to-get-promoted-any-time-soon-1.210874
[513] Montgomery, Nancy, February 27, 2013, "Case dismissed against Aviano IG convicted of sexual assault," *Stars and Stripes*, downloaded June 4, 2013, from:
http://www.stripes.com/news/air-force/case-dismissed-against-aviano-ig-convicted-of-sexual-assault-1.209797

[514] Montgomery, Nancy, March 11, 2013, "Hagel orders review of UCMJ after Wilkerson sex assault case," *Stars and Stripes*, downloaded June 4, 2013, from: **http://www.stripes.com/news/hagel-orders-review-of-ucmj-after-wilkerson-sex-assault-case-1.211333**

[515] Colonel (retired) Scott Cusimano, U.S. v Wilkerson, Record of Trial, pg 835

[516] U.S. v Wilkerson, Record of Trial, pg 834-838

[517] Montgomery, Nancy, November 1, 2012, "Brigadier general takes stand in Aviano sexual assault case," *Stars and Stripes*, downloaded June 4, 2013, from: **http://www.stripes.com/news/brigadier-general-takes-stand-in-aviano-sexual-assault-case-1.195550**

[518] Montgomery, Nancy, March 11, 2013, "Hagel orders review of UCMJ after Wilkerson sex assault case," *Stars and Stripes*, downloaded June 4, 2013, from: **http://www.stripes.com/news/hagel-orders-review-of-ucmj-after-wilkerson-sex-assault-case-1.211333** and Montgomery, Nancy, April 12, 2013, "Overturning verdict was right decision, general says," *Stars and Stripes*, downloaded June 4, 2013,, from: **http://www.stripes.com/news/overturning-verdict-was-right-decision-general-says-1.216406**

[519] Montgomery, Nancy, February 27, 2013, "Case dismissed against Aviano IG convicted of sexual assault," *Stars and Stripes*, downloaded June 4, 2013, from: **http://www.stripes.com/news/air-force/case-dismissed-against-aviano-ig-convicted-of-sexual-assault-1.209797** and Montgomery Nancy, April 25, 2013, "Air Force plans to investigate new allegations against Wilkerson," *Stars and Stripes*, downloaded June 4, 2013, from: **http://www.stripes.com/news/air-force/air-force-plans-to-investigate-new-allegations-against-wilkerson-1.218182**

[520] US v Wilkerson, OSI report, pg 32/34 at **http://www.foia.af.mil/shared/media/document/AFD-130403-029.pdf**

[521] Lieutenant Colonel James Wilkerson, interview with author, June 6, 2013

[522] Colonel Don Christensen in email to Lt. Gen. Richard Harding, USAF, November 5, 2012, downloaded September 3, 2013, from: **http://www.foia.af.mil/shared/media/document/AFD-130821-018.pdf**

[523] U.S. v Wilkerson, OSI interview with Lt. Col. Wilkerson from the Air Force Freedom of Information web site at: **http://www.foia.af.mil/reading/thewilkersonfoiacase.asp**

[524] CBS Evening News, viewed June 6, 2013, from: **http://www.cbsnews.com/video/watch/?id=50142769n**

[525] "Sex assault clemency surprised prosecutor," *Air Force Times*, April 22, 2013, Staff writers, downloaded, June 6, 2013, from: **http://www.airforcetimes.com/article/20130422/NEWS/304220007/Sex-assault-clemency-surprised-prosecutor**

[526] "Sex assault clemency surprised prosecutor," *Air Force Times*, April 22, 2013, Staff writers, downloaded, June 6, 2013, from: **http://www.airforcetimes.com/article/20130422/NEWS/304220007/Sex-assault-clemency-surprised-prosecutor**

[527] "Sex assault clemency surprised prosecutor," *Air Force Times*, April 22, 2013, Staff writers, downloaded, June 6, 2013, from: **http://www.airforcetimes.com/article/20130422/NEWS/304220007/Sex-assault-clemency-surprised-prosecutor**

[528] "Sex assault clemency surprised prosecutor," *Air Force Times*, April 22, 2013, Staff writers, downloaded, June 6, 2013, from: **http://www.airforcetimes.com/article/20130422/NEWS/304220007/Sex-assault-clemency-surprised-prosecutor**

[529] Montgomery Nancy, April 25, 2013, "Air Force plans to investigate new allegations against Wilkerson," *Stars and Stripes*, downloaded June 4, 2013, from: **http://www.stripes.com/news/air-force/air-force-plans-to-investigate-new-allegations-against-wilkerson-1.218182**

[530] Friedman, Dan, March 13, 2013, "Sen. Kirsten Gillibrand ripped into top Pentagon lawyers during Senate subcommittee hearing, charging military has been too slow to stem tide of sex crimes in ranks," *New York Daily News*, downloaded June 6, 2013, from: **http://www.nydailynews.com/news/national/senate-hearing-sex-crimes-military-article-1.1287979**

[531] Email from Frank Spinner, March 13, 2013

[532] Stepman, Jarrett, May 6, 2013, "3rd AF commander victim of politically-correct witch hunt," HumanEvents.com, downloaded June 4, 2013, from: **http://www.humanevents.com/2013/05/06/commander-of-3rd-air-force-victim-of-politically-correct-witch-hunt-2/**

[533] Dao, James, April 17, 2012, "Panetta Proposes New Sexual Assault Rules for the Military," *The New York Times online*, downloaded June 2, 2013, from: **http://atwar.blogs.nytimes.com/2012/04/17/panetta-proposes-new-sexual-assault-rules-for-the-military/**

[534] Colonel Don Christensen, Trial Counsel, U.S. v Wilkerson, Record of Trial, pg 533

[535] Doyle, Michael and Taylor, Marisa, "Bureaucracy has blossomed in military's war on rape," McClatchy Newspapers, November 28, 2011, downloaded June 4, 2013, from: **http://www.mcclatchydc.com/2011/11/28/131524/bureaucracy-has-blossomed-in-militarys.html#.UauEKZzD-M9**

[536] Doyle, Michael and Taylor, Marisa, "Bureaucracy has blossomed in military's war on rape," McClatchy Newspapers, November 28, 2011, downloaded June 4, 2013, from: **http://www.mcclatchydc.com/2011/11/28/131524/bureaucracy-has-blossomed-in-militarys.html#.UauEKZzD-M9**

[537] Doyle, Michael and Taylor, Marisa, "Bureaucracy has blossomed in military's war on rape," McClatchy Newspapers, November 28, 2011, downloaded June 4, 2013, from: **http://www.mcclatchydc.com/2011/11/28/131524/bureaucracy-has-blossomed-in-militarys.html#.UauEKZzD-M9**

[538] Doyle, Michael and Taylor, Marisa, "Bureaucracy has blossomed in military's war on rape," McClatchy Newspapers, November 28, 2011, downloaded June 4, 2013, from: **http://www.mcclatchydc.com/2011/11/28/131524/bureaucracy-has-blossomed-in-militarys.html#.UauEKZzD-M9**

[539] Doyle, Michael, September 13, 2012, "Tough talk by Marine Commandant James Amos complicates sexual-assault cases," McClatchy Newspapers, downloaded June 4, 2013, from: **http://www.mcclatchydc.com/2012/09/13/168410/tough-talk-by-marine-commandant.html**

[540] Doyle, Michael and Taylor, Marisa, "Bureaucracy has blossomed in military's war on rape," McClatchy Newspapers, **http://www.mcclatchydc.com/2011/11/28/131524/bureaucracy-has-blossomed-in-militarys.html#.UauEKZzD-M9**

[541] Doyle, Michael and Taylor, Marisa, "Bureaucracy has blossomed in military's war on rape," McClatchy Newspapers, **http://www.mcclatchydc.com/2011/11/28/131524/bureaucracy-has-blossomed-in-militarys.html#.UauEKZzD-M9**

[542] Lerman, David, May 16, 2013, "Polling Experts Question Pentagon Sexual Assault Survey," downloaded May 16, 2013 from: http://www.bloomberg.com/news/2013-05-16/polling-experts-question-pentagon-sexual-assault-survey.html

[543] King, Casey, "Sexual Assaults Plague Military and Obama Administration," June 1, 2013, *The Guardian Express*, downloaded June 4, 2013 from: http://guardianlv.com/2013/06/sexual-assaults-plague-military-and-obama-administration/

[544] Lerman, David, May 16, 2013, "Polling Experts Question Pentagon Sexual Assault Survey," downloaded May 16, 2013, from: http://www.bloomberg.com/news/2013-05-16/polling-experts-question-pentagon-sexual-assault-survey.html

[545] Lerman, David, May 16, 2013, "Polling Experts Question Pentagon Sexual Assault Survey," downloaded May 16, 2013, from: http://www.bloomberg.com/news/2013-05-16/polling-experts-question-pentagon-sexual-assault-survey.html

[546] Department of Defense Annual Report on Sexual Assault in the Military, Fiscal Year 2012, pg 3

[547] Lerman, David, May 16, 2013, "Polling Experts Question Pentagon Sexual Assault Survey," downloaded May 16, 2013, from: http://www.bloomberg.com/news/2013-05-16/polling-experts-question-pentagon-sexual-assault-survey.html

[548] Lerman, David, May 16, 2013, "Polling Experts Question Pentagon Sexual Assault Survey," downloaded May 16, 2013, from: http://www.bloomberg.com/news/2013-05-16/polling-experts-question-pentagon-sexual-assault-survey.html

[549] King, Casey, "Sexual Assaults Plague Military and Obama Administration," June 1, 2013, *The Guardian Express*, downloaded June 4, 2013, from: http://guardianlv.com/2013/06/sexual-assaults-plague-military-and-obama-administration/

[550] Wiki Answers, How many people serve in the US armed forces, *Wikipedia*, downloaded June 10, 2013, from: http://wiki.answers.com/Q/How_many_people_serve_in_the_US_armed_forces_presently

[551] *City-Data.com*, downloaded June 10, 2013, from: http://www.city-data.com/crime/crime-New-York-New-York.html

[552] Department of Defense Annual Report on Sexual Assault in the Military, Fiscal Year 2012, pg 16

[553] Department of Defense Annual Report on Sexual Assault in the Military, Fiscal Year 2012, pg 53

[554] Montgomery, Nancy, January 9, 2013, "Air Force strengthens sex assault prosecutions with new measures," *Stars and Stripes,* downloaded June 4, 2013, from: http://www.stripes.com/news/air-force-strengthens-sex-assault-prosecutions-with-new-measures-1.203291

[555] Doyle, Michael and Taylor, Marisa, "Bureaucracy has blossomed in military's war on rape," McClatchy Newspapers, http://www.mcclatchydc.com/2011/11/28/131524/bureaucracy-has-blossomed-in-militarys.html#.UauEKZzD-M9

[556] Doyle, Michael and Taylor, Marisa, "Bureaucracy has blossomed in military's war on rape," McClatchy Newspapers, November 28, 2011, downloaded June 4, 2013, from: http://www.mcclatchydc.com/2011/11/28/131524/bureaucracy-has-blossomed-in-militarys.html#.UbXtKZzD-M8

[557] Taylor, Marisa, and Adams, Chris, November 28, 2011, "Military's newly aggressive rape prosecution has pitfalls," McClatchy Newspapers, downloaded June 10, 2013, from:
  http://www.mcclatchydc.com/2011/11/28/131523/militarys-newly-aggressive-rape.html#.UbXto5zD-M8

[558] Taylor, Marisa, and Adams, Chris, November 28, 2011, "Military's newly aggressive rape prosecution has pitfalls," McClatchy Newspapers, downloaded June 10, 2013, from:
  http://www.mcclatchydc.com/2011/11/28/131523/militarys-newly-aggressive-rape.html#.UbXto5zD-M8

[559] Montgomery, Nancy, January 9, 2013, "Air Force strengthens sex assault prosecutions with new measures," Stars and Stripes, downloaded June 4, 2013, from: http://www.stripes.com/news/air-force-strengthens-sex-assault-prosecutions-with-new-measures-1.203291

[560] Taylor, Marisa, and Adams, Chris, November 28, 2011, "Military's newly aggressive rape prosecution has pitfalls," McClatchy Newspapers, downloaded June 10, 2013, from:
  http://www.mcclatchydc.com/2011/11/28/131523/militarys-newly-aggressive-rape.html#.UbXto5zD-M8

[561] Montgomery, Nancy, January 9, 2013, "Air Force strengthens sex assault prosecutions with new measures," Stars and Stripes, downloaded June 4, 2013, from: http://www.stripes.com/news/air-force-strengthens-sex-assault-prosecutions-with-new-measures-1.203291

[562] Taylor, Marisa, and Adams, Chris, November 28, 2011, "Military's newly aggressive rape prosecution has pitfalls," McClatchy Newspapers, downloaded June 10, 2013, from:
  http://www.mcclatchydc.com/2011/11/28/131523/militarys-newly-aggressive-rape.html#.UbXto5zD-M8

[563] Taylor, Marisa, and Adams, Chris, November 28, 2011, "Military's newly aggressive rape prosecution has pitfalls," McClatchy Newspapers, downloaded June 10, 2013, from:
  http://www.mcclatchydc.com/2011/11/28/131523/militarys-newly-aggressive-rape.html#.UbXto5zD-M8

[564] Taylor, Marisa, and Adams, Chris, November 28, 2011, "Military's newly aggressive rape prosecution has pitfalls," McClatchy Newspapers, downloaded June 10, 2013, from:
  http://www.mcclatchydc.com/2011/11/28/131523/militarys-newly-aggressive-rape.html#.UbXto5zD-M8

[565] Taylor, Marisa, and Adams, Chris, November 28, 2011, "Military's newly aggressive rape prosecution has pitfalls," McClatchy Newspapers, downloaded June 10, 2013, from:
  http://www.mcclatchydc.com/2011/11/28/131523/militarys-newly-aggressive-rape.html#.UbXto5zD-M8

[566] Taylor, Marisa, and Adams, Chris, November 28, 2011, "Military's newly aggressive rape prosecution has pitfalls," McClatchy Newspapers, downloaded June 10, 2013, from:
  http://www.mcclatchydc.com/2011/11/28/131523/militarys-newly-aggressive-rape.html#.UbXto5zD-M8

[567] Taylor, Marisa, and Adams, Chris, November 28, 2011, "Military's newly aggressive rape prosecution has pitfalls," McClatchy Newspapers, downloaded June 10, 2013, from:
  http://www.mcclatchydc.com/2011/11/28/131523/militarys-newly-aggressive-rape.html#.UbXto5zD-M8

[568] Taylor, Marisa, and Adams, Chris, November 28, 2011, "Military's newly aggressive rape prosecution has pitfalls," McClatchy Newspapers, downloaded June 10, 2013, from:
http://www.mcclatchydc.com/2011/11/28/131523/militarys-newly-aggressive-rape.html#.UbXto5zD-M8

[569] Taylor, Marisa, and Adams, Chris, November 28, 2011, "Military's newly aggressive rape prosecution has pitfalls," McClatchy Newspapers, downloaded June 10, 2013, from:
http://www.mcclatchydc.com/2011/11/28/131523/militarys-newly-aggressive-rape.html#.UbXto5zD-M8

[570] Taylor, Marisa, and Adams, Chris, November 28, 2011, "Military's newly aggressive rape prosecution has pitfalls," McClatchy Newspapers, downloaded June 10, 2013, from:
http://www.mcclatchydc.com/2011/11/28/131523/militarys-newly-aggressive-rape.html#.UbXto5zD-M8

[571] Cave, Philip, D., "UCMJ and Sexual Assault Accusations, It could happen to you," downloaded June 2, 2013, from: http://www.court-martial.com/Practice-Areas/Under-Investigation/UCMJ-And-Sexual-Assault-Accusations.shtml

[572] Floyd, John and Sinclair, Billy August 25, 2012, "Cry Rape: False Allegations Destroy Lives," downloaded March 21, 2013, from:
http://www.johntfloyd.com/blog/2012/08/cry-rape-false-allegations-destroy-lives/

[573] Captain Benjamin Beliles, U.S. v Wilkerson, Record of Trial, pg 1077

[574] Cloud, David S., June 7, 2013, "General suspended over handling of sexual-assault investigation," *Los Angeles Times online*, downloaded June 10, 2013, from: http://www.latimes.com/news/nation/nationnow/la-na-nn-general-suspended-20130607,0,7509086.story

[575] Taylor, Marisa, and Adams, Chris, November 28, 2011, "Military's newly aggressive rape prosecution has pitfalls," McClatchy Newspapers, downloaded June 10, 2013, from:
http://www.mcclatchydc.com/2011/11/28/131523/militarys-newly-aggressive-rape.html#.UbXto5zD-M8

[576] Rodman, Lindsay L., "Fostering Constructive Dialogue on Military Sexual Assault," April 2013, *Joint Forces Quarterly on line*, downloaded April 3, 2013, from: http://www.ndu.edu/press/military-sexual-assault.html

[577] Doyle, Michael and Taylor, Marisa, B"ureaucracy has blossomed in military's war on rape," McClatchy Newspapers, November 28, 2011, downloaded June 4, 2013, from: http://www.mcclatchydc.com/2011/11/28/131524/bureaucracy-has-blossomed-in-militarys.html#.UauEKZzD-M9

[578] Department of Defense Annual Report on Sexual Assault in the Military, Fiscal Year 2012, pg 79

[579] Hlad, Jennifer, May 7, 2013, "Obama to Hagel: Pentagon must 'step up our game' to reduce sexual assault," *Stars and Stripes*, downloaded June 4, 2013, from: http://www.stripes.com/news/obama-to-hagel-pentagon-must-step-up-our-game-to-reduce-sexual-assault-1.219995

[580] Major General Scott Zobrist, Commander, 31st Fighter Wing, as written on James H. Wilkerson, Officer Performance Report, signed April 24, 2013

[581] Montgomery Nancy, April 25, 2013, "Air Force plans to investigate new allegations against Wilkerson," *Stars and Stripes*, downloaded June 4, 2013, from: http://www.stripes.com/news/air-force/air-force-plans-to-investigate-new-allegations-against-wilkerson-1.218182

[582] "Air Force Commander Directed Investigation of Lt. Col. James Wilkerson," downloaded September 3, 2013, from:
http://www.foia.af.mil/shared/media/document/AFD-130823-055.pdf
[583] Davis, Kristen, June, 28, 2013, "Lawmakers want Wilkerson kicked out of the Air Force," *Air Force Times*,
http://www.airforcetimes.com/apps/pbcs.dll/article?AID=2013306280022
[584] U.S. Supreme Court, FERES v. UNITED STATES, 340 U.S. 135 (1950), About.com US Military, downloaded September 3, 2013, from:
http://usmilitary.about.com/library/milinfo/blferes.htm
[585] Secretary of Defense Chuck Hagel, memorandum to all Department of Defense personnel, August 6, 2013, downloaded August 12, 2013, from:
https://www.jagcnet.army.mil/852577C1004877F2/0/9933F316EA0D3227852 57BC50068FCFF/$file/SECDEF%20Memorandum%20on%20Integrity%20of %20the%20Military%20Justice%20Process%206%20Aug%2013.pdf
[586] Defense Finance and Accounting Service, military pay tables, downloaded November 16, 2013, from:
http://www.dfas.mil/militarymembers/payentitlements/militarypaytables.html
[587] Alexander, David, "Female U.S. general who overturned sex-assault ruling to retire," November 8, 2013, *Reuters*, downloaded November 16, 2013, from:
http://www.reuters.com/article/2013/11/09/us-usa-defense-sexualassault-idUSBRE9A800A20131109
[588] Colonel Don Christensen, email to Lt. Gen. Harding, November 4, 2012, downloaded September 3, 2013, from:
http://www.foia.af.mil/shared/media/document/AFD-130821-018.pdf
[589] Montgomery, Nancy, December 18, 2013, "Air Force Removes Lt. Gen. Franklin from Sexual Assault Case," *Stars and Stripes*, downloaded December 18, 2013, from: http://www.stripes.com/news/air-force-removes-lt-gen-franklin-from-sexual-assault-case-1.258268?utm_source=dlvr.it&utm_medium=twitter
[590] Cassata, Donna, December 20, 2013, "Senate OKs bill that cracks down on sexual assault in the military," *Associated Press*, downloaded December 20, 2013, from: http://www.boston.com/2013/12/20/senate-oks-bill-that-cracks-down-sexual-assault-the-military/1lQIk1ih1lF17bc3XbMxCL/story.html
[591] Rodman, Lindsay L., "Fostering Constructive Dialogue on Military Sexual Assault," April 2013, *Joint Forces Quarterly on line*, downloaded April 3, 2013, from: http://www.ndu.edu/press/military-sexual-assault.html
[592] Isikoff, Michael, June 14, 2013, "Victim of alleged rape at Marine base: 'I thought… I would be safe,'" NBC News, downloaded June 14, 2013, from:
http://openchannel.nbcnews.com/_news/2013/06/14/18940666-victim-of-alleged-rape-at-marine-base-i-thought-i-would-be-safe?lite
[593] Isikoff, Michael, June 24, 2013, "Victim of alleged rape at Marine base: 'I thought… I would be safe,'" NBC News, downloaded June 14, 2013, from:
http://openchannel.nbcnews.com/_news/2013/06/14/18940666-victim-of-alleged-rape-at-marine-base-i-thought-i-would-be-safe?lite
[594] Innocence Project: Facts on post-conviction DNA exonerations, as written in Respecting Accuracy in Domestic Abuse Reporting, mediaradar.org, downloaded June 2, 2013, from:
http://www.mediaradar.org/research_on_false_rape_allegations.php#sdendn ote1sym
[595] Angelucci, Marc, and Sacks, Glenn, 2012, "Research shows false allegations of rape common," *Los Angeles Daily Journal*, September 15, 2004, downloaded June 30, 2013, from: http://www.glennsacks.com/research_shows_false.htm

[596] Suzanne Berrong, email addressing prosecution threats, February 5, 2013; sent to this author and Lt. Gen. Franklin

[597] Suzanne Berrong email on prosecution threats, February 5, 2013; sent to this author and Lt. Gen. Franklin.

[dxcviii] Dao, James, April 17, 2012, "Panetta Proposes New Sexual Assault Rules for the Military," *The New York Times online,* downloaded June 2, 2013, from: **http://atwar.blogs.nytimes.com/2012/04/17/panetta-proposes-new-sexual-assault-rules-for-the-military/**

Made in the USA
Charleston, SC
24 May 2014